D0350778

Singing an
Indian Song

*For my very dear friend
Betty Rosenthal*

Dorothy R. Parker

Dorothy R. Parker

Singing an Indian Song

A Biography of

D'Arcy McNickle

University of Nebraska Press
Lincoln and London

Publication of this book was assisted by a
grant from The Andrew W. Mellon Foundation.

The paper in this book meets
the minimum requirements of American
National Standard for Information
Sciences—Permanence of Paper for Printed
Library Materials, ANSI Z39.48–1984.

Library of Congress Cataloging-in-Publication
Data
Parker, Dorothy R. (Dorothy Ragon), 1927–
Singing an Indian song : a biography
of D'Arcy McNickle / Dorothy R. Parker.
p.   cm.—(American Indian lives)
Includes bibliographical references and index.
ISBN 0-8032-3687-5
1. McNickle, D'Arcy, 1904–1977—Biography.
2. Novelists, American—20th century—
Biography.
3. Anthropologists—United States—Biography.
4. Indians of North America—Biography.
I. Title.   II. Series.
PS3525.A2844.Z83   1992
813'.52—DC20   [B]   92-7616   CIP

Frontispiece: D'Arcy McNickle at the
Newberry Library, ca. 1972.
Photograph by Peter Weil, courtesy of
the Newberry Library, Chicago.

Contents

ILLUSTRATIONS

Preface

In D'Arcy McNickle's last novel, *Wind from an Enemy Sky* (1978), the voices of Indians singing provide a kind of leitmotif. The Indians sing of the world's beauty, of courage in the face of adversity, and they sing to ward off death from an old man who knows that his end is near. McNickle described it this way: "The singing never stopped. It never swelled to loudness, and it never stayed the same. A few riders would start the chant and carry it along, others would take over, still another part of the group would pick it up, then it would spread to all voices. And after a while only a few would be carrying it along."

This singing of an Indian song might well be the theme of D'Arcy McNickle's life. Born in 1904, he was one of the first Native American historians to interpret the Indian's encounter with white people from the Indian's point of view; in fact, during his long career he wrote several Indian histories, one of which, *Native American Tribalism*, is still in print.

Much as he might have wished otherwise, however, writing was not the primary focus of D'Arcy McNickle's life. He also served as an administrator in the Bureau of Indian Affairs under John Collier in the 1930s and

1940s, was a university professor of anthropology, did field work among the Navajos, and provided training and encouragement for a generation of young Indian people, many of whom have become today's tribal leaders. Through the disciplines of the social sciences he worked tirelessly to restore pride, political autonomy, and self-determination to all Indian people.

But first among his various identities, and to some extent by choice, D'Arcy McNickle was an Indian. Born of Canadian Cree, French, and Irish ancestry, he was enrolled and allotted on the Flathead Reservation in western Montana, and as a boy he attended the off-reservation Indian boarding school at Chemawa, Oregon. His perceptive insight into his mixed heritage determined the path of his life.

McNickle is most widely known today for his novels, *The Surrounded* (1936), *Runner in the Sun: A Story of Indian Maize* (1954), and *Wind from an Enemy Sky* (1978). Published at twenty-year intervals, the novels provide unusual insight into his maturing awareness of his own Indianness and of the role of Native Americans in this country's history. All three novels have recently been reprinted by the University of New Mexico Press, and today they are reaching a second audience, one larger than they had originally known. He also wrote a biography of Oliver La Farge and numerous articles.[1]

My investigation into McNickle's family background began with the generous assistance of his niece, O. Jahala Currie, in Calgary, Alberta. Mrs. Currie had been tracing the family's roots for several years, and she did not hesitate to share her extensive findings with me. But the most important single source of material on D'Arcy McNickle was the collection of his personal papers at the Newberry Library in Chicago. Over the years, he had saved much of his correspondence and had kept an almost daily diary. In 1983, when the Center for the History of the American Indian at the Newberry Library was renamed in his honor, his daughter Toni donated those papers to the Center. This valuable collection reveals McNickle's intimate familiarity with people and events that significantly influenced the lives of twentieth-century Native Americans.

A fellowship at the Newberry Library in 1986 provided me with un-limited access to McNickle's papers. In addition, Newberry President Lawrence W. Towner and Frederick E. Hoxie, Director of the D'Arcy McNickle Center, were most helpful and eager to share with me their personal reminiscences. John Aubrey and his staff in the library's Special Collections also offered every possible assistance in making the uncatalogued collection available to me.

McNickle's activities at the Bureau of Indian Affairs were traced not only through his papers but also through those of John Collier, on microfilm at the University of New Mexico's Zimmerman Library, and in Record Group 75 at the National Archives in Washington, D.C. My superb guide into this latter intimidating resource was Robert Kvasnicka, who suggested more ways of finding pertinent material than I could have imagined. I was also assisted in Washington by James Glenn, at the Smithsonian National Anthropological Archives. He and his staff helped me find my way into the early records of the National Congress of American Indians. Financial aid for research later provided through the Student Research Allocations Committee of the Graduate Student Association at the University of New Mexico made it possible for me to investigate the Flathead Tribal Records at Pablo, Montana.

In the course of writing this book I have benefited from the counsel and encouragement of many people. Margaret Connell-Szasz and Ferenc Szasz, at the University of New Mexico, listened for hours as McNickle's story unfolded, then exercised their considerable editing skills as the writing progressed. I am indebted as well to Alfonso Ortiz for suggesting that I write this biography and for making his own collected material available to me.

I also wish to acknowledge the contributions of Louis Owens, now at the University of California in Santa Cruz, and A. LaVonne Brown Ruoff, general editor of the American Indian Lives series, for their enthusiastic support of my research into McNickle's novels. Owens has written several articles about McNickle's role as a Native American novelist, and for months while he was on the English faculty at the University of New Mexico we shared insights into both the writer and the public man. Such sharing was, I hope and believe, a mutual pleasure.

To those people who consented to be interviewed, and to those who took the time and trouble to respond to my inquiries by mail, I owe a special debt of thanks. Omer Stewart in Colorado, Harold Fey in California, and Richard Pope in Canada sent collections of material that proved invaluable. Other significant contributions came from Robert Bieder, Robert Bigart, Roger Dunsmore, E. Reeseman Fryer, Francis Jennings, Fred Margolis, Willard Rollings, Erma Hicks Walz, Arthur Warner, and Murray Wax.

While writing a book is an individual, and at times a lonely, effort, the cooperation of those mentioned above, and many others, has helped sustain my interest and bring the person of D'Arcy McNickle to reality in my own mind. I am grateful to them all. Any errors of omission or commission in this work, of course, are entirely my own.

A Place of Beginning

For generations, the great buffalo hunts of the Red River Métis and their Indian relatives had moved south and west from the Canadian settlements to the prairies that belonged to no one and to all, and then, later, across the invisible line that separates Canada from the United States. The hunters sought the vast herds of buffalo that provided them with the substance of their lives. For most of the nineteenth century, the Métis families of Wilkies, Dumonts, Laframboises, Delormes, and Parenteaus had gathered at Pembina, present North Dakota, or St. Joseph, present Minnesota, just south of the forty-ninth parallel. There they organized themselves by mutual consent under a temporary regime that established the rules of the hunt.[1]

The buffalo-hunting Métis (the word comes from the French "métisser," to mix breeds) were, for the most part, descendants of the voyageurs and Indians who had navigated the inland waterways of Canada in the seventeenth and eighteenth centuries. They worked first for the French traders, then for the great British fur-trading companies. They were people of mixed European and Indian ancestry, most often French and Cree,

Iroquois, or Ojibwa. It had not been uncommon for the French coureurs de bois to marry Indian women "after the manner of the country," and children born of such unions often married each other. Thus the degree of Indian blood became mixed and uncertain. True to their French heritage, however, the Métis people baptized their children into the Catholic faith. Many of them were bilingual, although perhaps nonliterate, and they lived more as Europeans than as Indians. Nevertheless, most of them continued the economic activity best suited to their environment; they hunted the buffalo, until there were no more buffalo to hunt.[2]

From the 1820s on, many of these mixed-blood families began to settle in satellite villages around the various posts of the Hudson's Bay Company. A large group joined the Earl of Selkirk's Red River Colony, which later became the city of Winnipeg.[3] By the 1860s, however, the buffalo hunters had become aware of a change in the grazing patterns of the great herds. The animals were moving more to the west in their annual migrations, and the herds seemed smaller than in times past.

The last great buffalo hunt was in 1880. After that, it was painfully evident to the Métis hunters that the rhythm of their lives had changed. No longer did their families congregate every summer for the southward trek. The silence of the prairies was shattered, not by the roar of the mighty buffalo herds, but by the shriek of coal-fired, smoke-spewing monsters that raced across the land on iron rails. The vast expanses of the Northwest Territory became the prairie provinces of Manitoba and Saskatchewan, where plows ripped the sod and settlers built fences around their land, and newly organized mounted police tried to keep a kind of rough frontier order. Some of the families at Red River, already anticipating the changes that were coming, reluctantly turned to farming to supplement their food supply.

Some of the Métis, however, began to chafe under the increasingly "civilized" life of the settlements, and these men and their families gradually moved west and north to a less crowded area on the south fork of the Saskatchewan River. Sites along the river, with their plentiful supplies of wood and water, had long been used by the buffalo hunters as temporary wintering places. In 1868 their friend Father Alexis André moved into the area as resident priest, and soon the villages of St. Laurent, Batoche, Duck Lake, and Prince Albert formed the nucleus of a permanent community. The Métis drew up plans for a local government, which they fashioned after the organization of the hunt. As their leader they elected the charismatic Gabriel Dumont, who had been chief of the hunt since 1863. Wily, fearless, incredibly strong, compassionate among his own people, and a superb strategist in frontier warfare, Dumont soon became the undisputed leader of the Métis people of the Saskatchewan.

The local government thus established was not recognized by the Canadian authorities, however, and for a few years, a couple of decades at most, chaos ruled instead of law. The Hudson's Bay Company had for two centuries been the sole voice of authority throughout the interior drainage territory of Canada. In the 1860s the Company had ceded this land to the British Crown, which in turn expected the newly formed Dominion of Canada to exercise control. But officials in Ottawa saw no need to hurry in the establishment of new provincial governments; they wanted the Northwest Territory, as they called it, to be surveyed first, and a railroad built. When settlers began to arrive, there would be time enough to talk about such things as land claims and courts of law.

Thus the Métis farmers, who were considered squatters, had no way of acquiring title to their land. They became increasingly concerned as railroad surveyors and immigrants from the eastern provinces arrived and encroached on their homesteads. From 1869 to 1885, first at Fort Garry on the Red River, then at Qu'Appelle to the west, then north to the forks of the Saskatchewan, the Métis people pressured the Canadian government to recognize their claims to the land.

Louis Riel, a young man from one of the Red River settlements, led the first active Métis protest during the fall and winter of 1869–70.[4] What some historians have called a relatively minor incident eventually led to the formation of the Province of Manitoba. One white Canadian was killed during the brief fighting, and Riel, wanted by the authorities for this murder, moved south across the border into present Montana. Many of his supporters decided that they too should put some distance between themselves and the local constabulary at Red River, and they joined forces with the people along the Saskatchewan. Among those who moved north was a young man, Isidore Parenteau, D'Arcy McNickle's grandfather (1849–1925), who had family ties with the settlers at Batoche. Isidore and his bride, Judith Plante, had married in June 1870 at Red River. Their first child, Marie, was born the following year at St. Laurent.[5]

The young family (Isidore was only twenty-two) quickly found a place among the Métis of the Saskatchewan, as would be expected in view of the network of family relationships that enveloped them. Isidore's older sister, Judith, had married Gabriel Dumont's brother, also named Isidore, and Baptiste Parenteau, Isidore Parenteau's cousin, was one of Gabriel Dumont's closest friends. Isidore's and Judith's relatives bore such surnames as Patenaude, Beriault, Sansregret, Laverdure, Gariepy, and Laframboise, names that identified them as members of Métis patriarchal families.

The Plantes and Parenteaus were also counted among this patriarchal group. Judith's father, Antoine Plante, had been a steersman for the Hudson's Bay Company. He was a maker of the famous Red River carts, indispensable for overland travel in the Northwest Territory. Her mother, Angelique Dumont, was Gabriel Dumont's second cousin. Judith herself was born in the Red River settlement of St. Francis-Xavier in 1857.

Isidore Parenteau also grew up in the Red River area, although he was born in the United States. Some records state that he was born in present St. Paul, Minnesota, but it is more likely, as he himself later told his grandson, that his birthplace was St. Joseph, about thirty miles east of Pembina.[6] Possibly he was born during the 1849 buffalo hunt, to one of the families that accompanied the hunters in the traditional way. He was baptized the following year in St. Boniface, another of the Red River communities.

Isidore and Judith must have been well informed about the first Riel incident in 1869–70, although Isidore seems not to have been an actual participant. Gabriel Dumont, who was at Red River at the time, may or may not have been actively involved, but records show that he offered Riel the support of Métis manpower from the Saskatchewan villages and was totally sympathetic to Riel's cause.[7] When Isidore and Judith set out for St. Laurent in 1870, Dumont may well have accompanied their party.

Métis unrest in all the settlements grew in the face of continued governmental neglect. Finally, in 1884, Dumont and several companions met in council and decided to ask Riel if he would once more lead them in an attempt to reach some solution to their land problems. They found him teaching school in Montana, and persuaded him to return to the Saskatchewan and take up the Métis cause once again.

Riel's diaries, which were not published until 1976, reveal the spiritual intensity of this man who made a number of extraordinary claims regarding his own destiny and that of his people.[8] Louis Riel believed that he was chosen to be the Métis' spiritual guide, to direct them as they established their own territorial government. As his followers grew in number, he appointed Gabriel Dumont to organize them under a military command. Rebellion had become a possibility that was soon to be realized, although it was doomed to failure almost before it began.

The events that followed Riel's return to Canada had a nightmarish quality of inevitability. Accounts of the several battles of the Riel Rebellion of 1885 are numerous,[9] and it is unnecessary to relate them here except to note that they changed Isidore's and Judith's lives forever. Isidore's brother-in-law, Isidore Dumont, who was Gabriel's brother, was one of five men killed in March 1885 at Duck Lake, and other friends and relatives also became casualties before the fighting ended at Batoche. According to the records, Dumont's leadership was superb, but time after time he subordinated his military instincts to Riel's increasingly unrealistic mysticism.

By mid-May the rebellion was over and the Métis cause was lost. Within a few months, Riel was captured, tried for rebellion, and hanged, even though some observers at his trial argued for leniency on the grounds that he was psychologically unbalanced. Dumont and many of his followers, including Isidore and Judith, straggled south across the border into the United States. Although some eventually became permanent residents of Montana and other border states, others returned to Canada the following year when the government declared a general amnesty for all who had been involved in the rebellion.

A whole way of life changed for Isidore and Judith when they left Canada. Although Isidore, now the father of five children, apparently had not taken part in the actual fighting at Batoche, he had lost his entire homestead, which by 1885 consisted of a log house, two stables, and a fenced pasture for five horses and fourteen head of cattle.[10] He claimed 160 acres, fifteen of them broken to the plow and planted. For that time and place it was a substantial holding, and it is not surprising that he was concerned about obtaining a clear title. But he had not anticipated the ravages of even a minor war. "At the time of the rebellion of 1885," he later declared, "I lost all my cattle, and even my house was ransacked so that I had to leave my place to find work to keep my family."[11]

To leave his place, to flee as one wanted by the police for sympathizing with Riel—this was what faced Isidore Parenteau. The border promised safety for his family, and before the year 1885 was over, he and Judith had moved south into the Flathead country of western Montana Territory. Were they part of a larger group of refugees to settle there? It is impossible to say. Of their immediate family, Marie, the eldest child, was fourteen. Julie was twelve, Leo nine, Philomene (D'Arcy's mother) three, and Eliza was not yet walking. They owned little more than the clothes they wore when they finally crossed the Continental Divide and arrived at the mission town of St. Ignatius in the lovely valley of the Flathead Indians. The massive front of the Mission range to the east seemed to offer shelter from the storms that had played such havoc with their lives, and once more they settled down to build anew.

I

Into a New World

"He had mounted that treeless, grass-blown, unnamed hill," D'Arcy McNickle wrote of Max Leon in his first novel, *The Surrounded*, "and at the summit he literally fell on his knees and prayed." What lay before him, awesomely beautiful, was the expanse of an almost deserted valley stretching away to the north for fifty miles. To the west the land was relatively open, and to the east the spectacular Mission Range dominated the skyline. "Without foothills, though with curving approaches which spread some distance out upon the valley floor, the mountains raised a magnificent barricade against the eastern sky, the highest jagged crests floating in morning mist 8000 feet above the valley floor." It was not surprising that, confronted by such a view, Max Leon felt humbled and contrite.[1]

The Flathead Indian Reservation in western Montana, where D'Arcy McNickle spent most of his childhood, lies between Missoula and Glacier National Park in spectacular Rocky Mountain country. Flathead Lake occupies the northern half of the long, narrow Mission Valley, and to the south a handful of reservation towns mark off the miles to Missoula. Today the interstate highway and the railroad provide easy access to Missoula and the towns to the north, but in 1885 the railroad was still a novelty, and the automobile was scarcely a dream.

The first mission among the Flathead Indians was established in the Bitterroot Valley south of Missoula by the Jesuit priest Father Pierre De Smet in 1845. Ten years later the church was moved north to the Mission Valley, to what is now St. Ignatius. That same year, 1855, the United States signed the Treaty of Hell's Gate with the Confederated Tribes of the Salish, Kalispell, Kootenai, Flathead, and Pend d'Oreilles peoples. The treaty essentially established the boundaries of the reservation, although Chief Charlo and his Flathead band remained in the Bitterroot Valley outside the reservation until 1891.[2]

St. Ignatius Mission soon became the focal point of the Indians living in the Mission Valley. Between 1875 and 1900, which was the "golden age" of the mission, the Sisters of Providence established a boarding school for girls, and the Jesuit Fathers added another for boys. The Fathers built a flour mill and a sawmill, and after acquiring a printing press they translated biblical narratives for the schools and compiled a Kalispell dictionary. In 1891 they laid the cornerstone for a new brick church.[3] An array of houses clustered around the church and the school buildings was not arranged on any street or path, yet the setting was not without a plan. As McNickle later described it, "each cabin faced the church. Each door—there were no windows—gave a full view of God's tall house and the cropped poplar trees around it."[4] Of those original buildings, only the church remains today, cared for as a National Historic Site.

The country was still largerly unpopulated in 1885, although the number of non-Indians living there grew slowly after the railroad came through in 1880. The valley was ideally suited for stock raising, and areas not under cultivation were open range. With sufficient rain, the land produced several crops of hay a year, and pasturage was plentiful. Horses and cattle grazed freely during the winter and were rounded up in the spring for branding and farm work. There was even the remnant of a buffalo herd. In 1880, Michael Pablo and Charles Allard, some local ranchers, had collected a herd of some thirty buffalo, which by 1907 had increased to

625 head.[5] Although most Indians near St. Ignatius lived in houses like the whites, they retained as many of the old ways as possible. White civilization, however, was forcing itself upon them. The transcontinental railroad brought new settlers, and talk of opening the reservation to homesteaders attracted even more.

It is impossible to know the details of how Isidore and Judith Parenteau adapted to their new environment on the reservation. They had been an integral part of the Métis community on the Saskatchewan River, where Isidore had developed survival skills that proved useful to him in this new place. Their speech was a blend of French and Cree; although they may also have understood English, they probably chose not to speak it unless it was absolutely necessary. The same blend of Indian and French appeared in Métis housing, dress, and other components of their daily lives. While as a rule the Métis were as deeply religious as their Indian forebears, their religious impulse found expression through Catholic Christianity rather than in native ceremonials. Yet dancing, essentially a religious act among the Indians, remained a vital part of Métis culture and possessed its own distinct character. Music to accompany their dancing evolved from old French folk songs, and was usually provided by fiddlers who frequently made their own instruments.[6] But among the Flatheads Isidore and Judith were strangers, with a culture that reflected their Canadian Métis heritage.

People of mixed Indian and French ancestry had been part of the Flathead population for several decades before the Riel Rebellion, as is evident from the many French surnames on early tribal census rolls. By the 1880s, fur trappers of European descent had been frequenting the area for more than a hundred years. However, most of the Canadian Métis who fled to the United States after the 1885 rebellion stayed in eastern and central Montana, where they remained landless and persecuted and were sometimes deported by the U.S. Army. In 1887, one of their leaders, Pierre Busha, appealed to the Confederated Tribes for permission to settle sixty Métis families on the Flathead Reservation, but his appeal was refused, because Chief Charlo's band was soon to relocate on the available land.[7]

It appears that Isidore and Judith acted alone in settling among the Flatheads, and just why they decided to stay there remains a mystery. Apparently they were never subjected to the broader harrassment inflicted on their kin to the east. In time the family established itself in one of the houses near the mission church, and Isidore, being an experienced farmer with no land, hired out for wages. Ties to their Métis families remained close, however, and Isidore and Judith returned when they could to visit friends and relatives in Saskatchewan. Baptismal records tell of the birth and subsequent death of a son, Joseph, in Batoche in 1890, and the family was included in the Canadian census of 1891.[8] (As decreed by the Indian Act of 1875, the Canadian government recorded all Métis who traced their paternal lineage to European origins as legally white, not Indian, and the 1891 census listed Isidore's family accordingly, although they had been listed on the Flathead census rolls of 1890 as Cree.) Isidore also spent the summer of 1893 on his homestead at Batoche, despite the fact that little remained of his earlier efforts. McNickle himself remembered that as a small boy he had visited Saskatchewan with his mother and grandfather.[9]

For reasons of their own, and despite their close ties to the Saskatchewan River, Isidore and Judith remained on the Flathead Reservation and became true Montana pioneers. They put their roots down at St. Ignatius, and it was there that Philomene, D'Arcy's mother, and her sister Eliza attended the mission school. It was there, too, that Philomene met William McNickle, whom she married in 1899.

D'Arcy's father, William James McNickle, the son of Irish immigrants, was born in 1869 (or in 1861—there is some discrepancy about the date) in Pittsburgh, Pennsylvania. He left home as young man, lived briefly in Winona, Minnesota, and moved on to Montana Territory in 1884. Like his father, James, William worked for the railroad and helped build the Northern Pacific through Montana in the 1880s. He possessed some mechanical skills, and for a number of years he farmed and worked for the mission schools at St. Ignatius as a "maintenance engineer."[10] In 1904,

Flathead agent W. H. Smead recommended to the Indian commissioner in Washington that William be appointed "industrial teacher" for the government boarding school at Jocko, south of St. Ignatius. Smead wrote to the commissioner, "McNickle has been on the reservation for a number of years, bears a good reputation, and is I believe entirely reliable."[11] The only apparent obstacle to his being hired was that he was not Indian. Although he was subsequently offered the position, William did not accept it. By this time he had land of his own, and he did not want to leave it. McNickle recalled later only that his father had worked in a janitorial capacity at the school in St. Ignatius.

William McNickle would have met the Parenteau family through school contacts sometime before he and Philomene were married in May 1899. She was not yet seventeen, he was around thirty. In accordance with Métis custom, her parents had arranged the marriage. As Philomene later told the Indian agent, she married William in order "to be a good girl." To her parents, William seemed a good prospect: he was Catholic, mature, owned some property, and was white, not Indian. As Métis, the Parenteaus did not consider themselves to be Indian, and they did not want their daughter to marry an Indian.[12]

Philomene and William had three children, Ruth Elizabeth, born in March 1900; Florence Lea, eighteen months later; and William D'Arcy, on January 18, 1904. The origin of the name "D'Arcy" is uncertain, although family tradition maintains that it was a placename in Canada. By the time D'Arcy was born, William had acquired considerable acreage several miles east of town, so one by one, as the children became old enough, they were enrolled as boarding students at the mission school in St. Ignatius. On the school rolls the McNickle children were listed as mixed-blood.[13] Although neither Philomene nor William had any intention of raising their children to be Indian, the youngsters spent their most formative years at school among their Indian peers.[14]

D'Arcy McNickle's enrollment as a member of the Flathead Tribe was, surprisingly, a rather circuitous gift from his Irish father. The Dawes Act, passed by the U.S. Congress in 1887, had provided for the individual allotment of reservation land among tribal members, with the hope that, through the ownership of private property, Indians might learn the joys and responsibilities of American citizenship. Establishing tribal rolls of those who would be eligible was the first step toward allotment. That, however, proved to be a tedious and time-consuming process. Preparations for a definitive enrollment of the Confederated Tribes were not begun until 1902, and the question immediately arose concerning the status of those living on the reservation who had other Indian blood and those who had none. The Indian commissioner wrote to Special Agent Charles McNichols in September 1902:

> Where persons of Indian blood other than of the five tribes have been on the reservation for more than ten years, and have been recognized by the Indians, . . . they may be enrolled. In all cases, if the Indians desire the enrollment of such persons, they should adopt them in regular council, records of the proceedings of which should be made by the Agent and transmitted to this office for submission to the Secretary of the Interior.[15]

The same process of adoption could be followed for those with no Indian blood whatever, if all parties agreed.

In April 1905, a new special agent, Thomas Downs, was appointed by the commissioner to make the final roll of the Confederated Tribes. He called a meeting of the tribal council, "with a view of having them pass on all claims of those persons mentioned who possess the blood of some other than the Five Confederated Tribes of this reservation." Sixteen chiefs and judges of the Confederated Tribes, including old Chief Charlo, convened to decide who should be adopted, and among those considered were Philomene McNickle and her three children. By a vote of nine to seven, the council gave its consent. On May 25, Downs reported to the commissioner, "It may therefore be accepted as a fact that every person enrolled has had his enrollment approved by the chiefs, judges and headmen of the tribe of which he is shown to be a member." The final roll, dated April 18, 1905, included 557 Flathead Indians, sixteen of whom were adopted as being "of other Indian blood." D'Arcy, his mother, and his two sisters were among those sixteen.[16] Their blood affiliation was listed as Cree.

In August 1962 Philomene wrote to her grandchildren that it was William who had placed the family names before the council for adoption, although the minutes of the council proceedings for April 18, 1905, indicate that "Philomene McNickle presented herself and asked that she and her three children be adopted."[17] It would not be surprising if the action had been taken with the support of agents Smead and Downs. Philomene's family was well known and accepted by the Indians, and by virtue of their adoption, she and the children became eligible for allotments of reservation land. When allotments were made, William saw to it that their eighty-acre parcels were adjacent to the land he had been farming for several years.

Despite the family's growing prosperity, however, William's marriage to Philomene was not a happy one. Since the children lived in St. Ignatius during the school year, they missed some of the unpleasantness, but they were certainly aware that all was not well at home. As D'Arcy later recalled, "I was too young to know what was going on between my parents, although I was aware of a great deal of mud-slinging both ways."[18] Philomene appeared to be quite unstable, at one point even threatening to kill her husband, and she left him more than once. The new Flathead agent, Major Fred Morgan, tried several times to mediate between them, but his efforts met with only temporary success and in 1912 he arranged a legal separation.

The terms of the separation provide some indication of the family's relative prosperity. Philomene, of course, retained her allotment, and she received five hundred dollars cash to build a house on her land. She was also awarded personal property that included a buggy, various items of household furniture, and "one lot of chickens." She was freed of all debts and obligations the couple had incurred, and she had custody of the children during the summer months of school vacation. William, in turn, retained all rights of homestead (he had filed for another 320 acres by this time), nine months each year of child custody, and "absolute control and sole authority" over the children's allotments.[19]

Unfortunately, Morgan's attempted arbitration was short-lived. In early 1913, Philomene wrote to him complaining of William's use of the children's land and requesting that her allotment and D'Arcy's be exchanged. She had not yet built on her own land and William had erected a house on D'Arcy's, which she apparently wanted. Morgan, however, refused to approve her request. By this time the children had been drawn into the struggle between their parents. Disgruntled by the terms of the separation, Philomene finally filed for divorce, although her attorney doubted that the court would be very sympathetic toward her efforts to gain custody of the children.[20]

The hearing for the divorce was held behind closed doors, suggesting that one or both parties had seriously violated the mores of the community, if not the law of the land. According to Morgan, Philomene admitted during the hearing that "she [was] keeping a hired man in the home with no others except herself and small child," and in itself that was incriminating evidence against her. Philomene's behavior was so unpredictable that her appeal for custody of the children had little chance of being granted. Morgan wrote to the commissioner, "McNickle may not be blameless, but from what I know of the case, she [Philomene] has been more responsible for their troubles than he has." He characterized McNickle as "a sober and industrious man who, at all times, worked hard and used the proceeds derived from the allotments of his children in caring for his family."[21]

The divorce decree, granted in April 1913, ordered that D'Arcy should spend summer vacations with his mother and Ruth with her father, and Florence was to divide her vacation between her parents. William retained control over the children's land, with instructions to cultivate it for their benefit.[22] The decree also ordered that the children continue to attend the mission school in St. Ignatius, if the Fathers and Sisters were willing to keep them there. If not, the children, by virtue of their being enrolled members of the Flathead Tribe, were to be placed in an off-reservation Indian boarding school. Although neither parent was to have custody of the children during the school year, both Philomene and William were given visiting privileges.

In reading the accounts of the court proceedings as reported by Fred Morgan, one must put the agent's rhetoric into context. Morgan had been appointed agent to the Flathead Reservation on November 30, 1908, in response to a demand by Father Louis Taelman, the Jesuit in charge of St. Ignatius Mission, that Smead be replaced. Just a month after Morgan's appointment, Father Taelman wrote again to Commissioner Francis E. Leupp, this time praising the new agent, "whom all the good people of this reservation already look upon as a first class agent. Many people have already spoken to me to that effect, and in their names and in the name of all the Mission people, I thank you for his appointment. We all feel happy over the great changes for the better."[23]

The problem that had alarmed the mission people before Morgan's arrival, and that had prompted Father Taelman's request to the commissioner for a new, morally responsible agent, was concubinage. Taelman had complained that the practice of sleeping with someone other than one's spouse had become epidemic on the reservation and Smead had refused to take effective action against it. Such behavior was a great disgrace to the good people of the mission. Leupp had replied that he could do little about the situation unless he had the names of those suspected of such behavior, whereupon Father Taelman sent him a list of names, along with this request: "I would ask you that in carrying out your plans [to put a stop to such immorality] the work appear to come simply from the Government, leaving out the Mission people. The results will be obtained just as well, and we shall not unnecessarily lose any influence upon these Indians, whose moral welfare we simply have at heart."[24]

Morgan's appointment was Leupp's response to Father Taelman's concern about reservation morality. With this background, it is not surprising that Philomene's behavior, which may have been quite innocent in this regard, evoked a negative response from the representatives of civil and religious authority. Sixty years later, McNickle recalled that "it was a hell of a society to grow up in."[25]

Frontier Montana at the turn of the century may well have been a "hell of a society" for a sensitive young boy. The Flathead country was unusually chaotic at that time because of its impending allotment and the opening of the reservation to white homesteaders. McNickle later recalled how, after homesteading, the range was fenced and the local people were forced to sell their herds because they could no longer support them on the land allotted to their families. The buffalo herd belonging to Pablo and Allard posed a particular problem, as buffalo were notoriously difficult to keep fenced. The herd was eventually rounded up and sold to a Canadian buyer.[26] Photographs of the roundup were widely distributed because, even then, the vanishing herds had become part of western mythology. Some years later, Karen Fenton, a high school teacher in Missoula, sent some of these photographs to McNickle. Writing to thank her, he told her that he had been a witness to that roundup. "I was especially pleased," he said,

> by the photos of the scenes at Ravalli, when they were shipping the Pablo-Allard buffalo herd. As a child of five or six I stood watching, amazed and terror-stricken, through the heavy timbers of the corral. One buffalo cow had been gored and her insides were pouring out. I either saw or was told about the great bull who went charging up the ramp and right through the other side of the stock car.[27]

The opening of the reservation had an impact on more than reservation landholdings. Local schools were also affected as the non-Indian population increased. Before the turn of the century, the mission school at St. Ignatius and others like it had been under contract with the federal government to provide educational services for Indian children. Although Congress terminated funding for contracts with church-affiliated schools in 1900, St. Ignatius managed to continue its program on a reduced scale for a number of years.[28] But there was almost no alternative for either Indians or whites on the Flathead Reservation. In 1903, the only government-operated boarding school on the reservation, at Jocko, was filled beyond capacity with forty-seven students.[29] By 1911, when D'Arcy was old enough to start first grade, three of the four federally supported day schools had been closed. In 1920 no government schools remained on the reservation, although delegates from the Flathead Tribe twice appealed for renewed government assistance for the mission schools.[30] By that time, however, federally supported church schools were out of the question. While a few locally controlled public schools had appeared when the reservation was opened to settlement in 1912, discrimination in their classrooms caused many Indian children to stay away.

Ruth, Florence, and D'Arcy McNickle attended the mission school in St. Ignatius until their parents' divorce in 1913. As children, D'Arcy and Florence were particularly close, and they spent much time together at their favorite pastime, fishing. McNickle later recalled that his mother discouraged his playing with Indian children, although they were among his schoolmates and part of his daily life. In the aftermath of the divorce, however, William decided that Philomene, who had remarried and stopped attending church, was a poor influence on the children. Superintendent Morgan (his title was changed from "Agent" shortly after his appointment) and the school officials concurred. It is not difficult to imagine that Morgan himself persuaded Father George de la Motte, Mission Superior at the St. Ignatius school, to refuse admission to the children when school opened in the fall of 1913. The Fathers and Sisters, thinking it best to separate the children from their mother, decided that they would not allow the children to return. Thus Morgan was obliged to place them in an off-reservation boarding school, as required by the divorce decree. Although Philomene objected strenuously, all three children were enrolled at the Salem Indian Training School in Chemawa, Oregon in the fall of 1913.

Philomene was far from reconciled to the fact that the children were being taken from her. She especially missed D'Arcy, who was apparently her favorite. During the next school year she tried through the courts to have D'Arcy returned to her. She sent train fare to Chemawa so that he might spend the summer of 1914 at home. When it was time for him to return to school in the fall, she encouraged him to run away, which he did. Although this tactic was only temporarily successful, it indicated how strongly she resented his being taken from her. She continued to pressure the mission school in St. Ignatius to admit D'Arcy, until finally the Mother Superior complained to Morgan. "We fear the mother's influence will destroy all our efforts toward the training of [the boy's] character," she explained. "Then, too, her reputation is such that her visits here would be a detriment to the good name of our Institution."[31]

Philomene's attempts to regain custody of D'Arcy resulted in a particularly nasty court hearing. She took him to court with her and encouraged him to make accusations about the school food and the supposed poor health of his sister Florence. At her urging, D'Arcy even implied that his roommate had had "improper relations" with Florence. None of D'Arcy's charges appears to have had any validity, however, and her appeal for modification was denied.[32]

At that point Philomene, who had remarried, went over the heads of her local adversaries and wrote directly to the Indian commissioner. "There is no reason what aver for Morgan to take that child way from me I am marred with a good respectable man we have a good home for him and want to raise him as white man we got a good publice school [he has] not got eneght Indian blood for them schools in the first place, my children are only one 8 Indian my wishis to raise them as white children."[33] She was fighting a losing battle against the white establishment, however, and all three children remained at Chemawa until 1916, the two girls even longer.

The Chemawa Indian School was the second oldest of the United States government's off-reservation boarding schools, having been established in 1880, and it was generally considered one of the better ones. Its founding reflected the same mentality that supported the Dawes Act a few years later. These schools (there were as many as twenty-five at various times) were designed to remove Indian children from their tribal cultures and teach them to become "civilized" American citizens. Nevertheless, it was Morgan's second choice for the McNickle children. He had first tried to enroll them in Haskell Institute, an Indian boarding school in Kansas, but Haskell refused to take all three and William did not want them separated. There was no question, however, about the children being qualified as Indians to attend an Indian school. Their tribal enrollment was in full compliance with the law; they were bona fide members of the Flathead Tribe.

McNickle rarely mentioned his three years at Chemawa except in his fiction. Initially it must have been a strange and lonely life for a ten-year-old boy, uprooted from home yet knowing, at the same time, that his family was shattered beyond repair. Other children from St. Ignatius also took the long train ride from Ravalli to Salem, but that was small comfort. D'Arcy and his sisters lived in separate dormitories, and their parents were far away. Regimentation was nothing new, however, and the school at Chemawa was probably no more strict than the mission school in St. Ignatius.[34] In McNickle's writing there is nothing to indicate that the school provided a more "Indian" experience or a routine that was much different from what he had known on the reservation. Chemawa was an Indian school, but so was the mission school at St. Ignatius, and his status as one of the students had not changed. When McNickle wrote about Archilde's life at the school in Oregon in *The Surrounded,* he did not include details or incidents that an outsider might consider as being uniquely Indian. Archilde was just a boy among boys at school, with experiences common to boys everywhere. D'Arcy's sister Florence never told her own children that Chemawa was an Indian boarding school. All they knew was that the boarding school their mother had attended was a very good school and she had enjoyed it.[35]

It is difficult to assess the impact that Chemawa had on McNickle. Our only insight into those three years comes from anecdotal material he included in his novels. In *Wind from an Enemy Sky,* written quite late in his life, there are several paragraphs in which Antoine, the young hero, who has just returned after four years away at school, recalls the unthinking brutality of the school administration and the atmosphere of fear that pervaded the lives of the students.[36] McNickle's account of Antoine's experience suggests that such incidents had indeed left their imprint on his memory.

In his nonfiction, however, McNickle impersonally related the usual description of Indian boarding schools as places where children were denied access to their cultural heritage and were punished for speaking their native language. D'Arcy must have been aware that such punishment was administered, but he himself probably escaped it. After all, he spoke only English, and he was probably more acculturated than most of his fellow students. Looking back at his own experience, he might well have considered his introduction to music as the most significant event of those years. In *The Surrounded*, which is largely autobiographical, he described in detail how Archilde first learned to play the violin and how a significant older person took the time to be interested in a young boy. Although McNickle must surely have witnessed the enforcement of various sanctioned behaviors, he appeared not to have been personally traumatized by extreme punishment.

The boarding school experience might well have had a deeper impact on the shaping of McNickle's personality, however. His parents' efforts to raise him as a non-Indian were more than countered by his association with Indian children at the mission school in St. Ignatius, and such contact became even more intense at Chemawa. His lack of interest in competition as an adult, his refusal to participate in materialistic one-upmanship, his nondirective management style, and his emphasis on consensus building, all of which are consistent with a Native American personality profile, reflected his reservation and boarding school childhood.[37] His sense of humor, especially, seemed more Indian than white.

Chemawa obviously was not a totally negative experience for McNickle, although he later commented that it did little to stimulate his love for learning. This was not surprising; off-reservation boarding schools for Indian children were programmed as vocational training schools, and they made little attempt to prepare their students for higher education. The McNickle children did well in their schoolwork, however, and Philomene and William both maintained close contact with them.

William sent spending money for holidays and excursions, and he spent Christmas of 1914 with them at Chemawa. His mother asked to have D'Arcy's eyes examined when he complained about headaches, and the school provided him with glasses. Even Philomene's new husband, Gus Dahlberg, wrote to D'Arcy, telling him how eager they were to have him and his sisters come home for vacation. Philomene, making the best of what she considered a bad situation, finally wrote to Chemawa's Superintendent Wadsworth about her son, "I must say that I am very well please of all is Report.—he is scurly doing fin since is been there I hop he will keep on."[38]

Finally, in 1916, Philomene succeeded in gaining custody of her son. By then D'Arcy had finished his three-year enrollment, and he returned to Montana to live with his mother and Gus Dahlberg. He seemed content to be part of a family again, and he took Dahlberg's name, although Gus never legally adopted him.

Court records detailing the McNickles' marital problems have provided more information about D'Arcy's mother than about his father, and much of that information is prejudicial. William, D'Arcy's father, on the other hand, appears in the rare glimpses we are given to have been an honorable, civic-minded man who tried to make a decent home for his family. Despite the fact that he never remarried, the house he built on his farm was seldom empty. Isidore and Judith, Philomene's parents, who had lived with the McNickles since 1911, remained there after Philomene left. Later, after her own divorce, Ruth and her four children moved in and Ruth worked beside her father on the farm. One of Ruth's children recalled that her grandfather was "a kind and compassionate old man, everything a girl could want her grandfather to be."[39]

McNickle's debt to his father was much greater than he was willing to admit. It was William who had taken the necessary steps to enroll his family in the Flathead Tribe before the allotment of the reservation, and because they were tribal members, Ruth, Florence, and D'Arcy were eligible to receive allotted lands and to attend school at Chemawa. D'Arcy's enrollment in the Flathead Tribe later opened the doors of the Bureau of In-

dian Affairs when he applied for employment in the 1930s. William may
have married Philomene partly in anticipation of her allotment—many
men at the time did just that—but he willingly accepted the responsibilities that came with marriage and he genuinely cared for his children.
Unfortunately, D'Arcy's position as a pawn in his parents' struggle de-
prived him of a potentially caring relationship with his father during
much of his boyhood. He may have lived with his father occasionally during summer vacations and helped on the ranch, but by this time father and
son had little in common.

D'Arcy's grandfather probably had a more immediate influence on the
young boy than did his father. During their periodic visits to Batoche and
St. Laurent, Isidore and Judith visited relatives and friends and remi-
nisced about the events of their common past. Gabriel Dumont was part
of this group, and what has been written of Dumont might well be said of
Isidore: "It was with the children of his nephews and his cousins, and with
their friends, that he was most at home, sitting at his cabin door and ex-
pounding like some patriarchal teacher the lore of the old West."[40] The
Métis had retained a strong oral tradition, and Isidore, too, regaled his
grandchildren with stories of buffalo hunts and Indian companions on the
northern plains. D'Arcy later retold Isidore's stories to his own grandchildren. His love for "fiddle music" might also have come to him from his
Métis grandparents.

D'Arcy returned from Chemawa in 1916 to live with his mother and
Gus Dahlberg, while Florence and Ruth remained at the school until they
graduated. From this time on, D'Arcy had little further contact with the
people he had known on the reservation. The family lived for a short time
in Pablo, ten miles north of St. Ignatius, then in 1918 they moved to Lang-
ley, Washington, where wartime shipbuilding offered more employment
opportunities for Gus. D'Arcy made an uneventful transition from an Indian boarding school to the public school in Pablo and then to high school
in a community with very few Indians. Florence, who graduated from
Chemawa in 1917, enrolled in nursing school at nearby Everett. She obtained her nursing certification without incident and moved to Canada.

There she married a Swede, raised four daughters and one son, and worked in the nursing profession for years. Ruth married a mixed-blood from St. Ignatius and raised her four children as members of the Confederated Tribes.

Gus Dahlberg was a relatively unskilled laborer who picked up work wherever it was available. In Pablo he had worked as a meat cutter, and in Washington he hired on at the shipyards. The family income was augmented by the periodic distribution of tribal funds to Philomene and D'Arcy, funds that accrued from the sale of reservation timber and other tribal assets. D'Arcy and Florence also received income from their allotments, which were leased and farmed by their father. Their various incomes were kept in trust accounts at the Flathead Agency, to be drawn on as needed.

Because the ever-paternalistic Indian Bureau required that tribal members justify their withdrawals, D'Arcy wrote occasionally to the agency office, and his letters provide what little information is available about his high school years.[41] Most of his withdrawals were for amounts of twenty-five or fifty dollars, primarily for clothing. Students in city schools, he informed the agent, dressed differently than did students on the reservation, and besides, he was more than ready to wear long pants. On occasion he also withdrew money for gifts for the family. Music lessons, too, constituted a legitimate expense. D'Arcy had continued his study of the violin, first buying his own instrument, then later paying for lessons and music.

While hardly extensive, the correspondence between D'Arcy and Flathead superintendent Theodore Sharp was revealing. The boy told of playing a lead role in the school's production of Shakespeare's *Twelfth Night*. He also reported winning a spot on the debating team and a prize in a short story competition. The city school obviously offered opportunities that did not exist on the reservation, and he seemed eager to take full advantage of them. Sharp complied with D'Arcy's requests for money and he was also generous with his praise. He was pleased that D'Arcy was doing well in school, getting good grades, and playing the violin. Although his letters were businesslike, they conveyed a genuine personal interest, and they tell us what little we know about D'Arcy's high school years.

The Dahlbergs moved back to Montana and settled in Missoula in time for D'Arcy to graduate from high school there in 1921. The following September, still as D'Arcy Dahlberg, he enrolled at Montana State University. He lived with Philomene and Gus until their divorce in 1924, at which time Philomene moved back to St. Ignatius. D'Arcy's letters to the agency after that bore several different addresses, all of them in the vicinity of the university, although he spent a few days in jail one summer when a misunderstanding with his landlady over some back rent led to his arrest. But he stayed on at the university, determined to finish the work for his degree.

D'Arcy's poor grades at the university do not reflect his growing commitment to scholarship and to the world of books. Throughout his life he would teach himself those things he considered really important. The university, however, offered him an opportunity to develop his talents as a writer. He had the good fortune to come under the tutelage of Harold G. Merriam, a Rhodes scholar who had recently become chairman of the English Department. In 1920, Merriam and his students, including A. B. Guthrie, Jr., and Dorothy Johnson, had founded the *Frontier: A Literary Magazine,* which, although small, later became an influential regional publication. D'Arcy served on its editorial staff for two years and he was senior editor for the 1924–25 winter edition. He also contributed poetry and several short prose pieces.[42] He even tried his hand at writing a play, a satire entitled "Fashion," in which he played the leading role as "T. Tennyson Twinkle, a Modern Poet."[43] Seeing his work and his name in print reinforced his growing determination to become a professional writer.

D'Arcy's interest in drama and literature was shared by a fellow student, a young woman named Joran Birkeland, who was also from western Montana.[44] Joran became circulation manager of the *Frontier* while D'Arcy served on the editorial staff, and she, too, contributed to several issues of that publication. Joran was much attracted to this classmate who wrote poetry and prose with such sensitivity, for D'Arcy had become a handsome young man. He was of average height and medium build, and his most striking feature was a shock of dark, wavy hair that swept back from his high forehead in a pronounced widow's peak. Behind his glasses, his heavy-browed eyes were dark and intelligent, and when his mouth laughed, his eyes laughed too. From time to time he experimented with growing a small mustache. Although his clothes were not stylish (he didn't know much about that), they were always clean and neat. He looked, in fact, much more French than Indian, and few people were aware of his Indian ancestry. A. B. Guthrie, Jr., who also served on the *Frontier*'s editorial staff, wrote in his autobiography, *The Blue Hen's Chick*, "It was fortunate that we had no Indians in the student body. Everyone knew about Indians. No prejudice, just a normal capacity for realism."[45] D'Arcy was not about to try to change Guthrie's mind.

In manner D'Arcy was usually quiet and serious, given to periods of introspection and at times painfully aware of his own shyness. He maintained a sense of personal privacy that few people were invited to enter. But somewhere, at some time, he learned to love books. He carried one or more around with him constantly, which was decidedly an unpopular thing to do on campus. Years later he told Carey McWilliams, the well-known editor of the *Nation* in the 1950s and 1960s who became an admirer of McNickle's Indian histories, that at the university "it was a sin to be caught carrying a book under your arm unless you were going to class."[46] But he liked to take a book, along with his fishing pole, and Joran, too, sometimes, and hike to a favorite spot along Clark's Fork, the river that ran down from the mountains alongside the university campus and through the city of Missoula. Those things represented the best life he could imagine.

In 1924 and 1925, however, D'Arcy was concerned primarily about money, or his lack of it, and how that would determine his future. Someone other than his father was now leasing his land, and he wrote several times to the agency to see if anything could be done to ensure more regular payments. Encouraged by Merriam, he began to consider the possibility of spending his senior year of college at Amherst. That would require cash, however, and his only tangible asset was his land. His sisters had already sold portions of their allotments and D'Arcy began to consider that possibility. If he could get two or three thousand dollars for his land, he could go almost anywhere.

With this in mind, he wrote once again to the agency and asked for help in obtaining a fee patent. His letter was a passionate one. He wanted to use his land as collateral for a loan, or even, perhaps, sell it outright, to further his education. "I'm into this thing heart and soul," he wrote to Superintendent Charles Coe. "I want to grasp every possible advantage in getting my education. It is the best thing I can get out of my youth . . . when everything I ever do in the future depends on how I train and equip myself now."[47] Because D'Arcy was not yet twenty-one, however, Coe advised him to wait one more year, then apply again. He had no choice—he would have to stay at Montana for his senior year. Perhaps he could go away for graduate study.

D'Arcy filed for the fee patent on his land just one month after his twenty-first birthday, on February 14, 1925. Once again he had to justify his request, and he wrote on his application that he hoped to go to an eastern college or to Europe to do graduate work.[48] This time his application was approved and, with few regrets, he sold his allotment.

But events conspired against him. His grandfather Isidore died early that spring and his death affected D'Arcy profoundly. He began to skip classes; he spent hours in the library instead, reading and writing poetry. Finally the dean put him on temporary suspension.[49] He would not graduate in June after all. Once again he was forced to rethink his options.

The hours D'Arcy spent in the library were not a total loss, however. He wrote a poem as a tribute to his grandfather and won first prize in a statewide contest sponsored by the *Missoulian,* the local newspaper.[50] Entitled "Old Isidore," the poem celebrated the old man as a Montana pioneer, one whose life had given shape to the frontier, and it was by far the best thing he had yet written. An eloquent goodbye to his grandfather, it was also to be his farewell to Montana.

Despite D'Arcy's failure to graduate, Professor Merriam was eager to have his talented pupil expand his horizons. The fact that D'Arcy had not graduated made little difference; he could earn his bachelor's degree at Oxford. The more he and D'Arcy discussed the possibility of such a trip, the more real that possibility became. The several thousand dollars D'Arcy had received from the sale of his land seemed enough to take him anywhere. In the letter of introduction that Merriam wrote for him to present at Oxford, his mentor described D'Arcy as "a student of sincere purpose, of considerable promise, and of devotion to literature, . . . who as a writer of verse reveal[s] penetrating imagination, delicate fancy, strong and controlled emotion, and originality. He [writes] prose of quiet energy and subtlety of expression."[51] When D'Arcy finally applied for his passport, everything that needed doing had been done. The summer seemed endless as he waited until it was time to go.

2

Surrounded No More

D'Arcy McNickle (a.k.a. Dahlberg) sailed for England on the North German liner *Columbus* on September 30, 1925. The German ship provided his first encounter with foreigners en masse, and he was not above a degree of condescension as he observed the beer-drinking propensities and social characteristics of his fellow passengers. He noted smugly that a string quartet played at dinner with "Teutonic heaviness," and "the fiddle notes are full of wobbled bowings and slivers and yes, even bridge-riding." After a week of listening to the quartet's music making, he produced a diagnosis—"Beer and music! I wonder what manner of philosophical or chemical arrangement makes for such a combination." His critical observations, however, did not prevent him from enjoying the company of an attractive young fraulein whom he dubbed "a sister to the original Eve."[1]

As the ship approached England, he could barely contain his excitement. "This last night out," he wrote back to Missoula, "I shall not forget it soon. Moonless, starless, mist-hidden. A wind blowing neither warm nor cold but softly penetrating. And within myself these voices of song . . ." Then, impatiently pacing up and down the deck, he invoked the spirit of Walt Whitman: "And I was dreaming, sentimentally, of the day when Americans would be walking under strange stars, singing the songs of their own adventure. And I heard how Whitman has whispered down the ages—'I hear America singing—.' And it seemed, then, that such things would happen. Well, England tomorrow."[2]

Despite D'Arcy's high hopes for accomplishment in England, however, Oxford was a great disappointment. Perhaps Merriam had encouraged unrealistic expectations. D'Arcy had anticipated becoming part of a community of scholars, but he soon found himself discomfited by his fellow students' use of language itself. While his own writing, as Merriam had pointed out, was strong and subtle, he was ill prepared for the kind of sophisticated word games and verbal sparring that seemed to delight the others. He was homesick and lonely, and handicapped by his shyness. The damp cold of England's climate only added to his misery. As he recalled many years later, "The only time I felt warm at Oxford was when I drank steaming tea beside a glowing fireplace stacked with channel coal."[3] The luxury of such a fire was, however, beyond his modest means and he did not often indulge.

McNickle became even more unhappy when he discovered that Oxford would not accept all his academic credits. He was dismayed when he learned that it would take at least two more years to complete the work for his degree. Since he knew that he did not have enough money to stay in England that long, he never matriculated. He remained in England only through December, auditing lectures, exploring the libraries, and taking advantage of what study opportunities he could find on his own. By the end of the year he had moved to Paris, where he mingled with other expatriates of the "lost generation." He remained in Paris until the following May, then returned to New York. Although he apparently kept a diary during his months in Paris and later used some of the material in his writing, the diary itself was lost. The trip to Europe was not a happy experience, and he seldom referred to Oxford in later years except to say that he had been there.

McNickle spent most of the next decade in New York City, with only a brief seven-month interim in Philadelphia. During those Depression years he developed a political conscience and, writing in his diary, he gave shape to some of his ideas. As economic conditions worsened he became convinced that neither the Republicans nor the Democrats offered a real solution for the social and economic chaos that afflicted the country. The Bonus March of World War I veterans on Washington in 1932 and its violent aftermath provided stark evidence of the tragedy that faced the nation. What was needed, he thought, was a new devotion to selflessness, a new set of values to replace the grasping after "things" that had become the primary characteristic of American society. He was not, however, a radical political animal. He offered no panacea for how society ought to be organized, no theories of economic recovery that might take place without the assistance of increasingly acquisitive consumers. Nevertheless, he was convinced that the form of capitalism developing in the United States held no real promise for the American people. The forces of true happiness, he believed, were to be found elsewhere.[4]

Six years after his return, on a hot, steamy August afternoon in 1932, he began to write an assessment of his experiences since he had left Montana. By that time the country had reached the lowest point of the Great Depression, although it was not yet obvious to those living through it that the economy had bottomed out. Republicans and Democrats had just selected their presidential candidates, and Herbert Hoover and Franklin Roosevelt prepared to face each other in November. Although Hoover's attempts to promote economic recovery appeared bankrupt, no one knew whether Roosevelt could offer an alternative that would restore confidence and hope to millions of Americans.

Perhaps it was Walter Lippmann who provided the incentive for D'Arcy to begin his evaluation of those New York years. Lippmann wrote regularly in the *New York Herald Tribune* about the political and economic issues of the day, and D'Arcy read his column avidly. On July 26, 1932, in an article titled "Crisis and Renewal," Lippmann had stepped back from the day's events to take a longer view of the disruptions that the Depression had brought to American society. "This is a hard time," he wrote,

> for those who are irrevocably committed to . . . old arrangements, old prestige, old reputations, and old interests. It is a cruel and bitter time for those who are the present victims of disorder. But for the young and for those who are free in spirit it is a time of liberation and of opportunity. For them there remains, come what may, their own energy, and the richness of the earth, the heritage of invention and skill, and the corpus of human wisdom. They need no more.[5]

D'Arcy read Lippmann's words as a challenge. He was both young and free in spirit, and he was eager to seize the opportunity that Lippmann described. Two weeks later, in his diary, he began to frame his response. He wrote about where he had been and where, perhaps, he was going. He wanted to explore his own values in the light of recent history and to see how those values fit into the American scene.

As he began his account of the years that followed his return from Europe, McNickle recalled most clearly his sense of confusion about how he was going to make his way in a world that was so totally different from the world of his childhood. As his ship had approached New York, the city appeared in a haze, reflecting, so it seemed, his own lack of direction. He had no clear definition of who he was or what he wanted of life. Instead, he viewed himself as "an undesigned, unaccountable, unwitting accident in the laws of causation." Only two things stood out from that confusion. He knew that he wanted to write and that he did not want to return, as he put it, "to the scenes from which I had fled."[6] The past was painful, and the trauma of his parents' divorce still lay heavily upon him. He refused even to consider going back to St. Ignatius. In fact, the only remaining link to his life in Montana was Joran Birkeland.

When D'Arcy had departed for England in 1925, Joran remained at the university in Missoula where she received her B.A. degree in English the following June. Then she decided, after some urging by D'Arcy, to join him in New York City. She also hoped to become a writer, and New York was the publishing center of the country. In what D'Arcy later considered further evidence of his confused state of mind, he talked to her of marriage. Joran, perhaps, was wiser than he; she was reluctant to make the commitment. She wanted time to live alone and establish herself in a job, "to gain a sense of control over her own future," as D'Arcy later wrote.[7] He was persuasive, however, and finally won her over. In November 1926, financed only by the money from a pawned watch, they were married.

The pressing need for a dependable income led McNickle to accept a job in Philadelphia as an automobile salesman, a far cry from what he really wanted to do, and he soon discovered that an income based on commissions was not very dependable. Even more important, he realized that selling automobiles represented the antithesis of his own personal values; it forced him into what he called "a daily betrayal of my birthright in opposition." This was his first experience in the world of high-pressure salesmanship aimed at a consumer society, and he was appalled and outraged at what was expected of him. "Everything I was called upon to do," he recalled, "was a violation of instinct and desire."[8]

Even after six years, writing about those months of trying to sell automobiles brought only bitter memories. High-pressure salesmanship as he experienced it was "unintelligent, wasteful, ruthless, animal, intent on driving every vestige of individual preference in matters of taste, modes of living, and cultural pursuits out of existence." And more than salesmanship itself was tainted. "Ideas of loyalty to a boss, of being on time, of 'boosting' God, country, and cowboy, of wearing a smile, of being 'regular,' of eschewing all mental activity that did not have to do with 'getting ahead'"—all these attitudes, it seemed, had evolved into a kind of national religion. They revealed a society "bent on exploiting every inch, every microscopic entity, of the known world in the interest of money."[9] He realized that he was somehow out of step with the modern economic rat race. He lacked the essential acquisitive instinct, and he held a set of values that were apparently contrary to those of most Americans.

Although several years had passed since his disastrous experience as an automobile salesman, D'Arcy's anger about it and about America's economic system was still very close to the surface as he began writing his response to Lippmann's challenge. He was particularly indignant about how some of the country's large corporations had cynically adopted a policy of "welfare capitalism," a prime example of what he called "the intellectual prostitution" of modern industry. It seemed to him that welfare capitalism, which combined the money-making motive with humanitarian doctrines of progress and social enlightenment, had produced a system which constituted the ultimate betrayal of the workers. Its seemingly benevolent tactics on behalf of employees, establishing such things as cafeterias, lounges, and employee newspapers, were "executed with such a magnanimous flourish and so successfully that intelligent people were convinced that our captains of industry were about to create an age of material well-being and universal happiness such as the world had never known." But the stock market crash and subsequent depression had shown America's industrial leaders to be "blundering opportunists, welchers, babbling panderers, senile optimists, contemptible bluffers."[10] The greed of its practitioners had revealed all the weaknesses of modern American capitalism.

McNickle had the advantage of hindsight, of course, when he confided these thoughts to his diary in 1932. All the anger, disappointment, and frustration of the past six years were contained in this single diatribe. By that time he realized that it was the nation's values, not his own, that had been misplaced. The rest of the country, not he, had embraced the wrong criteria for success, and from then on he claimed his "birthright in opposition." While a materialistic, consumer-oriented society could produce a great many "things," it could never produce enduring happiness for its people. If he had learned anything at all in the past six years, he told himself, it was to trust his own instincts as to what was good, even if it meant sacrificing money or position. He would hereafter follow his own inner voice. He agreed with Lippmann; new opportunities were at hand. He would be ready, but for what he could not yet imagine.[11]

McNickle had endured the job of selling automobiles for only seven months. Then, wisely, he returned to New York and switched his efforts to the publishing field. His income was not much improved, but at least he could maintain his personal integrity and be in touch with the world of letters. He worked briefly for the *Encyclopaedia Britannica* and for E. F. Houghton and Company, learning the details of the publishing trade. Then in 1929 he became an assistant to the managing editor at James T. White and Company, publishers of the *National Cyclopedia of American Biography*. In this new job he wrote and edited biographical articles and supervised proofing and book make-up. He especially enjoyed an assignment that gave him the opportunity to query his old mentor, Harold Merriam, about the origins of the *Frontier and Midland* (as the *Frontier* had become), which by then was a significant regional literary publication.[12]

Despite his financial concerns, McNickle was fascinated with the teeming life of New York City. He rode the subway and the ferries and walked the streets, collecting images for his writing in the little pocket notebook he always carried. He described the moods of the sky, and even in the city he anticipated the changing seasons. Babe Ruth was a national hero, and he and Joran cheered for the Yankees whenever they could afford a ticket to a ball game. They also went on picnics, and one particular outing rated a page in his diary. They had crossed the Hudson River to Lake Hopatcong, in New Jersey, looking for a little solitude. A policeman directed them to a road that led to the backside of a nearby hill, but, he warned them, "there's nothing there but trees." They found the spot and, as D'Arcy noted, "the trees were very good company."[13] They were unfamiliar with poison ivy, however, and Joran suffered the misery of a severe attack for the next several days.

D'Arcy and Joran found their greatest pleasure during those lean years in music, and whenever possible they attended the free concerts in Central Park. Music had been important to McNickle since his violin lessons at Chemawa, and it continued to be a source of delight. He and Joran bought their first radio in 1933 and shortly thereafter were thrilled as they listened to a live broadcast of Arturo Toscanini conducting Wagner's *Parsifal*. Beethoven's *Ninth Symphony* was equally moving, and Tchaikovsky's

Pathétique, D'Arcy wrote many years later, "came to me with new meaning, an immense power that I had never before appreciated."[14] He never lost his love for classical music, especially that which was written for the violin, and during those difficult years it provided food for his soul. His observations in his diary about various performances reveal him as a knowledgeable and sensitive critic.

Despite his experience in England, McNickle had not given up his desire to earn a college degree. In the spring of 1929 he enrolled in classes at Columbia University, where, for the first time since high school, he studied American history. Required reading for the course included V. L. Parrington's *Main Currents in American Thought* and Charles and Mary Beard's *Rise of American Civilization.* Not surprisingly, he preferred Parrington's approach to history through literature because, as he observed, Parrington "analyzes with a keenness and writes with a clarity that few historians of the American adventure have possessed." Not even the Beards, he thought, provided such "well-defined, reasoned, logical conceptions of the fundamental content of ideas which our country has enjoyed."[15]

Frederick Jackson Turner's essays describing the impact of the frontier on the development of American character were also required reading, and Turner's insight proved a revelation for D'Arcy. He had been aware since writing his grandfather's memorial that his family had themselves been pioneers on the western frontier, and now he was able to put them into a larger historical context. He also began to realize that western Montana and the Flathead Indians could provide endless material for his writing. Turner's influence was evident in what he later told John Collier (whom he would work for at the Bureau of Indian Affairs) about his work: "I am interested in writing about the West, not in the romantic vein in which it has been dealt with in the past but with the object of revealing, in fiction, as it has been revealed by historical writers of the past generation, the character which was formed by the impact of the Frontier upon the lives of the people who settled it."[16] Unfortunately, economic pressures forced an end to his course work at Columbia, and he never earned the degree that seemed so important to him.

D'Arcy and Joran were able to take one long vacation during the lean years they lived in New York. In the summer of 1931 they went to France, where McNickle attended classes at the University of Grenoble. How they financed such a trip, considering their hand-to-mouth existence, is puzzling, but William McNickle, D'Arcy's father, had died in November 1929, and the timing of their trip suggests that some of his estate went to D'Arcy.[17] Such an inheritance would have made the trip possible. He and Joran spent six weeks in France, and by the time they returned, he had acquired a fair command of the written and spoken French language.

Even though living in New York and traveling to Europe had broadened his horizons considerably, McNickle was hardly the urbane, civilized man he had hoped to become. Still awkward and shy with other people and lacking words for light conversation, he was painfully certain that his ineptitude was obvious to those around him. His self-consciousness surfaced in his diary as he recalled an incident that had occurred when he and Joran were in France. Some kind of unpleasantness had arisen between them when they were entertaining guests at dinner, and he had fled the house to escape his humiliation and to dissipate his anger. "It came to me suddenly as I walked," he recalled, "that I am in fact far from achieving ease of manner and speech. Why embarrassment and fright should seize me I cannot understand. Intellectually I am at ease with myself. But when I am confronted by strangers and must contribute to the occasion a ghastly ineptness overcomes me. I cannot find a single word to utter—or if I do I stutter."[18]

The incident gnawed at him for days. Aware of his lack of social graces, he wanted desperately to remake himself into a cultured man of the world. At first he had believed that he would automatically outgrow what he called "the crudities of youth," but they were still with him. In his own eyes he was a "breed" from the frontier, untutored in the ways of the world, and socially disadvantaged. He would have to come to terms somehow with his past before he could overcome his sense of inadequacy. Although he was dimly aware that respect for his own selfhood was the key, how to achieve that self-respect remained a mystery.[19]

The episode in France was but one incident that revealed a growing tension not only within D'Arcy himself but in his marriage. Neither he nor Joran had been prepared for their venture into matrimony, and he began to realize that Joran had been the wiser in her desire to postpone it. Their impetuous action had not been good for either of them. He was aware that many couples faced the same kinds of problems, but their own situation seemed singular. "I am quite sure," he wrote, "that our instance was unique in that we were both so miserably educated . . . in ways of living, of meeting people, of conducting ourselves even before each other."[20]

McNickle's personal problems were aggravated by economic ones as the Depression brought increasing financial hardship. He and Joran fell into arrears with the Internal Revenue Service and finally arranged to pay their twenty-eight-dollar tax obligation at five dollars per month. It was, as D'Arcy observed wryly, more tax than J. P. Morgan had to pay. Both he and Joran did pickup work, writing and editing, working part-time at home, and sometimes not working at all. They were increasingly aware of the despair that surrounded them. One morning D'Arcy narrowly missed being struck by a despondent victim of the stock market who had hurled himself out of an apartment window to the sidewalk below. It was an unnerving experience.[21]

Fortunately, use of the New York Public Library was free, and McNickle continued to read, both for pleasure and for edification. Like keeping a diary, reading had become an enduring habit. Benjamin Franklin's *Autobiography,* with its imperative for self-improvement, struck a responsive chord, but D'Arcy's interests were broad. They ranged from Keith Anderson's play, *Night over Taos,* to Jeliffe White's *Diseases of the Nervous System*. He also read any and all newspapers and magazines that came to hand. Among contemporary columnists, Walter Lippmann and Heywood Hale Broun spoke to him most directly, and he often quoted or paraphrased them in his diary as he tried to make sense of the political and economic turmoil around him. With little background in either political science or economics, he found himself intuitively agreeing with Lippmann's interpretation of events. He followed Lippmann into the ranks of

Roosevelt supporters after the presidential election of 1932, although before Roosevelt's nomination he had favored the other Democratic contender, Al Smith.[22]

Even though McNickle's personal fortunes were more or less at the mercy of the Depression, he remained determined to become a good writer and a caring husband. He scraped together enough money to enroll in a poetry class taught by Robert Frost at the New School for Social Research, and out of that class came a poem that reflected his hunger for a renewal of his relationship with Joran. It was titled "Gifts to Joran."

> The time has passed somehow. We sit here
> And time has passed with us. How is it so?
> All lovers should be matched like fighters in
> A ring where a gong marks off in sharp command
> The passing time. They can't forget that way
> To stand up to each other, pass and dodge,
> Give and take. All games, to be played right,
> Require rules and some impartial one
> To stand as arbiter of decisions, right or wrong.
> Lovers are lacking that and they forget.
>
> .   .   .   .
>
> These passing months should find us knowing more
> The sweetness and the thrill of freedom
> That first we knew exploring and delving into
> Friendship. Instead, these last months are monotone.
> We've tried to progress in as straight a line
> As possible; we've fought off curvature
> Of effort and resisted undue stress.
>
> .   .   .   .
>
> This morning you are in the hot city
> Bearing the madness of a usual day.
> And I, for a moment only, have time to pause
> And think on this. The months have passed and I

Have made no startling gift to bear against
The monotone, I have not made you laugh
With star-tears in your eyes. The time has passed
And it is easy to forget to love.

. . . .

This morning as I sit a moment here
My thoughts fly through the green world and away.
I go searching everywhere for gifts
To Joran, High Street in Oxford-town,
The ancient villages of France, the broad
Parisian boulevards; I search for words
Of beauty and delight; I think of strange
Alluring scents and things to feel and see,
And have upon the skin, or things to taste—
To find a gift for Joran—O, to pile
Silks and gems and soft perfumes and all
That gives the secret fancy warm delight.

. . . .

Enough and more my wandering thought brings home!
But these are not enough. There is no end
To fancy. Riches and mortal strength
Have limits at their best.
One gift I have for Joran. That today
I have remembered to love.[23]

Although McNickle produced other poetry and several short stories during the years of the Depression, his major literary effort at the time was focused on his first novel.[24] He did not realize it then, but writing the novel was to become his therapy. Imagining his past as fiction forced him to face the unhappy memories of his childhood and to understand and accept those memories as part of himself. Earlier he had run away. He had changed his name, sold his allotment, and wandered in far places. But through the act of returning in his imagination to Montana, he reclaimed a childhood that he had earlier rejected. The novel provided an essential step toward the development of his mature identity and his freedom.

McNickle began writing his first novel in the late 1920s, and he worked on it for at least five years. There is evidence in his papers of a number of revisions with different titles, as well as a complete handwritten manuscript titled "The Hungry Generations." The central plot originated in an actual event on the Flathead Reservation, and many of the characters were drawn from people he had known as a boy. The entire novel, in fact, is largely autobiographical. Archilde Leon, the hero, bears a striking resemblance to the author himself. He is a mixed-blood—his mother is Salish, his father Spanish—and he learned to play the violin when he was a student at an Indian boarding school in Oregon. He is, in fact, able to earn a living with his music, so he returns to St. Xavier, on the reservation, only to bid a final goodbye to his mother and to visit the mountains and streams of his childhood for the last time. He has little to say to his father, Max Leon, who is estranged from his mother and no longer lives with her.

Acceding reluctantly to his aging mother's desire that he accompany her on a last ritual hunt into the mountains before he goes away, Archilde becomes involved in the disappearance of a game warden. Archilde is at first suspected of foul play, although his mother actually kills the warden during their hunt. It is the second killing in as many minutes—the warden has just shot Archilde's brother, Louis, and his mother's action is instinctive. Before they return home, Archilde digs a shallow grave for the warden's body, which is soon covered with snow; Louis's body they carry with them for proper burial. Although the warden's body is not found until spring, his disappearance focuses suspicion on Archilde. Meanwhile, however, Archilde's father dies, leaving his estate to Archilde, who leaves Montana for France. Paris seems an odd choice within the context of the narrative, but "everyone" has told him that Paris is the center of the civilized world. He takes his violin with him, having grandiose visions of becoming a concert violinist. He intends to concentrate on his music.

Gradually, however, Archilde begins to doubt the conventional wisdom that took him so far from home. For several months he wanders through the streets and alleys near his rented room, trying to decide whether to continue his musical studies or return to Montana. He becomes increasingly unsure of his potential as a violinist, and eventually he is no longer attracted by the possibility. Painfully shy and self-conscious, he has only his books and his violin to keep him company. Although he meets an American girl, Claudia, who eases his loneliness, he finally realizes that Paris has nothing more to offer him.

Archilde returns to the Montana ranch, which was part of his inheritance, and there he becomes totally absorbed in the seasons of planting and harvesting. The warden's body has been found, however, and now Archilde is suspected of murder. He is eventually arrested and jailed for his presumed complicity. When the facts of the murder finally emerge during the trial and prove his innocence, he once more takes up his life on the ranch. There he reaps the summer's harvest and, in the novel's romantic conclusion, awaits Claudia's arrival on the next train. Far from being "surrounded," Archilde's hopes for the future are sustained by his faith that the white man's justice and his own hard work have triumphed over adversity.

This romantic and patently autobiographical story provides an unparalleled source of information about McNickle's early years, because almost every incident clearly derives from some element of his own childhood. Archilde's learning to play the violin in boarding school, his estrangement from his parents, his love of music, his disenchantment with the church, his brief encounter with prison life, and his Parisian adventure, all were part of D'Arcy's past.

This early draft of his novel, however, contains far more than boyhood recollections. It provides a number of clues relating to his personal growth and development during that period. That Archilde, for instance, discovers prejudice in an anti-Jewish context while he is in Paris and becomes aware of prejudice as a universal phenomenon, speaks to McNickle's own experience of it. Archilde also becomes aware of overt homosexuality for the first time. The derivation of other anecdotal material from McNickle's early years strongly suggests that the Paris episodes, too, depict actual events that had occurred while he was there.

One clue to McNickle's development through writing "The Hungry Generations" is his description of Archilde's changing response to history. Archilde recalls that he had read history in school as though it were a work of imagination; it had seemed to him that history consisted of stories someone had made up. While in Paris, however, Archilde arrives at a new perception of history. "It finally stuck in his head," McNickle wrote of Archilde, "that he was learning about actual happenings in the past." Historical reality acquired new meaning for Archilde, as it did for D'Arcy himself while he was reading Turner and Beard and praising Parrington's insights into the American past. From that time on, Archilde read history "with breathless excitement and complete absorption."[25] The roots of McNickle's later historical narratives about American Indians may well be found here, in Archilde's new understanding.

Another incident of particular interest in the manuscript results from Archilde's relationship with Claudia. When she discovers that he is part Indian, she inquires about his past, and her questions lead him into a painful recollection of his Indian mother. Archilde is disturbed particularly by the fact that he can no longer communicate with his mother, who had encompassed his whole world when he was a child. He asks himself how and why she has changed so much and finally he is forced to admit that it is he, not his mother, who has changed. "Not that I meant to or tried to in any particular way," Archilde recalls. "I wasn't ashamed of my blood to begin with because I never even thought about it. I didn't think about anything. It is only now that I have grown ashamed of it, now that I have seen things, as it were, for the first time. Now I do want to be somebody else."[26] He recalls the odor of smoked buckskin, which evoked her presence so strongly, and it has become intolerable.

Archilde's estrangement from his mother in "The Hungry Generations" suggests a change in McNickle's relationship with his own mother. Although he and Philomene had been very close when he was a boy, he had failed to maintain contact with her during his years in New York City, and he had no idea where she was. By the same token, his family did not know where he was living. When his father died, his sister Ruth had told the local newspaper that he was in Chicago, a wild guess. There had been no communication with any of his family for years—he had fled from them all.

As McNickle worked through the several revisions of the novel, however, Archilde's perceptions of his mother begin to change. Finally, in *The Surrounded* (the novel "The Hungry Generations" eventually became), he admits that when he was a boy his mother had become an embarrassment to him. But when he returns to say his final goodbye, he notices for the first time the respect given her by her Indian relatives. Gradually he comes to appreciate the reality of her life, a reality that is again evoked by the smell of smoked buckskin.

What seems evident in the series of manuscript revisions that led Archilde to a reevaluation of his mother and her people is that McNickle himself was discovering a new dimension of his own past. He became curious about his tribal origins, as he had never been before. He wrote to the Flathead Agency to inquire into his mother's whereabouts (she was in Milwaukee, Wisconsin, at that point), and asked for information about the nature of the tribe's income, a share of which he had continued to receive from time to time.[27] He took advantage of the opportunities available to him for research at Columbia University and began to read about the Indians, the fur traders, and the early explorers. The creative process was leading him to the discovery of his own place in history.

McNickle first submitted the novel to Harcourt, Brace and Company in 1929, the same year that Oliver La Farge's *Laughing Boy* won a Pulitzer Prize. At that time he was optimistic about its chances, for there appeared to be a growing interest in Indians in the public press. Although his first manuscript was not accepted, the editorial comments were encouraging. They described the novel as "the story of an Indian wandering between two generations, two cultures; excellent. . . . A new territory to be explored, ancient material used for a different end." Then they added prophetically, "Perhaps [it is] the beginning of a new Indian literature."[28] The editor did not, however, believe that the work was ready for publication.

Over the next five years, as McNickle wrote and rewrote the story of Archilde Leon, a number of publishers looked at the manuscript, and they all rejected it. Their editorial comments were often positive, however, and McNickle was willing to put in whatever time was needed to perfect his craft. He could see that with each revision the work was better than it had been before. He continued to revise it, and eventually he hired an agent on a contingency basis to submit it to publishers.

But he faced a growing collection of rejection slips. In 1931, K. S. Crichton, of Scribner's, wrote to him, "This is one of the most baffling stories we have read in a long time. In spots it is distinctly amateurish, but in essence it has something organically alive which shows a real narrative sense. Unfortunately we cannot use it, but we are very much interested in your work, and hope that you will send us anything you may do."[29] Such praise, faint though it was, kept him going.

Editorial comments from Macmillan in 1933 confirmed his belief that he was making progress. Several members of the staff read the manuscript this time, and they considered it at length before rejecting it. In a letter addressed to "Miss D'Arcy Dahlberg," they wrote, "We feel that you have a very vivid piece of work, and that Archilde is a most appealing figure. We liked a lot of things about the book, but we could not fit it in with our list."[30] It was some small comfort that the editors at Macmillan, like those at Scribner's, asked to see whatever he might produce in the future.

Macmillan's rejection arrived just days after Christmas, and D'Arcy was very disappointed. But he soon had a new distraction, as well as a new incentive. Joran gave birth to their first child, a girl, on January 2, 1934, and with that as inspiration, he began working on yet another revision.

Two significant changes occurred in D'Arcy's life about this time, one before and one after the baby's arrival. The first sheds additional light on the gradual resolution of his inner conflict about his own identity, as well as on the naming of his first child. In October 1933, with the baby on the way, D'Arcy changed his surname from Dahlberg back to McNickle.

The desire to return to his legal name was undoubtedly intensified by his work on the novel. He was registering to vote in the November 1933 mayoral election in New York City when, on a seeming impulse, he signed his name D'Arcy McNickle, not D'Arcy Dahlberg. Some time later he tried to explain the matter to John Collier. It happened, he said, because of his anticipated fatherhood. "The change would better have been made some years ago," he admitted, "but until the time came to consider which name was to be perpetuated, I had not thought much about it."[31] This echoes Archilde's observation that he had "never even thought about" his Indian identity. But writing about Archilde as a mixed-blood had heightened his awareness of his own heritage, and when the baby arrived, she was named Antoinette Parenteau McNickle, which included *both* of D'Arcy's family names. Her parents called her Toni.

McNickle's resumption of his legal name furthered the healing process within him. His parents' divorce and his assumption of the Dahlberg name had broken the original family bonds, but a partial restoration was taking place through the creation of "The Hungry Generations." As he revised the novel and Archilde Leon moved toward reconciliation with both his mother and his father, McNickle was doing the same. Although his father had died, McNickle never again lost track of his mother. The family itself had disintegrated, however, and despite D'Arcy's resumption of the McNickle name, he made no attempt, then or later, to restore his relationship with his sisters.

At another level, too, McNickle's name change was significant. Using his legal name opened the way for a reaffirmation of his Indian ancestry. D'Arcy Dahlberg had not been even partially an Indian. In fact, D'Arcy Dahlberg was a legal fiction. But D'Arcy McNickle had inherited Indian blood through his mother, and this was an essential part of his identity. Not only was he D'Arcy McNickle, he was also an enrolled member of the Flathead Tribe.

Even so, he chose to remain at a distance from the reservation. He was not a native son but an adopted one and he did not involve himself in tribal affairs. There is also the possibility that ongoing family conflicts kept him away from St. Ignatius. Although Indians generally claim tribal membership as their primary identity, McNickle was more "Indian" than "Flathead." This perception of nontribal "Indianness" was later reflected in his labors on behalf of such pan-Indian activities as the National Congress of American Indians and the American Indian Chicago Conference. Nevertheless, writing "The Hungry Generations" had ignited his interest in his Indian ancestry, and this in turn led to important changes in the direction of his life.

D'Arcy's resumption of his McNickle name in 1933 was followed within a year by a second major change as the focus of his novel continued to shift. He had taken the earlier title, "The Hungry Generations," from Keats's "Ode to a Nightingale," in which the poet envies the bird's freedom to escape the world where old age, decay, and death seem inevitable.[32] Archilde, as one of the "hungry generation," does indeed escape what seemed to McNickle to be the final dissolution of the Indians' ancient life. McNickle used another phrase from the same ode, "amid the alien corn," as the title of one of the short stories he wrote during this period.

But with each revision of the story, he had narrowed and altered the novel's plot and worked deeper into Archilde's situation as a mixed-blood Indian entangled in the clash of cultures. These changes reflected the circumstances of his own birth and childhood. By exploring the various possibilities open to Archilde, as well as his own emotions and his determination not to return to the scenes of his childhood, McNickle ultimately created a new story that was quite different from the original narrative.

The fantasy ending of "The Hungry Generations" had reflected the American dream and, by implication, the fulfillment of D'Arcy's father's expectations. It was also an attempt to resolve the inner conflict that had resulted from his parents' divorce. But in revising the work, McNickle began to question the validity of Archilde's experience as he had written about it. What if Archilde had not left the reservation and gone to Paris? What if he had decided to stay on the reservation? What happened to those boys he had known at school who did stay at home? What was their future? He knew the answers to those questions instinctively; that was why he had fled, and why he refused to go back to Montana. There was no future there for the young men who remained. The essential truth about Archilde's situation was not a "happily-ever-after" fairy tale but a deeply moving tragedy. He himself had escaped, but he knew that if he had gone back to the reservation his future would never have been as he had imagined it for Archilde. He would have been surrounded, by the mountains, by the old traditions, and by the white people's culture and institutions. By 1934 that was the story he had written. He called it *The Surrounded*.

The much-revised novel, with the entire Paris section deleted, was only about half the length of the earlier one. The plot lines of the two versions ran roughly parallel until Max's death. From there on, McNickle wrote a new story. Instead of going to Paris, Archilde stays in Montana and in the spring, when the body of the game warden is discovered, the search for the murderer is renewed. Once again Archilde is the prime suspect. Unfortunately, his mother dies before the facts are revealed and Sheriff Quigley, the archetypal enemy, is convinced that Archilde is the guilty party.

Archilde's mother, Faithful Catharine, is the prime mover of the story to this point, and as she dies she reaffirms her renunciation of Christianity. After her death, Elise La Rose, Archilde's distant cousin and granddaughter of old, blind Modeste, a tribal elder, carries the action forward and precipitates the final scene. Elise is the complete opposite of Claudia in "The Hungry Generations," and very different also from Faithful Catharine. She had been a student at the boarding school in Oregon when Archilde was there, but, true rebel that she is, she had run away. Scornful of all authority, Elise drinks, smokes, and swears, and she has an unsavory reputation among both the Indians and the whites of St. Xavier. Also, Elise is estranged from her world; the old ways will not serve her, nor will the new. As Modeste had explained to the others in a scene where Catharine was ceremonially whipped to atone for killing the game warden, "The old law is not used, and nobody cares about the new."[33] Elise's vitality, wildness, and sensuality, however, attract Archilde, who is strangely passive in her presence, just as he had been when faced with his mother's demand that he accompany her on the hunt. When Sheriff Quigley finally closes in, Elise spirits Archilde away into the mountains, and in the final episode of the novel it is she, not Archilde, who kills the sheriff. But in the end, "Archilde, saying nothing, extended his hands to be shackled."[34] Nevertheless, while Catharine and Elise are the actors and Archilde passively responds to them, it is Archilde's growth and his fate that remain the core of the novel. The young ones are still the hungry generation, and they are surrounded by an alien world.

McNickle was confident that the novel was much improved, and he took the chance of resubmitting it to publishers who had previously expressed an interest in his work. One of those publishers collected the various comments of his editorial staff and summarized them in a "Manuscript Report," which he sent to McNickle. The report began this way: "This book, submitted to us originally under the title The Hungry Generations, is back again, vastly improved over its original version. As a matter of fact, the novel is so much improved that many of the defects which it originally had but which were obscurely imbedded in the book because of its general confusion, can now be seen in true perspective."[35]

The report then suggested four main points for consideration. First, the basic conflict between an emerging religious theme and the earlier generational theme needed to be resolved or integrated. Second, while McNickle had skillfully pared the narrative down to a basic skeleton and eliminated much of its confusion, he now needed to flesh it out and give it shape. Third, the non-Indian characters needed clearer definition as an effective balance to the more finely drawn Indians in the story. And fourth, the climax should be more fully developed so that the "tragic implications of Archilde's failure" could carry the full impact of the plot. The publisher concluded, "There are other smaller matters, but these are the important points. I believe McNickle can carry out these changes successfully and that with them the book stands an excellent chance of making a real mark. It will be one of the best novels ever written about the American Indian, and the essential poignancy of its theme will find a wide audience."[36]

Even before he had a chance to work through these changes, however,

McNickle believed, for a brief moment, that his dreams for publication were about to be realized. One of the publishers who had received the latest revision was Civici, Friede. On October 29, 1934, he received a letter from their editor Harry Block, along with an unsigned contract, to begin negotiations to publish. His hopes soared. A few weeks later, however, on February 5, Block wrote to tell him that the editorial board had changed its collective mind and decided not to publish the novel after all. Block was almost as disappointed as McNickle. He believed in D'Arcy's talents and in the novel and he had fought for its acceptance, but the board had decided otherwise. He was unable to give McNickle any real reason for its rejection and McNickle was devastated. Publication had seemed assured, but once again the possibility had evaporated.[37]

Nevertheless, McNickle knew by now that he had a good story, and he had come closer than ever to having a signed contract. Now he would get to work on those latest editorial suggestions. He began by integrating the two main themes. Max Leon, Archilde's Spanish father, assumed a pivotal role, and relating to Max in different ways were Father Grepilloux, the Jesuit priest at St. Xavier, and George Moser, the white trader who had been the primary villain in "The Hungry Generations." These three represented the white people's culture. McNickle now realized that all of the "civilizing" institutions of white society—the trader, the church, the white settlers, and the government—were the true antagonists. By realigning these relationships and more clearly depicting the various non-Indian characters, he defined the basic conflict in the story as ethnic and cultural, white versus Indian, rather than narrowly religious or generational. The new focus allowed him to define both the Indian and the non-Indian characters in the story more fully.

This was particularly true of Archilde's Salish mother, who in "The Hungry Generations," had been a relatively minor character. Her role in *The Surrounded,* however, is crucial. In her smoked buckskin, she becomes the primary carrier of the old Indian culture. Faithful Catharine was a small child when the friars first came to the Mission Valley. Baptized at that time and educated in the mission school, she has been, in the church's view, a model convert. But although she has followed precisely the rituals and teachings of the church, she has also clung to the old ways of living, and as a result she is much revered by her own people. Through her, Archilde gradually becomes aware of the life she represents, and he learns to value the stories and ceremonies that, he comes to realize, are part of himself. As he watches his mother prepare his nephew Narcisse for a tribal dance, he senses the ancient traditions that guide her hands. He sees that in this setting she is "pleased with her duties in the way that only an old art or an old way of life, long disused, can please the hand and heart returning to it." From that time on, he begins to appreciate her place as a matriarch within the community of her own people. In one scene, he watches the old ones dance: "[Archilde] felt those people move in his blood. There in his mother's tepee he had found unaccountable security. It was all quite near, quite a part of him: it was his necessity, for the first time."[38]

Catharine conveys the traditional Salish culture throughout the novel, and her estrangement from Archilde's father provides one element of the story's basic conflict. Even more significant is her eventual estrangement from the church. Although she confesses her role in the murder of the game warden, the church's absolution fails to give her the peace of mind she seeks. Finally she dreams three times of the white man's God telling her that in order to go to the Indians' heaven she must renounce her baptismal vows. This she does when she asks Modeste to administer the traditional expiation of the whip. "In the old days you were whipped and no one spoke of it again," she tells him. "The heart was free." Modeste and the elders finally agree; the old way was best in some circumstances. After Catharine is ceremonially whipped, they are all renewed. "Those old people turned back on the path they had come and for a while their hearts were lightened. The old lady, with the red stripes of the whip on her back, slept without dreaming."[39]

McNickle turned to traditional Salish folk stories and ethnographic material to fill in what the "Manuscript Report" had called the skeleton of the story. Here he drew on material he had discovered in the library at Columbia University, transcriptions of Salish folk tales that recalled stories he had heard as a child. He used several of them at crucial points in the novel, where they are told in a traditional setting by the tribal elders. In a perceptive analysis of the role of this material in the novel, the literary scholar John Purdy has described McNickle's innovative skill in recreating the context of a ceremonial feast for the old people's storytelling. While such a setting had always been an integral part of the storytelling event, it was generally lost in the reproduction of anthropological transcriptions.[40] McNickle's traditional setting for those stories provided yet another dimension of the disappearing Salish culture that he was describing in *The Surrounded*.

As McNickle worked his way through repeated revisions of Archilde's story, he was inevitably forced to question the rationale of his own flight from Montana and his determination not to return. As Father Grepilloux had pointed out to Max, Archilde had come to a place where the road of his life divided. "He belongs to a new time," the Father had said. "He may not stay in the valley, and it makes no difference whether he does or not; it is what he makes of himself that will count. It will be felt by all."[41] In his fiction, McNickle explored those options. He himself could have stayed in Montana, farmed his allotment, lived as his father had lived before him, and perhaps become a successful rancher. True, there probably would have been little place in his life for music if he had stayed. He had never played the violin at home—his father might have laughed at him if he had. But it would not have been a bad life, to become a respected landowner. In fact, that was what the Indian Bureau had wanted for all Indians since the time of the Dawes Act, and in "The Hungry Generations," McNickle had chosen that road for Archilde.

Another road for young men on the reservation was to revert to Indian ways, to go "back to the blanket," as Max scornfully described it. The most crucial element in D'Arcy's revision of the novel was to have Archilde, along with his nephews Mike and Narcisse, follow this road rather than the white man's. Archilde does not deliberately choose this alternative; he seems, rather, to be moved by forces that gradually overcome his ability to choose otherwise. The two versions of the novel explore these options, the one romantic and unrealistic, the other tragic but all too possible from McNickle's point of view. McNickle had pointed to divergent roads, and neither held hope for Archile's future.

A third option, one McNickle only alluded to in fiction, was the one he himself chose. He actually did the romantic, implausible thing. Like Archilde, he went to Paris. But he did not return to the reservation. Since his high school days he had been oriented toward an urban rather than a rural environment. He had learned to love music and drama and the excitement of the city. Although he could envision no possibilities for his future in either place when he returned to the United States, he knew that he would not go back to Montana. His description of himself in 1926 as unformed and accidental was perceptive. He believed in his ability to become something else, a good writer perhaps, but even if he failed, he would not return to the place from which he had fled.

These were the options that McNickle explored as he wrote first "The Hungry Generations" and then *The Surrounded*. As he finished the novel, he could look back with some perspective and see both his boyhood and the reservation in a new light, not as a child but as a man. Those ten years since he left the reservation had been painful, but they were vital and creative in his life. The published novel shows how far he had come.

McNickle was not the only mixed-blood to be aware of the literary possibilities of reservation life at that time. Mourning Dove's *Cogewea, the Half-Blood: A Depiction of the Great Montana Cattle Range,* published in 1927, is a far cry from McNickle's more sophisticated novel, yet they are both set on the Flathead Reservation in western Montana.[42] The protagonist in both is a mixed-blood, or "breed," and both authors innovatively use folk material to elucidate their characters and plot. Other Native American authors who published novels in the 1920s and 1930s were John Milton Oskison (Cherokee), who wrote three novels about the Oklahoma frontier, and John Joseph Mathews (Osage), who published his only novel, *Sundown,* in 1934. Scant evidence exists that any of these authors knew of the others' work at the time they were writing, however, and there is little similarity between their work and McNickle's.

Critics of modern Native American literature have found a likely source for McNickle's narrative style in the work of Ernest Hemingway and others of Gertrude Stein's "lost generation." Particularly suggestive of Hemingway is a quote taken by John Purdy from "The Hungry Generations": "Archilde had a knack of speaking in simple plain phrases that brought his story before his listeners with the greatest clearness."[43] McNickle wrote as Archilde spoke, in concise, straightforward, unambiguous prose. Much of McNickle's dialogue in *The Surrounded* brings Hemingway's work to mind. McNickle was undoubtedly familiar with the work of America's expatriate writers, some of whom he had perhaps met while he was in Paris. He knew the work of contemporary regional authors as well and would have included himself among them. The general outlook of "The Hungry Generations," however, shows little evidence of the disillusionment that characterized the "lost generation." Only as he had his disastrous adventure as a car salesman and then worked through revisions of the manuscript did he begin to question the values of mainstream America. McNickle's narrative style, as critics have pointed out, was undoubtedly influenced by his contemporaries, and so, perhaps, was the "return of the native" theme. But his subject matter, the mixed-blood Indian's discovery of his essential identity through returning to the reservation, and his subsequent recasting of tribal culture in a positive light, was uniquely his own.[44]

McNickle's frustration in getting his novel published was matched over the years by his growing pile of rejection slips. Deciding that a new agent might be able to offer a fresh approach to the market, in April 1935 he gave the manuscript to Ruth Rae, a young New Yorker whose enthusiasm and faith in his work provided a welcome antidote for his bruised ego. Rae was optimistic about selling the novel and perhaps some of his short stories as well. Her first success for him was to place a piece called "Meat for God" with *Esquire* magazine. *Esquire* not only ran the story in its issue of September 1935, it also named McNickle "Esquire's Discovery of the Month."

McNickle received the grand total of seventy-five dollars for that effort, and despite his own need, he was so excited about having something published that he offered half of it to Rae. He knew that she had worked very hard on his behalf, and he was grateful. Rae accepted her 10 percent commission but refused his further generosity. She would not accept it now, she told him, because she expected to make lots of money on him in the future.[45]

Then, not content to rest with her success, Rae took several of his stories to Constance Lindsay Skinner, an editor at Farrer and Rinehart. Skinner immediately shared Rae's enthusiasm for McNickle's work. Skinner's father had been a fur trader, and she, too, had grown up on the frontier. McNickle's stories captured the essence of people and places she herself had known firsthand. Writing directly to him, she praised the stories she had read, then asked if he would be interested in contributing to a series of books that her publisher was preparing on the rivers of North America. Of course he would be interested, McNickle replied; he would especially like to write about the Columbia and Saskatchewan rivers and the fur traders who had explored them. His mother was Cree, he explained, and her family, too, had participated in the fur trade. Although he could not identify the specific Indian element of his heritage, he told Skinner, "The stories and songs of those people were the first I ever heard."[46] The opportunity to write about them was immensely appealing.

Although Skinner was impressed with McNickle's narrative sense and his creative ability, she realized that his writing skills were still in a formative stage and that he seemed torn between telling a good story and delivering a sermon. Her observation about the nature of his writing was prophetic. "I can't foresee yet whether you'll go 'artist' or 'preacher,' creativist or scold, but I hope, of course, that you'll hitch your wagon to a star."[47] McNickle recognized the truth of her assessment. He decided, for the moment at least, that whatever his message, it could be conveyed more effectively through the dramatic power of his art than through overt sermonizing. He began to plan his research for the river book and Skinner promised to do what she could to get his other stories published.

Despite the energetic efforts of Rae and Skinner, however, a contract to publish *The Surrounded* still eluded him. The unhappy fact was that the Depression had dealt a near-mortal blow to the publishing industry, and very little new work was being accepted, even that of authors who already had books in print. Those years were the worst possible time for McNickle or anyone else to try to sell a first novel.[48]

The money from *Esquire* did not, of course, go very far toward paying the bills for his growing family. To make his financial situation even worse, he had a terminal falling-out with James T. White and Company, and he was not able to find enough free-lance editing to pay the rent. Although he had applied to John Collier for work with the Bureau of Indian Affairs, nothing had come of his application. By August 1935, he was so desperate that he borrowed twenty-five dollars from the Authors League Fund (he had joined the League in February 1934) to keep a roof over his family's heads.[49]

Even though the summer and fall of 1935 were the worst months of the Depression for D'Arcy and Joran, the publication of "Meat for God" that September marked the beginning of their recovery. His work on Skinner's rivers project was short-lived, however. He had submitted his application for the new Federal Writers Project (FWP) being organized under the Works Progress Administration, and early in September he received notice that he had been accepted. The FWP assigned him to the administrative staff in Washington, D.C., and by the end of that month, he had moved his family to the nation's capital. He could barely contain his excitement. He wrote jubilantly to Constance Skinner that he would be involved in writing and editing the new State Guide series, working primarily with material relating to Indians and anthropology. "We're going to have a lot of Indian material and I'll have a chance to take a hand in it, probably working under a trained anthropologist," he told her. "And this, as I have just learned, will probably result in a permanent job at the Indian Office."[50] His annual salary of twenty-six hundred dollars was more money than he had seen in quite some time.

More good news was yet to come. Early in December, Ruth Rae wrote that she had finally sold *The Surrounded*. Dodd, Mead and Company had bought it and had announced a publication date of February 14, 1936. McNickle could hardly believe that the months and years of hard work had paid off, and that he would finally see his novel in print. Unfortunately, in the six years since Oliver La Farge had won the Pulitzer Prize for *Laughing Boy,* public concern for Indian affairs had been largely eclipsed by the Depression. Potential buyers were too full of their own problems to be interested in Indians, and sales were disappointing. After its initial publication, *The Surrounded* was ignored until its reprinting by the University of New Mexico Press in 1978. By that time an entirely new audience was ready for it.

Nevertheless, McNickle found some consolation in the reviews. La Farge himself wrote in the *Saturday Review* that *The Surrounded* should be added "to the small list of creditable modern novels using the first Americans as theme." He concluded, "Perhaps the most interesting aspect of Mr. McNickle's book is his success in catching the whole in small compass, by the exercise of a thoroughly artistic selection and writing of such sort that the reader is primarily interested in an excellent story as such, and only secondarily in the background, which he gets in proper balance." Mary Heaton Vorse, who was editor of the Indian Bureau's newsletter *Indians at Work,* reviewed the story for the *New Republic* and called it "one of the few Indian novels where the Indian has not been treated with sentimentality and where the whole course of life on an Indian reservation is portrayed with unfailing truthfulness."[51]

However, not all the reviewers responded positively. Florence Milner wrote in the *Boston Transcript:* "The book is full of interesting information, [but] some of it is not clearly related to the main trend of action. . . . Stories are introduced, more for preserving bits of folklore than as a moving part of the story, which is often held up by the telling."[52]

Fred T. Marsh, reviewing the book for the *New York Times,* was more perceptive: "For all its deftly interpolated bits of background and folklore, this is a very modern, very youthful novel. . . . Without losing sight of his people, Mr. McNickle makes us think we understand them because he relates them to universal problems, intensified here in a special situation."[53]

Marsh considered the work an unusual and finished first novel, not without its faults but well worth the time needed to give it a careful reading. Archilde's story, he felt, was a tragedy that raised questions with no answers, but which nevertheless needed to be asked.

Constance Skinner read the book straight through and wrote to McNickle as soon as she finished. It was two o'clock in the morning, she told him, and she had just turned the last page. Very perceptively, she had picked up on the crucial symbol of Archilde's estrangement. "I smelled smoke-tanned buckskin suddenly in your book. The odor was in my nostrils some time before I was wholly aware of it, sniffed, and queried, '*What* is that smell?'" His treatment of the church, she thought, was especially effective:

> The priests are true, like the other people, and one pities them at their unselfish, holy & profitless task of "spoiling good pagans to make bad Christians." . . . It is the life itself, (as I know, not from books), the kind priestly mind, desiring to understand, *believing* it does, while unable, of course, to change the scent, to overcome smoked buckskin (50,000 years in the smoke) with medieval incense.[54]

To Skinner, the story was so honest in its depiction of the Indians' dilemma that it gave her "a bad heartache" (she forgave him for inflicting such pain), and once again she promised to do what she could to ensure the author's success.

McNickle's narrative about the mixed-blood Indians on the Flathead Reservation elicited interesting comments from some of the whites who had been McNickle's neighbors on the reservation. J. Verne Dusenberry, who had moved to St. Ignatius in 1934 and so had not met McNickle at the time, wrote to applaud the novel and to tell him of the local response. Not surprisingly, *The Surrounded* had created quite a stir locally, with everyone trying to identify the characters and scenes. Most of those who read the novel thought that it was an honest, if somewhat painful, depiction of life as it really was on the reservation. George Beckwith, a prominent local storekeeper who declared that it was "sympathetic, searching, and utterly honest," claimed to have identified all the characters except the merchant Moser who, according to the amused Dusenberry, was drawn in part from Beckwith himself. The local people who remembered D'Arcy as a boy were eager to claim their acquaintance with one of their own who had achieved some degree of celebrity. The only disapproval, and Dusenberry knew of it only through hearsay, came from Father Taelman, the Jesuit priest, who reportedly thought that D'Arcy had "gone completely mad."[55]

Dusenberry urged McNickle to return to the reservation, if only for a vacation. Changes were coming swiftly, and at the same time there was resistance to change. A newly formed tribal council was moving the people toward self-government, and, he reported, "Some of the mixed-bloods are reacting rather unfavorably to the responsibility, all of which merely deepens the antagonism between them and the whites. The old ones are simply bewildered. I do think that there is going to be some good material out of this for another story."[56]

Despite Dusenberry's urging, McNickle put the invitation aside. He did not return to St. Ignatius until 1946, and then only for a brief visit to attend his sister Ruth's funeral. He had little reason to go back. His other sister, Florence, had moved to Canada in 1921. His father, William, was dead. His mother, Philomene, who had never settled down, was living by this time in Portland, Oregon. McNickle's growing interest in the Native American cause would lead him far away from St. Ignatius and the valley of the Flathead Indians, although he would devote the rest of his life to their well-being.

3

The Collier Excitement

As McNickle had anticipated, his job with the Federal Writers Project, coupled with his growing concern about Indians, soon led to his employment by the Bureau of Indian Affairs (BIA). His interest in Indian anthropology, which had begun in the late 1920s with his work on *The Surrounded,* achieved clearer definition while he was writing biographical sketches for the *National Cyclopedia of American Biography* (NCAB). His contact with Harold Merriam at the University of Montana had offered him a look back over his shoulder at the past, but his future direction was presaged by a brief but intense correspondence in 1934 with William Gates, the subject of another NCAB essay.

William Gates was an anthropologist associated with Johns Hopkins University.[1] A specialist in linguistics, he was best known for his field work on the Mayan culture in Mexico, and NCAB had solicited him for autobiographical information. McNickle wrote the biography based on the data Gates submitted, then sent it to him for correction before passing it on to the next level of NCAB editors. Gates returned the essay to McNickle with appropriate comments and corrections. He apparently considered himself an iconoclast among anthropologists, and his writing revealed an original cast of mind that appealed to McNickle, who impulsively decided to do something entirely beyond the scope of his position. He wrote to Gates, asking for employment.

McNickle was aware of the breach of protocol, and he apologized to Gates for his "hell of a nerve" in writing. Nevertheless, he hoped that Gates would at least read his letter. "[It has been my very good fortune]," he explained, "to have poured over the rich material you sent us for compiling a biography of yourself. . . . This letter has nothing to do with James T. White & Co., but I hope it will have something to do with me, and that you will not count it an imposition—that you will withhold it from the waste paper basket at least until you have read it." He then introduced himself to Gates as "one of the original Americans." "I am an Indian, a breed rather, for I had a Scotch-Irish father and a French-Canadian (that is, French-Cree) mother. I do not know the proportion in which the bloods are mixed on my mother's side, and probably no one will ever resolve the question."[2]

McNickle then tried to explain the impulse that had led him to write. He told Gates that he was attracted to the anthropologist's work with the Maya and to his "vigorous, gristled" writing about it. Would there be any possibility at all that he might need some kind of service that McNickle could provide? McNickle admitted that he was not an anthropologist, nor would he be able to leave his young family to work in the field. "I have not the special training which the work requires," he told Gates, "and I don't believe I have the kind of mentality which gets pleasure out of unknotting perplexities. . . . But I wonder if there might be something I could do, if you should find this application creditable."[3]

He then told Gates of his own writing and of his growing desire to work creatively with Indian material. "Are there any separate tales or episodes which might be exhumed and saved from a second burial in a Ph.D. thesis?" he wondered. "I could not undertake to write learnedly in the field, but neither do I mean to vulgarize the material for Boy Scout publications and their kind." Although he had no clear idea of how his skills might be put to use in anthropological field work, he would offer his services to this man whom he admired and see what might come of it.[4]

Gates was slow in replying, because McNickle's letter had followed him from Baltimore to Yuma, Arizona. He was obviously touched by McNickle's admiration, and by his impetuous, naive plea for a job: "Of course I liked your letter, every damned word of it; all you say about your people's firstness, and all that. Also, what I very much liked was the way you put your pen on the critical descriptive word of the guts of things. You first hit it when you acknowledged [to] me that the necessary "official" statement [as prepared for the NCAB biography] just isn't what for."[5]

Gates's response to McNickle's query, although somewhat rambling, was warm and enthusiastic. As far as a job was concerned, however, it was a disappointment. The only opportunities Gates could see were in field work, which McNickle had ruled out. Gates assured him that concern over Indians was growing and the future would be different, but for now there was nothing. "Do I thus reward your 'hell of a nerve,'" he apologized. Nevertheless, he was very pleased that McNickle had written, because he recognized the response of a kindred soul. "Some day, when chance allows," he told D'Arcy, "I shall have a fine set-to of council-fire talk if I can meet you." McNickle already felt warmed by the prospective encounter.[6]

The timing of McNickle's correspondence with Gates is significant. McNickle first wrote on March 25, 1934. Gates's reply was dated May 14. In the interim, McNickle had sent his first letter applying for employment to John Collier, commissioner of Indian affairs.[7] Collier's office responded almost immediately with an application form, which McNickle returned on May 25, shortly after he heard from Gates. What McNickle had learned from Gates's reply was that Gates and Collier had known each other for years, and that Gates was a member of the Board of Directors of the American Indian Defense Association, which Collier had established in the 1920s.

Gates mentioned Collier when he explained to McNickle what he was doing in Yuma. Collier, it seems, had recommended to Interior Secretary

Harold Ickes that Gates be appointed as a consultant, and Gates was en route to Arizona at Collier's request, "to see what [he] could find to do for the Yumas. Just a '$-a-year man' for a while, with total freedom of movement and digging. And getting results."[8] Although the establishment of Collier's Applied Anthropology Unit in the Indian Bureau was still two years away, the commissioner was already making tentative moves toward the use of professional anthropologists in developing Indian policy. Gates was among the first to be appointed.[9]

When McNickle had first written to Gates, he had been unaware of any connection between the anthropologist and Collier. He did not, therefore, mention Collier or the BIA in his letter. Nor had Gates's appointment as a dollar-a-year man been included in the information he had submitted to NCAB; it had occurred too recently. McNickle was somewhat surprised to learn of the connection between Gates and Collier, but perhaps it could be useful. When he returned his formal application to Collier's office, he decided, on the basis of Gates's warm response, to suggest him as a reference. He admitted to Collier that he had not met Gates personally, but explained, "It is possible that he might have an impression of me which would help you decide what to do with this application. . . . If Mr. Gates needs some one to carry his portfolio while in your service, couldn't you give me the assignment?"[10]

The formal application McNickle submitted contained some questions that he thought were irrelevant, if not ridiculous, although he dutifully answered them. In response to a query about his drinking habits, he replied, "I am very fond of wine and beer with my meals, but to say that I drink intoxicating beverages steadily sounds as if I should rate myself a confirmed toper. I have been intoxicated but once or twice in my life but never at all since coming to the age of reason. I hope the government service does not frown upon healthy eating habits." His arrest record, he felt, was equally insignificant. Yes, he admitted, he had once been arrested; when he was a college student his landlady had once had him arrested over a misunderstanding about his rent. It was so trivial a matter that he would not have mentioned it had not dire consequences been threatened for not doing so.[11]

Collier's office responded once more, this time to inquire about McNickle's specific qualifications for employment—he might be Indian, but what could he *do?* McNickle was indignant, and when he wrote to Gates a second time, he complained about the whole application procedure. Was this Collier's touted "hire Indians" policy? It was fine to hire Indians, but only if they were "qualified"? The only Indians he knew "had no special training above the degree of mule-skinning." If they were qualified for anything else, he told Gates, there would be no need for an Indian Bureau.

Nevertheless, he tried to answer the Bureau's questions truthfully. He also made one concrete suggestion on his own behalf. If there was to be a genuine reorganization of Indian education as authorized by the Indian Reorganization Act of 1934, he might be able to offer a unique perspective to that reorganization. He was, after all, a product of the current system. "Might there not be good reason for using experience derived from personal association, as a student, with the present type of Indian boarding school?" he asked. "It seems that here at least I might find a use for my experience, such as it is."[12]

To McNickle, the rationale of the questionnaire was totally frustrating. "A bureau is a bureau, no matter how much life blood is pumped into it," he complained to Gates.

> What I want to know is, if Mr. Collier is in earnest about building up an Indian staff. . . how is he going to manage if his Bureau won't take a chance on any but "specifically qualified" applicants? . . . Somebody will have to be a little reckless, if the intention is sincere, and try to teach them a job. Maybe they could learn to fold letters or carry messages. They might even put little kegs of rum in their mouths and send them out to succor benighted congressmen.[13]

Even though Gates sympathized with McNickle's frustration and appreciated the irony of his suggestions, he was realistic. He believed in what Collier was trying to do through the redirection of Indian policy, but it would take time to break the present system. He and Collier, "a few of us," would eventually like to put the Bureau out of a job, but they would have to use the Bureau to do it. He urged McNickle to be patient. Meanwhile, he would inquire about D'Arcy's application when he went to Washington the following week.[14] Whether he did so is not known; McNickle heard nothing further from the BIA at that time.

These four letters between McNickle and Gates were more significant, however, than the discussion of employment possibilities might indicate. In them, Gates introduced McNickle to the art of linguistics and did much to spur his growing interest in cultural anthropology. Words and language had always fascinated McNickle, and he had become intrigued with the possibility of translating or transcribing the kind of Indian folk material he had discovered as he was writing *The Surrounded*. Joran was also interested in these matters. Her parents had come originally from Norway, and she was working on a translation of a book from the Norwegian. She and D'Arcy had discussed the cultural dimensions implicit in the translation of thought from one language to another, and they were struggling with the difficulties of conveying the original intent of a word in the absence of precise equivalents. Gates's work with Mayan linguistics prompted McNickle to ask about the possibilities and the problems involved with direct translation from one language to another.

Gates replied by sending McNickle a copy of a journal he had published at Johns Hopkins University. McNickle read it avidly. Then he began to ask himself about the cultural specificity of language and how it reflected the particular experience of reality unique to any single culture. Gates's writing had introduced McNickle to the Sapir-Whorf theory of the relationship of culture to language, and he began to understand how translation from one language to another must involve more than word equivalency.[15] The translator must find some intuitive way to perceive the imaginative mind of the poet or storyteller.

But if this was correct, how could Gates justify his attempt to translate from an ancient Mayan language into English? McNickle asked Gates if there was a "missing link," some key to getting inside another culture's thought patterns so that the songs and stories of that culture could become accessible to the translator. He wondered what kind of expertise was required to communicate across the cultural abyss, and whether a valid translation was, in fact, really possible. McNickle would like to use folk material in his writing, he told his new friend, but the articles in Gates's journal had raised all kinds of questions about the difficulties of legitimate translation.

McNickle admitted that what he had proposed in his first letter was just that sort of thing—doing some kind of translation or interpretation of Mayan material. Now he was beginning to doubt the validity of that suggestion: "I was perhaps contemplating doing the very thing which, in reading, I have distrusted and felt antagonized by: I mean those 'translations' one finds of Indian poetry in which the 'translator' has made the Indian singer over into a kind of sonneteer or at worst a *vers librist,* and on top of that has asked us to admire the individuality of Indian poetry."[16] It was obvious that he would have to give much more thought to the use of Indian material in his own writing if he were to avoid violating the integrity of its origins.

Gates replied thoughtfully to McNickle's query. Different cultures experience the same phenomena of reality differently, he explained. Artistic perspective, musical rhythm, mathematical concepts, all are culturally determined; none are absolute. There was no missing link, he wrote, but "you do not just 'step across' as one makes a translation literal and therefore wholly false; [you must] go upstairs in the mental ambient to the thought, and then bring that down." People, he explained, are conditioned to perceive reality within the framework of their own language, which provides a way of sharing that perception with others. The difficulties of translation occur because the perceptions themselves, expressed by language, are determined culturally, not absolutely.[17]

Gates's ideas provided a touchstone for McNickle's developing awareness of cultural relativity. To go "upstairs" and explore the "mental ambiance" of another culture before attempting an interpretation or a translation—this was to become the essential element of his understanding of human interaction. In his later Indian histories, he would reveal an unusual empathy with both sides of cultural conflict as he sought to bring mutual understanding to Indian-white relations. He became increasingly reluctant to make absolutist judgments and he avoided taking adversarial positions, preferring instead to work toward consensus. He sought common ground where divergent forces could meet and communication could begin. Twenty-five years later, in a paper he presented to a conference on Indian affairs in Canada, McNickle repeated the message that he had received from Gates. "Reality is not an absolute state of things as they are," he told his audience. "The observer sees what his culture has taught him to see [and] language itself compels the particular abstract [he makes] of reality." In comparing Indian and white experiences, he explained that "the worlds in which different societies live are distinct worlds, not merely the same world with different labels attached."[18]

The four letters between McNickle and Gates are the extent of their correspondence in McNickle's papers. One wonders if the two men ever met for that "council-fire talk," or if Gates did, in fact, try to use his influence with Collier on D'Arcy's behalf. Gates himself had a falling-out with Collier the following year and withdrew his services from the BIA.[19]

Nevertheless, McNickle's correspondence with Gates is important because it reveals the direction of D'Arcy's thought about the essential nature of Indian-white conflict. His last novel, *Wind from an Enemy Sky,* which was published posthumously in 1978, showed the depth of his concern about the difficulty of cross-cultural communication. His correspondence with Gates had quickened his interest in cultural anthropology, and his work with the Indian Bureau would bring him into a close professional relationship with people at the cutting edge of the field.

Although McNickle's 1934 job application languished, his correspondence with Gates reinforced his determination to do whatever he could to get a job with the Bureau of Indian Affairs. Specifically, he wanted to work with John Collier. He knew that Collier had supported Montana senator Burton K. Wheeler's effort to protect Indian ownership of a proposed dam site on the Flathead Reservation in 1932. He followed with great interest the newspaper accounts of Collier's appointment as Indian commissioner and his ensuing struggle with Congress over passage of the 1934 Indian Reorganization Act, also called the Wheeler-Howard Act. In a draft of his first letter to Collier, McNickle had written, "At the risk of appearing to court your interest, I must say that it gave me great pleasure to hear of your appointment to the Indian Bureau, as I had been aware of your efforts on behalf of the Indians for several years. It would be a real privilege to take part in the work of reconstruction you are carrying forward."[20] Although he had no clear idea of what Collier might accomplish if the Indian Reorganization Act was passed, he was convinced that the new commissioner would make significant improvements in the Indian Bureau.

Circumstances other than Gates's possible intervention, however, led to McNickle's eventual employment by the BIA. As he had anticipated in his letter to Constance Skinner, it was his new job with the Federal Writers Project, working on Indian material for the State Guide series, that put him in a position of high visibility vis-à-vis the Indian Bureau. He submitted a new application to the Bureau shortly after he arrived in Washington.

This time McNickle's application was more formal than his first letter to Collier had been eighteen months earlier. He started with the required questionnaire, indicating that he was one-quarter Flathead Indian, enrolled and allotted. In response to questions about his education, he listed private study at Oxford and his two courses at Columbia—he did not mention Grenoble. He admitted having a slight musical gift and said that he enjoyed the theater, baseball, fishing, and the outdoor life. His preferred reading was in books about the history of the Northwest; as for magazines, he noted, "[I] read anything that comes my way." In response to a question about what he had done between the ages of twelve and twenty-one (a rather odd question, in his opinion), he reported that he had been a farm worker, garage helper, steamboat fireman, railroad worker, logger, and elevator operator. There may have been a little tongue-in-cheek humor in this list—such work, although not impossible, has not been documented. To the final question, "Give any further information about yourself which you think significant," he responded, "You have plumbed the depths."[21]

McNickle's second application was well timed. The Indian Reorganization Act had passed in June 1934 and the process of Indian reorganization was moving into high gear. Collier was searching for articulate people who could explain the complicated process to both Indians and whites. The commissioner had become frustrated, however, because many Indians were suspicious of what they perceived as just one more arbitrary policy being imposed on them by the Bureau of Indian Affairs. McNickle, being Indian, might be especially effective in explaining the new program to the various tribes and putting to rest some of that suspicion. The BIA forwarded McNickle's application to the secretary of the interior, and his appointment was confirmed in February 1936, just three days after Dodd, Mead released *The Surrounded*.[22] McNickle was almost in a state of shock. Within six months he had moved from the ranks of New York City's unemployed to the tumultuous offices of one of Washington's busiest bureaus and he had published his first novel.

In his work for Collier, McNickle found his mission, the cause that would claim his devotion for the rest of his life. But he became so caught up in his new work that he had little time or energy for his own projects. In September he sent another short story to Ruth Rae. "Here is the first story I've attempted in about a year," he told her. "In one way or another this has been a year of distraction and I want—and need—very seriously to come to terms with a working routine." Perhaps he would have more time to write in the winter. Already, it seemed, he anticipated a promotion and a raise in salary. He was also eager for a financial accounting on *The Surrounded*. "It must be about time for Dodd, Mead to give us the lowdown, isn't it?" he asked Rae. "I hope it makes a fine jingle when they finish."[23] The "fine jingle" from the sale of only twenty-nine copies of *The Surrounded* could scarcely be heard when his first accounting arrived the following January, however, and the novel never did sell very well.

Unfortunately, the McNickles' move to Washington and their improved financial situation did little to alleviate the stresses that had been
building for years within D'Arcy and Joran's marriage. Joran had seemed
to enjoy her new role as mother when Toni first arrived, but she grew increasingly restless. Ruth Rae had succeeded in placing her translation of
Norwegian country life with E. P. Dutton for publication in 1937, but
that good news did little to help.[24] D'Arcy was away from home a good
deal with his new job, and another man had come into her life. She also
wanted very much to see Norway. Finally, leaving four-year-old Toni with
D'Arcy, she departed for a prolonged visit to Norway, and his life became
infinitely more complicated.[25]

McNickle's diary for much of this period is missing, so it is impossible
to know in detail how he coped with the responsibility of caring for a
small child. He and Joran were divorced after her return in 1938, but he
did not remain single for long. In the course of his work he had met Roma
Kauffman, a Phi Beta Kappa graduate from Grinnell College, who was an
accomplished writer and editor for the United States Office of Education.
Her work had often brought her to the Indian Bureau's public relations
office, where she had met D'Arcy, and they were married soon after his divorce from Joran became final. Even though they were in their mid-
thirties, Roma and D'Arcy both wanted "their" child. They lost a son,
born prematurely in 1940, but the arrival of a girl, Kathleen, the following
year soon eased the pain of their loss. Roma wanted to keep her career position with the government, so they hired a housekeeper to help care for
Toni and Kay.[26]

With two professional salaries, McNickle's growing family lived comfortably. D'Arcy's transfer to the BIA in February 1936 allowed him the
same salary he had had working for the Federal Writers Project, twenty-
six hundred dollars annually. A year later, as he had anticipated, it was
raised to twenty-nine hundred dollars, which was a comfortable income
in the 1930s. In 1938 only 4 percent of the Indians working for the BIA
earned over two thousand dollars, so McNickle considered himself very
well paid indeed.[27] He was classified as an "administrative assistant," a cat-

egory that allowed Collier considerable flexibility in determining where he would be most useful.

By the time McNickle started working for the BIA in 1936, Collier's policy of Indian reorganization had assumed a definitive shape. His plan was to provide Indian tribes with a constitutional base that derived from within the context of traditional tribal authority. After they verified their enrollments, the tribes voted on whether to accept reorganization under the terms of the Wheeler-Howard Act. If they voted in favor, they adopted a constitution based on a model drawn up by the BIA, which presumably was modified to accommodate individual tribal structures. As a constitutional body the tribe could then incorporate itself, thus obtaining further benefits and legal protection.

But first Collier was determined to stop the steady alienation of the tribal land base, which was each tribe's primary corporate asset. Indian land had been diminished severely since the allotment program began in the 1890s. As soon as he took office Collier stopped the sale of unallotted "surplus" land and began to consolidate tribal holdings through buy-outs and trades of reservation land that had passed into private ownership. During his administration the amount of tribal land increased notably.

This entire process of reorganization was lengthy, complicated, and outside the experience of most reservation Indians and many of the Indian Bureau personnel. McNickle's initial assignment as junior administrative assistant was to help Allan Harper, director of tribal organization, explain the new program to various tribes. As he became more familiar with the particulars, he assumed responsibility for reviewing the new constitutions and for preparing correspondence relative to tribal ordinances and resolutions. Working directly under Fred H. Daiker, who headed the Indian Organization Division, McNickle also dealt with problems of tribal enrollment.[28] In this area he attempted to define and restore tribal identities to individuals as well as groups. Unfortunately, the "paper trail" of McNickle's early work with the Bureau is faint. Although numerous letters and memos were routed across his desk, they reveal few traces of his specific activities. His efforts were submerged in the nameless anonymity of the lower echelons of the Indian Bureau.

Much of McNickle's work at this time was done in the field. Because of his background, Daiker sent him to Montana and North Dakota to talk with the "landless" Indians along the Canadian border, many of whom were Métis like himself. His efforts on their behalf resulted in the first of a number of articles he would write for the Indian Bureau's house organ, *Indians at Work*. "Hill 57," which appeared in the February 1937 issue, was a plea for understanding the problems of the people he had met along the northern border. "The background," McNickle wrote, "is Great Falls, Montana, or rather, sharpening the focus, what is locally called 'Hill 57'—in dubious tribute to the enterprise of a pickle manufacturer." That "dubious tribute" derived from the fact that the people living on Hill 57 were of mixed and uncertain ancestry—part Cree, part Chippewa, part European, neither Canadian nor United States citizens, belonging nowhere. Their European ancestry, however, was generally traced through the female line rather than the male, and because of this they were living on the ragged edge of survival, with no land and no treaty recognition. McNickle was tremendously moved by their situation. He realized that their basic poverty was symptomatic of economic and social problems within the larger society and could not be alleviated overnight, but their most pressing need, which could be met immediately, was for productive land so that they could at least feed themselves.[29]

In writing this article, however, McNickle was preaching to the choir. The Indian Bureau had already obtained a forty-acre tract of land for use by the people on Hill 57, but the non-Indian residents of Great Falls were opposed to such "coddling." They did not want any Indians, full-blood or mixed, occupying valuable land nearby. These were the people who really needed to hear McNickle's message. Unfortunately, they created so much opposition to any idea of settling the disinherited people on land of their own that the Bureau's plans came to nothing.[30] Sensitized by his own Métis ancestry, McNickle could not help but internalize some of the scorn that had been heaped on the people on Hill 57.

McNickle's work on tribal enrollment for the Montana Indians unexpectedly provided him with new insight into the processes of his own adoption and enrollment. He was shocked when he learned that his tribal adoption as an infant had not required proof of any blood quantum whatsoever. The routine documentation of his enrollment, which he had received from the agency in Montana to support his job application, had attested to his having one-quarter Indian blood. Now he learned that no "hard" proof had been required, and that some of those enrolled claimed no Indian blood whatsoever. Once again he was brought face to face with the puzzle of his own ancestry and the legitimacy of his claim to being Indian.

After writing "Hill 57," McNickle contributed frequently to *Indians at Work,* writing feature articles and reviewing books that were of general interest to Indian Bureau employees. He was often "borrowed" from Allan Harper's Tribal Relations Division by the publication's new editor and public relations director, Floyd LaRouche, to help respond to the growing number of requests for information about Collier's program. But as pressures mounted in other areas, Harper increasingly called him back to work on the new tribal constitutions. LaRouche finally complained to Collier, "The services of D'Arcy McNickle, who was extremely valuable in fields of research and writing . . . have been entirely lost to us."[31] Although McNickle still contributed an occasional article, LaRouche was forced to solicit most of his material thereafter from the Bureau's field agents.

McNickle enjoyed working in both public relations and tribal relations. Writing about Indian affairs was exciting and stimulating, but so, too, was his assignment with Harper. When he first began working for the government, McNickle had looked forward to associating with anthropologists such as William Gates, and now more anthropologists were being brought into the Bureau to assist in reorganization. Collier believed that it was possible to develop a science of humankind that would establish objective criteria on which to base the policies and programs of Indian affairs. He thought that social scientists would be able to advise the Indian Bureau about "the contemporary social organization of each group of Indians that want[ed] to organize under the IRA [Indian Reorganization Act] so that the constitution drawn up [would] be based on the actual social life of the group."[32] Following such tentative first steps as hiring William Gates and a few others as dollar-a-year consultants, Collier established the Applied Anthropology Unit (AAU) in January 1936, a month before McNickle arrived.

McNickle was thus able to observe at first hand the role anticipated for professional anthropologists, as well as the difficulties they faced in trying to initiate effective change toward tribal self-government. Controversy developed almost immediately over the nature of, and the need for, social scientists in the Indian Bureau. Unfortunately, the model constitutions used in tribal reorganization had been formulated before the AAU was established, and the anthropologists' recommendations were often made after the constitutions had been adopted by the tribes, rendering the anthropologists' efforts irrelevant.

There was great resistance to the anthropologists among many old-line field personnel who resented the presence of professional social scientists in the Bureau. Almost from its inception, the Indian Bureau had been staffed by political appointees rather than by those with experience in dealing with Indian people, and the entrenched bureaucracy resented the implication that they were in any way unqualified for their work. To make matters worse, anthropologists often wrote in a professional jargon that was unintelligible to field agents who were not schooled in the discipline. There were also jurisdictional problems—no one knew what branch within the Indian Bureau the AAU was ultimately responsible to. Such questions were brought to the attention of Congress, endangering the already fragile bureaucratic structure that Collier had created to implement Indian reorganization. The AAU struggled to overcome the impact of jealousies from within the Bureau and the congressional attacks from without, but by the end of 1937 the unit was dismantled.[33]

Nevertheless, McNickle, who was an observer of these events, had become convinced that anthropologists could indeed make an important contribution to Indian reorganization. Although he had been with the

BIA for less than eighteen months, he wrote a memo to the commissioner in which he referred to a recent report by Felix Cohen, one of the attorneys who had assisted in developing the Bureau's model constitution. Returning from the Fort Belknap Reservation, Cohen had reported on some of the difficulties the Indian tribes there were experiencing as they attempted to implement their new programs. In light of that report, McNickle was concerned that the failure of the Bureau to follow through in dealing with some of those problems might negate the advantages offered by reorganization. He pointed out that the Bureau had been in close contact with the tribes before they voted to accept the program, but once they had adopted their new constitution, the Bureau had departed and left them on their own. "The pressure from Washington is taken off," McNickle observed, "and the tribe, after being in the spotlight, feels itself cast again into the outer darkness. In selling the idea of reorganization, I suppose we never did make clear enough that this was the tribe's own concern and that it would be dealing with problems which, if the solutions were to be its very own, it must handle alone."[34]

McNickle then suggested that the Bureau shift the emphasis of its program from tribal reorganization to maintenance and support. Ideally, field agents should be instructed in tribal culture by anthropologists who were knowledgeable about that particular tribe. The agents would then be prepared to work directly with the newly organized tribal councils to put the constitutions into effect. McNickle also recommended the development in Washington of a trouble-shooting squad that could be moved from place to place whenever its assistance and encouragement seemed advisable. He predicted, "The farther away we get from the initial impulse which brought about tribal organization, the more difficult it will be to rescue the program."[35]

McNickle's memo was timely, but no such maintenance was established. A program such as he suggested would have assisted many tribes in developing the political concepts necessary for the effective application of constitutional government. The constitutional model presupposed a majority party and a loyal opposition, concepts that inherently contravened the Indians' traditional development of consensus. "It is probably not surprising," anthropologist Nancy O. Lurie later observed, "that those who assisted and advised tribes in developing their constitutions neglected to discuss the ground rules of organized, loyal opposition and the stability of bipartisan policies along with partisan issues. These things were simply taken for granted." The lack of planning beyond the initial phase of reorganization was symptomatic of some of Collier's limitations as Indian commissioner. His son, John Collier, Jr., later pointed out that his father's view "only focused sharply on distant circumstances. It was as if he could not comprehend or directly involve himself with life directly before him."[36] Like Cohen, McNickle understood the need to follow through on organizational reform, but Collier was not much interested, and a skeptical Congress refused to provide funds for implementing the kind of program that would have made additional support possible.

Although McNickle gave unqualified support to Collier's program, he never shared entirely the almost mystical philosophy on which it was based. Collier was a visionary. He had dreamed for years of an ideal human community grounded on nonmaterial values that would somehow emerge from within the community itself. He thought he saw this kind of social organization among the Pueblo Indians of the Southwest, and he extrapolated from them to all Indian communities in the western world. As he wrote shortly after he retired from the BIA, "The controlling fact of Indian life today, and of present governmental enterprise, is the triumph of the *group life* of the Indians. This triumph contains within itself the future of the Indians and their renewed power to benefit mankind."[37]

Collier's vision of community, however, ran counter to America's obsession with individual achievement and responsibility. To some observers, his policies appeared to isolate the Indians in a permanent condition of hopeless, helpless dependency. Collier obviously erred in extending his vision of community to include all the Indians of the Western Hemisphere, thereby denying their great cultural diversity.[38] His concern for tribal governments derived as much from a belief in their potential for saving the world as from his concern for the Indian communities themselves. But not all Indians wanted to preserve their ancestral traditions; many had successfully integrated into American society and had no interest in reviving a communal past. His belief in self-determination was thus distorted by his conviction that what he wanted for the Indians was what they wanted for themselves. Nevertheless, his concern that Indians should recover the power to determine their own future as tribes if they chose to do so was very sincere, and it was this concern that captured McNickle's imagination and his loyalty.[39]

McNickle, however, was of a more pragmatic mind than Collier. Although he shared the commissioner's antipathy toward American consumerism and his desire to restore the Indians' political and social autonomy, he did not share Collier's romantic vision of Indian communities as the ultimate hope for humankind. Indians, like other Americans, should simply have access to all possible opportunities for self-realization, individually or collectively. If Indian people chose to maintain tribal identity and tradition, he would fight to help them keep their land and culture. If they chose to assimilate into white society, he would assist them in achieving that goal as well. The obligation was to ensure freedom of choice, not the forced continuance of some mystical "community" as the ultimate hope of Western people.[40] Despite his philosophical differences, however, McNickle consistently supported Collier's reforms because he felt they were moving in the right direction.

It is not surprising that strong opposition arose almost immediately to Collier's policies of land acquisition and tribal autonomy. During the 1920s, he had been engaged in running battles with a number of small groups, both Indian and white, over those very questions. In 1934, shortly after his appointment as Indian commissioner, several of those opposing groups merged to form the American Indian Federation (AIF), whose sole purpose was to discredit him and his Indian reorganization program. The membership of AIF consisted primarily of three groups: assimilated Indians who were more or less successfully managing their own property; Indians who had been converted to Christianity by conservative Protestant missionary sects; and followers of men like Carlos Montezuma, a Yavapai from Arizona, who wanted to see the BIA put out of business entirely. Many of these people viewed Collier's effort to reconstitute the tribes as a threat to their own hard-won independence. Others asserted that his interest in preserving tribal organizations was communist-inspired, and that his refusal to grant special privileges to various churches and their missionaries in Indian boarding schools was anti-Christian.[41]

By 1936 the American Indian Federation had launched a full-scale attack on Collier; Interior Secretary Harold Ickes; and Roger Baldwin, director of the American Civil Liberties Union, who was a close friend of both Collier's and Ickes's. According to AIF publications, the entire Indian administration was part of an atheist-communist international conspiracy. The only solution, in the federation's view, was to abolish the Bureau and free the Indians from federal wardship and control.[42]

The dues-paying membership of AIF probably never numbered more than a few hundred people. Nevertheless, it was exceedingly vocal and had access to the daily press. As a result, it proved to be an annoying gadfly. One of the group's most articulate critics was Alice Lee Jemison, a Seneca from New York State, whose articles precipitated a deluge of negative commentary about Collier and the Bureau. Her accusations so alarmed a number of church groups that their missionary societies threatened to withdraw their support from government Indian policies thus tainted with communist ideology. As the Indian Bureau was flooded with inquiries and complaints, Floyd LaRouche and his public relations staff were assigned the chore of answering Jemison's denunciations and the ensuing correspondence. Once again McNickle was called upon to help. Collier himself responded to her attacks as often as possible, but none of them were able to stem the rising tide of her rhetoric, which Collier at one point called "glimmerings on the lunatic fringe."[43]

Collier and Jemison finally clashed head-on at a congressional hearing in June 1940. The hearing had been called to clarify a committee report on Senate Bill 2103, supported by Jemison, which would exempt certain Indian groups from the Wheeler-Howard Act. According to Collier, the

Senate committee's report on the bill, which had been sent to the House, had included Jemison's charges made during an earlier hearing, but had deliberately omitted the Indian Bureau's response. Collier, who was accompanied by McNickle and LaRouche, insisted at this second hearing that the Bureau's position also be made part of the record.[44]

Jemison presented to the hearing what she considered irrefutable evidence of the Indian Bureau's communistic, anti-Christian policies. As evidence in support of her position, she read from an article that she had written for publication in 1938:

> Through his [Collier's] program of atheist-communism, in less than five years time, he has largely destroyed the Christian efforts which preceeded this administration. His attitude toward Christianity, Christians, and Christian efforts among the Indians was well summarized in a book review which he published in [the] December 1937 issue of his government-financed propaganda sheet called Indians at Work.[45]

The book in question, she pointed out, was Oliver La Farge's latest novel, *The Enemy Gods*. The review was written by an administrative assistant named D'Arcy McNickle.

McNickle had taken great pleasure in reviewing La Farge's book, which he considered to be an even more profound evocation of Indian spirit than the earlier *Laughing Boy*. *The Enemy Gods* was the story of a young Navajo, Myron Begay, who was brought up by Christian missionaries. Begay had initially accepted the teachings of the missionaries and had even considered becoming a missionary himself. In the book's most memorable scene, he renounced the religion of his Navajo ancestors. Gradually, however, Begay began to doubt the tenets of Christianity, and by the end of the story he had returned to the religion of his people.

In his review, McNickle had tried to put Begay's experience into historical context. "The Indian," he wrote,

has always had "friends" and it has sometimes seemed that the "friends" have been his worst enemies. The abolitionists, the humanity lovers, out of employment after the Civil War, found the naked, hounded red man and cuddled him close. They offered Bibles instead of bullets, and there were Indians who thought it was a poor exchange. A dead Indian, they would say, is better off than La Farge's Myron Begay, at the moment when, frenzied by the cheap rascality of Christian soul-saving, he stood up in a kind of missionary pep-meeting and denied his Gods.[46]

McNickle had been impressed with the honesty of the story and with La Farge's ability as a non-Indian to convey the nature of the conflict within the young man as he made his spiritual pilgrimage. On the other hand, as McNickle pointed out, such a search for religious truth was not exclusively an Indian experience but a universal one. "This 'passion in the desert,'" as he called Begay's quest,

must have been old stuff when the Cro-Magnon were getting the spirit of things into imaged reality on their cavern walls. Why, then, label it as Indian or heathen? Why call it picturesque? Why, on the one hand, try to stamp it out, or, on the other, simper about it? Truly, it is one with the frenzy imaged by the prophets of Israel. It is in the stream of race consciousness. Amen to that.[47]

But Jemison was not about to say "amen" to that. She quoted at length from McNickle's review, then demanded that it be inserted into the record as evidence of the Bureau's anti-Christian position. She maintained that McNickle's reference to missionary efforts as "the cheap rascality of Christian soul-saving" was convincing evidence of the Bureau's anti-Christian attitude, and ultimately it was John Collier, not D'Arcy McNickle, who was responsible for it. As Indian commissioner, Collier was the chief editor of *Indians at Work,* and it was he who had allowed this review to be printed. "'The cheap rascality of Christian soul-saving,'" Jemison raved, "all the venom, hatred, and contempt of the atheist-communist for Christianity finds vent in that statement, which must have had the full approval of the Commissioner of Indian Affairs."[48] She returned again and again to McNickle's phrase as she continued to read her prepared testimony.

"The cheap rascality of Christian soul-saving," sneers the Government publication *Indians at Work*. Christians! Where are you, that by your silence you deny your Christ and abandon your wards to the onslaught of the atheist-communist program . . . designed to aid in the overthrow of this Government and the Christian religion in America? How long will you let your Congressmen and your Senators ignore the pleas of the first Americans for the removal of these people from public office?[49]

Jemison then pointed out that McNickle was only one of a number of young Indians hired under Collier's "Indian Civil Service" who were being subjected to the same evil influence. "Assailed by constant anti-Christian propaganda in the discussions of those around them, these young and amenable Indians soon mimic the attitudes and the viewpoints of their superiors," she declared. "Their Christian parents would shudder in horror to hear them expressing such views."[50]

By this time, McNickle himself shuddered at what Jemison was saying. He had been reading her attacks on the Bureau for several years and had considered them little more than a nuisance. But her personal diatribe, here before a congressional committee, was different. She had attacked his writing and his intellectual and moral integrity. Jemison had pointed her finger at him, and he felt painfully vulnerable.

Collier, however, came to his defense. He agreed with Jemison that the ultimate responsibility for the contents of *Indians at Work* was his. Nevertheless, as he explained to the committee, he had delegated this responsibility and did not read every word of *Indians at Work* before publication. He admitted that McNickle's choice of words was unfortunate, and that he, Collier, would not have allowed the phrase had he known of it. Then he offered for the record two letters the Bureau had received from clergymen who had become alarmed by Jemison's accusations, along with his (Collier's) replies. The offending words in McNickle's review, he explained, were written "by a man who, because he is himself an Indian, has deep and sincere emotions concerning any interference with what he calls "'the stream of race consciousness.'" He assured the committee that McNickle was an excellent worker who had given no evidence of being anti-Christian. McNickle himself, he told them, had prepared a statement explaining his intent in using the offending words, and Collier requested that McNickle's statement, too, be entered into the record.[51]

Finally, McNickle himself was questioned about his background and his religious philosophy. Yes, he told the committee, he was a baptized Catholic and an enrolled Flathead Indian. He had attended a Jesuit mission school on the reservation; the off-reservation Indian boarding school at Chemawa; the University of Montana; and Oxford, Grenoble, and Columbia universities. No, he certainly did not consider himself anti-Christian. He then admitted that the offending phrase in his review of the La Farge book was poorly chosen, but explained, "I was trying to describe something which I thought people were not fully enough aware of. I was trying to show in the book review that Indians have not always been satisfied with the white man's ways or his religion, and that there were Indians who feel that an Indian who denied his gods was betraying his people."[52] McNickle had, of course, made a similar point in *The Surrounded*. He was relieved when he realized that Jemison had not read that novel, since it, too, contained some very unflattering portraits of Christian missionaries. He was also grateful for Collier's intervention on his behalf. It had probably saved his job.[53]

Collier's concern about these attacks on the Bureau from the ideological right had another dimension, however, and the discussion of McNickle's book review was a relatively minor matter during the congressional hearing. Since 1936, Collier had accumulated a great deal of evidence indicating that the American Indian Federation had direct personal and financial ties with the German-American Bund, a pro-Nazi organization that was attempting to exploit internal suspicion and unrest in the United States. He had become convinced that the federation's attack on the Bureau was supported in part by a fifth-column propaganda invasion from Nazi Germany.

Collier's view is understandable. In December 1938 he had been an American delegate to the Eighth International Conference of American States in Lima, Peru. A major theme at that conference had been Hitler's increasing menace to democratic Europe and the danger that he posed for the democracies of the western hemisphere as well.[54] Secretary of State Cordell Hull had warned the delegates of the immediate threat of infiltration and subversion by Axis agents. It appeared to Collier, on the basis of substantial evidence, that the close relationship between the American Indian Federation and individuals who were associated with the German-American Bund was part of Germany's subversive efforts.

Although Alice Lee Jemison seemed unconcerned that she had been supported by funds from that questionable source, Collier viewed her as part of a larger hemispheric threat. Jemison and her associates were unimportant, he told the House committee, but Hitler and Mussolini were of the utmost importance, and the federation had let itself be used.[55] At the very moment of the hearing, Hitler was rampaging through France and threatening Great Britain, a fact that contributed to the urgency of Collier's testimony and charges of collusion. The Indians of the Americas, he believed, were vulnerable to Nazi propaganda designed to foment revolutionary sentiments. Such a threat might seem unlikely to the congressmen, but it appeared quite real to those who were knowledgable about the unhappy conditions of Indian life in much of North and South America.

As a result of the hearing on S.2103, Collier's refutation of Jemison's testimony became part of the record, and the bill was subsequently defeated. Collier's testimony outlining the connections between AIF and the German-American Bund also became a matter of record, and several key figures, including Jemison's contacts, although not Jemison herself, were soon indicted. The American Indian Federation, which had already lost much of its following, disappeared in the rush of events that led up to World War II.[56]

The importance of the International Conference of American States that Collier had attended in 1938 extended beyond Cordell Hull's warning about possible German propaganda activities in the Western Hemisphere. In its final session the conference had passed a resolution urging the establishment of an inter-American Indian organization to serve as a clearing-house for research and information concerning the hemisphere's twenty to thirty million Indian people. Collier had dreamed for years about creating such a body, and he immediately began marshaling U.S. support for the idea. A preliminary organizational meeting of such a group was scheduled for April 1940 in Pátzcuaro, Mexico, and President Roosevelt appointed Collier to lead the American delegation. McNickle accompanied the group as a technical adviser.[57] This meeting, held on the fiftieth anniversary of the First International Conference of American States and the thirtieth anniversary of the Pan-American Union, marked the founding of the Inter-American Indian Institute.

By the time the Pátzcuaro delegation returned to Washington, Collier was committed to organizing a United States affiliate of the inter-American organization. President Roosevelt agreed and in 1941 he issued an executive order that established the National Indian Institute (NII). It was to be headed by a policy board consisting of representatives from the State, Interior, and Agriculture departments; the Smithsonian Institution; the Library of Congress; the National Research Council; the Social Science Research Council; and the American Council of Learned Societies. Oscar Chapman, assistant secretary of the interior, was the board's first chairman, and Collier was ex officio director until 1946. McNickle was appointed as its mandated Indian member.[58]

From its inception NII was a bureaucratic stepchild, and funding for its operational budget was not regularized for years. There was a question of whether the institute, international in its approach, should be considered part of the Bureau of Indian Affairs, which had no mandated overseas role. Perhaps it fell more logically within the purview of the State Department. Although its establishment by executive order gave it treaty status, Congress was understandably reluctant to include it as a line item in the Indian Bureau's budget. Most of the institute's initial funding was obtained through the Commerce Department with the assistance of John D. Rockefeller, Jr., who was coordinator of inter-American cooperation.

During the war N II's activities were practically nonexistent, and later, as Congress cut funding for all administrative programs, the institute became even more forlorn. Collier, however, was unwilling to let the program die. After resigning as Indian commissioner in the spring of 1945, he became founder and director of the Institute of Ethnic Affairs, a privately funded group that adopted N II and supported it until 1950. McNickle, who by 1949 had become the N II's acting director, obtained funding from Congress through the B IA for one more year.[59] A sum of $22,500 allowed the institute to maintain a director, a professional field worker, and two clerks, but it was a temporary reprieve.

McNickle's defense in 1949 of the National Indian Institute before the House Appropriations Committee echoed Collier's testimony during the hearings involving the American Indian Federation. After explaining N II's purpose to the committee, McNickle appealed for congressional support on the basis of the institute's contribution to hemispheric democracy. The institute provided an opportunity to disseminate accurate information that would "counteract the propaganda being released in South America by Communists or other subversive groups trying to show us up to the world as being unfair and unjust in our handling of the Indian population."[60]

McNickle assured the committee that from its inception the institute had refrained from policymaking activities or other interference in Latin American matters. Its role in providing information about Indian affairs was solely to educate and promote the welfare of the Indians and thereby to counter communist propaganda. Pragmatically, he based his argument for support on the grounds that the institute provided an exploitable opportunity for waging war against communism. Even so, congressional interest was not sustained for very long. McNickle succeeded in convincing the legislators that the institute should be funded for one more year, but that was the end of its support through the Bureau of Indian Affairs.

However, McNickle's interest in the activities of the N II continued through the next decade. In 1949 he was again technical adviser with the American delegation at the Second Inter-American Indian Institute Conference in Cuzco, Peru, and he represented the American Anthropological Association at the fourth such conference in Guatemala City in 1959.[61] He also contributed an occasional article to *America Indigena,* the institute's quarterly publication. But his interest in N11 became largely academic after 1960. He was more concerned about the local problems of Indians in the United States. Where Collier had been interested in the larger hemispheric view, McNickle wanted to work with Indian people on a smaller, more intimate scale.

4

The Making of
an Applied
Anthropologist

John Collier's tenure as Indian commissioner, from 1933 to 1945, was the longest in the Bureau's history, and during that time he put his own imprint on the Indian Bureau. One of his most significant contributions was his continued insistence on involving the social sciences in the development of Indian policy. Despite the failure of the Applied Anthropology Unit, he was not dissuaded from the attempt, and in 1941 he set in motion a pilot study among the Papago Indians that initiated what he considered "beyond comparison the most important enterprise ever carried forward in the Indian Service."[1]

The Indian Personality, Education and Administration Research Project began in September of that year with a contract between the Department of the Interior and the University of Chicago. The goal of the project reflected Collier's interest in the cohesive structure of Indian community life. Researchers hoped to discover those elements of child rearing within Indian society that created the uniquely Indian child. Using the techniques of the social sciences, they anticipated achieving some degree of understanding of the dynamics of individual personality formation and its relation to the larger society. Results of their work would be published initially as a series of tribal monographs, then synthesized into a more general study of implication and application.

The second phase of the project would attempt to apply the field studies to administrative policies, so that the future development of Indian societies could take place from a base of Indian culture rather than that of whites. As Robert J. Havighurst, one of the project's planners, explained, "The hope was that the studies would allow further modification of policies to benefit Indian societies and their efforts to cope with the modern world."[2] The whole project was conceived as an exercise in cultural anthropology.

An impressive array of people from the University of Chicago and the BIA cooperated in designing the methodology and supervising the field work of the project's first phase. Named as coordinator was Laura Thompson, a highly regarded anthropologist who had spent most of the past decade in the Pacific and had returned to Chicago for post-graduate study.[3] From the university's Committee on Human Development came Robert J. Havighurst and W. Lloyd Warner. Ralph Tyler represented Chicago's Department of Education. Eugene Lerner, professor of psychology at Sarah Lawrence College, was also among the planners. Government personnel included Willard Beatty, director of Indian Education; Assistant Indian Commissioner Joseph McCaskill; Réné d'Harnoncourt, director of the Indian Arts and Crafts Board; and of course Collier himself. The commissioner assembled this distinguished group in November 1941 to discuss preliminary research procedures. Five Indian groups were selected to be included in the study: the Navajo, Papago, and Sioux tribes and Hopi and Zuni pueblos.

Early planning for the project was interrupted, however, by the onset of World War II, and although the pilot program got underway as planned, for some months the major efforts of the Bureau were directed elsewhere. Collier appointed Joseph McCaskill, who had already begun working on the personality study, to coordinate all activities that might contribute to the war effort, and McNickle served as McCaskill's administrative officer. They dealt with such questions as whether reservation schools, hospitals, road repair equipment, etc., would be needed if there were a general evacuation from coastal areas. The Bureau also considered the possibility of enlisting the Indians' help in dealing with saboteurs, should the need arise.[4]

Fears of invasion gradually subsided, but as the war gathered momentum the BIA faced two major changes in its operations, both of which affected the personality study and involved major shifts in personnel. The first was the Bureau's move to Chicago, which was completed during the summer of 1942. That was a major undertaking; the office furniture, equipment, and two thousand file cases filled more than thirty-two box cars. Collier, who took Assistant Commissioner William Zimmerman with him to Chicago, then appointed McCaskill as a second assistant commissioner. He and McNickle were to remain in the nation's capital, with a staff of ten. Together, McNickle and McCaskill functioned as the Washington office and became the primary liaison between the Bureau of Indian Affairs and the larger war effort. Collier, Zimmerman, and most of the Indian Bureau spent the rest of the war quartered in the huge Merchandise Mart in Chicago.[5]

The other major change caused by the war was the Bureau's supervision of one of the ten Japanese relocation centers that were established throughout the West in 1942. The role of the BIA in administering one of those centers was something of an anomaly. The War Relocation Authority (WRA), originally directed by Milton Eisenhower, had been established by executive order in March 1942 as an independent government agency. In its search for large tracts of land that might be used as sites for the resettlement centers, the WRA had turned to the Interior Department, which administered the public domain as well as the Bureau of Indian Affairs.

Of the ten sites that were eventually selected, one, by far the largest, was on the Colorado River Indian Reservation in Arizona. In a memorandum of understanding signed on March 18, 1942, between the WRA and the Interior Department, the WRA contracted for its use for the duration of the war. The memorandum provided that the several tribes living on the Colorado River Reservation would make available twenty-five thousand acres of undeveloped but potentially irrigable land for the establishment of one of the relocation centers. The memorandum also gave the Interior Department the sole administrative responsibility for this one center, with the option of choosing the administrative agent.[6]

Interior Secretary Ickes offered the job to the Bureau of Indian Affairs, and McCaskill, as coordinator of the BIA's war effort, urged Collier to accept. "The Indian Service's long experience in handling a minority group eminently equips it to direct this program," he told Collier. "The Interior Department's War Program could be expanded to make this contribution to the protection of the public, the successful prosecution of the war, and the salvaging of dignity and self respect of a group of our population, two thirds of whom are loyal Americans, who find themselves, against their wills, identified with a country with whom we are at war."[7]

Collier was finally persuaded, and according to an agreement signed on April 12, 1942, between the Interior Department and the Bureau, this one center, to be known as Poston, came directly under the authority of the Bureau of Indian Affairs, with the War Relocation Authority involved primarily as procurement agent.[8]

Collier saw in this assignment an opportunity to assist the war effort and at the same time to advance several of his pet projects within the Indian Bureau. One such project, under consideration since the 1930s, would open some of the Colorado River Indian Reservation to settlement by Indians from other Southwest tribes whose land bases were insufficient to support their growing populations. For several years Collier had considered the possibility of relocating Navajo and Hopi families to the area. If the Japanese, with their agricultural expertise, could initiate irrigated farming on at least part of those twenty-five thousand acres and grow most of their own food, his postwar resettlement plan might come to early fruition. Such improvements would serve in place of rent, to reimburse the Colorado River tribes whose land was being used.

Although some people within the Bureau questioned the wisdom of having the evacuees build an irrigation system that would ultimately benefit only the Indians, Collier brushed their arguments aside. He also refused to consider the possibility that the land developed by the Japanese Americans might be transferred to them after the war. Indian ownership of that land, he maintained, was inalienable. Nevertheless, he wanted Congress to fund, and the evacuees to build, permanent irrigation works and public buildings that could be used later by Indians. The evacuees themselves expressed resentment at being so used, and Dillon Myer, who replaced Milton Eisenhower as director of the War Relocation Authority in June 1942, strongly objected to the expenditure of funds for development of the area under these circumstances.[9] Nevertheless, Collier was increasingly eager to exploit the possibilities suggested by the B I A's administration of Poston.

The development of permanent facilities at Poston was not the only benefit that Collier anticipated. He also considered refocusing the personality study to include a sociological analysis of the problems of community development that might surface as the evacuees reorganized themselves in a community. Although he eventually decided that a direct connection between the center and the personality study was not feasible, he strongly urged Eisenhower to employ social scientists in the management of all the relocation camps. At Collier's suggestion, Eisenhower named John Provinse, who had just been elected president of the newly established Society for Applied Anthropology (SAA), to coordinate all W RA activities in its Community Management Division. (After the war Provinse became assistant commissioner of the B I A and was McNickle's immediate superior for a short time.)

In line with Collier's thinking about the research potential of the situation, McNickle drew up a policy draft that was used as the basis for the B I A's administration of Poston.[10] Collier then began reassigning personnel. This task became increasingly difficult as many of the B I A's younger people left for service in the armed forces. Wade Head, superintendent of the Papago Agency at Sells, Arizona, who had had previous experience with Japanese people in the Pacific, was named as Poston's director, to be assisted by Ralph Gelvin and John Evans, the son of an old Taos friend of Collier's, Mabel Dodge Luhan. Head's wife, Beulah, who had been his official assistant at the Papago Agency, remained at the Agency as superintendent. Collier then recruited Alexander Leighton, a young Navy doctor who was interested in social psychology, to direct a sociological research project at the center. That project was jointly sponsored by the United States Navy, the War Relocation Authority, and the Bureau of Indian Affairs. Congress funded this project on the grounds that it would help the government gain insight into problems that might develop in the management of Japanese territories after the war.[11]

While the personality study and the sociological research project were conceptually different, the two projects became closely identified when the University of Chicago asked Dorothea Leighton, Alexander Leighton's wife, to participate in the personality study. Dorothea Leighton was a social psychiatrist who had received her training at Johns Hopkins University. Just before Pearl Harbor, she and her husband had completed a field study on the Navajo Reservation under a Social Science Research Council grant. When the personality study researchers began their field work in 1942, about the time that the WRA centers were receiving their first evacuees, Dorothea was hired to oversee the psychological testing of Navajo and Zuni children. While she was analyzing the development of Indian children within the tribal context, her husband was tracing other processes of community development and their impact on the Japanese-American evacuees settling at Poston.

Not surprisingly, Collier gathered together a number of young professional anthropologists to work on these projects.[12] Edward and Rosamond Spicer were another husband-wife team—Edward was Alexander Leighton's assistant, and Rosamond worked with Dorothea Leighton in testing the Navajo and Zuni children. Gordon MacGregor, John Adair, Alice Joseph, Jane Chesky, and Clyde Kluckhohn were all involved in one way or another with the tribal studies. These people all developed a working relationship with Collier in Chicago and with McNickle and McCaskill in Washington.

Wade Head's appointment as director of the Poston relocation center
had a particular impact on McNickle. Although Wade's wife Beulah was
well qualified to replace him as superintendent on the Papago Reservation, her husband's transfer created a gap in that agency that had to be
filled. The reservation covered a huge desert territory, and Sells, the
agency headquarters, was sixty miles from the nearest town. With a relatively large Indian population, it clearly needed two administrators. Beulah and Wade Head, therefore, asked Collier to assign McNickle as her assistant for as long as Wade remained at Poston.

Collier did not respond immediately to the Heads' request. Instead, he
sent McNickle to Arizona to "look around." He told the Heads only that
McNickle was coming in an official capacity to visit Sells and Poston, and
he asked for their help in showing him around the agency. "What he
needs," Collier explained, "is to get a better concept of the possibilities of
developing the district organization toward profounder tasks, and . . . to
get the flow and meaning of the personality study." Laura Thompson was
already at Sells, completing the three-month pilot project that would initiate the personality study, so Collier wrote to her, too, about McNickle's
impending visit. "While McNickle is with you at Sells," he told her, "you
might be observing him from the standpoint of his role in either or both
the personality research or the scientific phase of the Japanese research
job." Collier's response to the Heads' request was deliberately ambig-
uous, because the Papago Reservation was to be included in the personality study research, and assigning McNickle to Sells could include work
on that project. Collier had not yet decided just where his administrative
assistant would be most useful.[13]

McNickle visited Sells and the Poston site in Arizona (there was no
construction at the center as yet) at the end of April. Then he continued
on to Santa Fe, New Mexico, for a three-week training seminar designed
to launch the first phase of the personality study. It is possible that Collier
arranged this entire trip as a way of offering McNickle a choice. Either he
could go to Arizona as assistant superintendent to the Papagos, or he
could become more broadly involved with the various anthropological

studies and still help with the w RA by remaining as coordinator in the Indian Bureau's Washington office.

The relationship between Collier and McNickle had deepened steadily after McNickle began working for the Bureau in 1936. Just a year later, when Collier recommended McNickle for a Guggenheim Fellowship, he had described his assistant as "a true man of letters and a scholar." In addition, said Collier, "he is at present holding a responsible position with the Indian Service in the field of Indian organization, and has met every test of a difficult job."[14] Collier was also impressed with McNickle's talent for putting words on paper; he readily admitted that McNickle was a better writer than he.[15] Collier's prose was often convoluted and given to overwrought generalizations, but McNickle's was direct and straightforward. McNickle was also a peacemaker. Whereas Collier could be abrupt, abrasive, dogmatic, and impatient with those who disagreed with him, McNickle recognized that both sides of any issue possessed a measure of truth. Those qualities made him a very effective administrator. Collier increasingly recognized the complementary nature of their relationship and he appreciated McNickle's integrity and clarity of thought.

Collier's growing regard for McNickle was also evident in his appointing D'Arcy as one of several Indian delegates to a 1939 Canadian conference on North American Indians that was jointly hosted by the University of Toronto and Yale University. Other Indian delegates from the United States had included Arthur C. Parker (Seneca), Louis Bruce (Mohawk), Archie Phinney (Nez Perce), David Owl (Cherokee), and Ruth Muskrat Bronson (Cherokee). This conference, which was overshadowed in the newspapers by Hitler's invasion of Poland, was nevertheless noteworthy because the Indian delegates from both the United States and Canada staged a walkout on the last day. They had begun to realize that even though they were Indians, they had become so acculturated that they no longer truly represented their fellow tribal members who still lived on the reservations and reserves. So they met as a separate group and went on record calling for an all-Indian conference on Indian welfare, to be limited to "bona fide Indian leaders actually living among the Indian people of the

reservations and reserves."[16] Then the following year, Collier had included McNickle in the delegation to the Inter-American Indian Institute
in Pátzcuaro, Mexico. By 1942, when the Heads suggested his transfer to
Sells, Collier was relying heavily on McNickle's presence in the Washington office as McCaskill's assistant. But McNickle had, on occasion, expressed an interest in field work, and he could be useful in Arizona, as well.
Collier apparently gave him the choice.

The seminar in Santa Fe that McNickle attended after leaving Sells was
primarily a training session for those BIA teachers, nurses, soil conservation experts, clerks, and administrators who had volunteered as researchers for the personality study. Many of them were initially skeptical
about the value of what they would be doing. Laura Thompson and the
project's advisors, however, had worked through the pilot study on the
Papago Reservation and were able to define the goals and techniques to be
applied in the field. The volunteers learned the theories behind the various
tests they would be using, which were the most sophisticated yet developed for analyzing personality development, and they had a chance to
perfect their interviewing techniques by practicing on each other.[17] Incredible as it seems, many of the volunteers had had little personal interaction with the people whose affairs they administered. They had never
been inside an Indian home, where much of the testing was to be done, or
attended an Indian ceremony. The initial prospect of having the intimate
contact required by the testing procedures was frightening to many, but
as the volunteers familiarized themselves with the techniques to be used,
they became increasingly enthusiastic about the possibility of genuine
community involvement.[18]

W. Lloyd Warner, who read the evaluations submitted by participants
when the seminar was over, reported to Collier that all the volunteers
were enthusiastic, and some were "positively lyrical." "It became clear that
what had happened was that a lot of these people had been stirred emotionally by gaining insight into their own lives and feeling somehow or
other they had got a new grip on the kind of life they wanted.[19]

McNickle, too, was caught up in the excitement of the seminar, and he returned to Washington to write an article entitled "Toward Understanding" for *Indians at Work* about what had happened in Santa Fe. "There is always the chance," he began apologetically, "that one will speak or write with a naive enthusiasm about what one has felt and seen and lived through. . . . Nevertheless, there are occasions when one must make the effort to speak deeply and truly. The Seminar held at Santa Fe from May 17 to June 5 . . . has been such an occasion, a time of profound experiences."[20] Then he explained the purpose of the personality study itself. It was an attempt first, he said, to learn how human personality was formed, and then to gather data that would make Indian administration more effective.

Even that data, however, would be a by-product. In his summary he reflected some of Collier's mystical perception of human potential. "The research, in actuality, is projected on the assumption that there are in human personality certain primal, earth-old powers which, if understood and developed and used, can make for that mastery of the soul which men have longed for but have lacked the skill to achieve."[21] He wrote as if he were talking about a religious experience, one not unlike Myron Begay's "passion in the desert" that he had described in his review of La Farge's *Enemy Gods*. He was obviously one of those who had been moved by the seminar experience. If he stayed in the nation's capital, he would have an opportunity to observe the full spectrum of the research and help evaluate its results. He decided to stay in Washington.

From his Chicago vantage point, Collier was able to maintain even closer contact with the University of Chicago and the personality study. The field work for the project was completed within the year, as expected. The University of Chicago then sponsored two seminars, in March and June, to begin the preliminary analysis of the data that was to be incorporated into the various tribal monographs. McNickle attended both sessions, then once again in *Indians at Work* he described the next phase of the project. He explained how the tribal monographs, written on each of the five tribes included in the study, were to be followed by a major publication dealing with the application of the research to problems of Indian education and administration. Such application, he reminded his readers, was the ultimate goal of the project.[22]

The contract between the BIA and the University of Chicago for the first phase of the study expired in late 1944 and for a variety of reasons it was not renewed.[23] Instead, the BIA negotiated a new contract with the Society for Applied Anthropology to complete the second phase of the study. The SAA appointed a Committee on Administrative Research, which included John Provinse as chairman; Paul Fejos, director of the Viking Fund (later the Wenner-Gren Foundation for Anthropological Research); Alexander Leighton; Edward Spicer; and D'Arcy McNickle, to complete the work. Laura Thompson stayed on as project coordinator. At D'Arcy's suggestion, his wife Roma served as publications editor and was also a member of the committee. The Viking Fund agreed to contribute six thousand dollars toward the completion of the project.

At that point the first of the tribal monographs, *The Hopi Way* by Laura Thompson and Alice Joseph, was ready for publication, while the others were in various stages of preparation. Collier, who by then was thinking seriously of resigning, became increasingly impatient with the inevitable delays in making the other studies available. Since the project was his legacy, he wanted the final analysis and policy recommendations printed and in the hands of Bureau personnel before he left office.[24]

Despite the committee's impressive roster, however, the impetus for completing the project spent itself with Collier's resignation. John Provinse, in writing to Laura Thompson about the committee's final report in 1947, admitted that the research had not been implemented anywhere "except in the attitudes of a few individuals who have taken time to read the reports." Nevertheless, as the historian Lawrence Kelly has since pointed out, Collier's insistence on using the insights of the social sciences to develop administrative policies was catching on, and other government activities became the beneficiaries of his foresight during the war.[25]

Although McNickle's specific contribution to the personality study remains difficult to assess, his unique position probably made him the most knowledgeable person in Washington on all aspects of the project. He and

Roma spent much of 1944 and 1945 preparing the various manuscripts, and despite cutbacks in funding that followed the end of the war, all of the tribal monographs were eventually published.[26] Only one volume of the second phase of the study was completed, however. That was Laura Thompson's *Culture in Crisis,* which was published in 1950. Meanwhile, the Committee on Administrative Research had disbanded. Although D'Arcy's and Roma's names appear in the acknowledgments, McNickle's labor on behalf of another publication perhaps provides a better indication of the nature of his involvement.

Before their involvement with the Indian Bureau projects, Dorothea and Alexander Leighton had prepared a manuscript, based on their prewar studies of Navajo healing practices, that described the problem of crossing cultural barriers in health education. They had shown the text to Edna Gerkin, a health education supervisor for the Bureau in Colorado, and Gerkin in turn had recommended it to Collier. She was obviously impressed with the Leightons' work, much of which was concerned with how to make modern information concerning health and hygiene relevant to the still-isolated and uneducated Navajos. A book such as the Leightons had written, she told Collier, would provide invaluable assistance for all Indian service workers in the health field, not just those on the Navajo Reservation, and she urged him to assist in its publication.[27]

After reading the manuscript Collier agreed with Gerkin's assessment. As he would write in the book's foreword, the authors' study was the product of people who had, without being inhibited by cultural preconceptions, "moved into the center of the Navajo's world view." As a result, their discoveries and generalizations about the problems of cross-cultural health education had far-reaching implications not only for the Indian service but for colonial administrations wherever they happened to be.[28] He wanted the book published, and he assigned to McNickle the task of preparing the manuscript.

McNickle was involved with the Leightons' book for over a year, and without his assistance it probably would not have been published. His editorial skill helped him identify and correct some of the problems of its internal organization, and he offered to rewrite the chapter on administration. The Leightons were more than happy to have him do so. His attention extended even to the end papers, which replicated a map prepared by the Bureau's Navajo Human Dependency Survey of the 1930s. He edited Collier's foreword as well. Unfortunately, commercial publishers who examined the manuscript thought that it lacked general interest and were reluctant to publish it. McNickle therefore decided to try various university presses, and when Dumas Malone at Harvard expressed interest, he was delighted. He forwarded Malone's letter to Alexander Leighton, who was still at Poston, with a brief comment: "Attached is a copy of a letter from Dumas Malone which should be cheering, in case everything else at the moment is going to pot."[29]

The letter from Malone was indeed cheering, but it was far from a contract. Harvard Press wanted a definite commitment from the Bureau as to how many copies it would buy, and McNickle patiently acted as go-between while Collier tried to avoid giving a specific answer. The negotiations with Harvard took months, but McNickle's efforts finally paid off. When *The Navajo Door: An Introduction to Navajo Life* was published, Collier was pleased with every aspect of the book, from its content to its cover. He wrote to the publishers, "The 'Door' is a most beautiful piece of book-making throughout. The cover is perfect. I believe that this book ought to have a really good market if it can be brought to people's attention, and I shall do what I can to help."[30] McNickle's work on *The Navajo Door* was patient, detailed, and effective, but, typically, he received little credit except for a line in the authors' acknowledgments.

Despite the lack of specific information about McNickle's contribution to the personality study, there is little doubt that his work on that project, as well as on *The Navajo Door,* played a major role in his education as an applied anthropologist. Although he never studied the subject formally, research on the project and subsequent work with the Committee on Administrative Research provided a unique opportunity for him to learn from those scholars who were most committed to work among American Indians. Parallel to those efforts, his various activities with the Indian Bureau had required intimate contact with individuals and tribes who were trying to make new adjustments to the modern world. His job offered a superb opportunity for his own field work. Although he never lost his self-consciousness about not having earned a college degree, those who were familiar with his background knew that a piece of paper could add nothing to his already profound and growing knowledge of social and cultural anthropology.

The war years, especially from April 1942 through December 1943, were inevitably hectic, and were made more so by the Bureau's involvement with the War Relocation Authority. Milton Eisenhower, who had worked out the initial cooperative agreements with Ickes and Collier, had soon found that he had no stomach for the heart-wrenching job of dispossessing and relocating more than a hundred thousand people. By June 1942, just three months after his appointment, he became ill from the stress and he asked President Roosevelt to reassign him.[31] As his successor he suggested Dillon Myer, a self-assured midwesterner who had been employed by the Soil Conservation Service since 1933. Before then, Myer had worked as a county agricultural agent. He and Eisenhower knew each other through the Department of Agriculture, where Myer had acquired a reputation as an able administrator.

There was no question that the relocation program needed competent administration, and Roosevelt gladly accepted Eisenhower's recommendation. Unfortunately for the Japanese-American evacuees and for the BIA's work at Poston, Myer had had almost no contact with any ethnic group other than his own, and he was totally committed to the melting-pot concept of American society. He was unfamiliar with the idea of cultural pluralism, and he would have rejected it had he known about it.[32]

Given the personalities involved and the terms of the initial agreement, it was inevitable that the Indian Bureau and the War Relocation Authority would collide over the policy and management of Poston; it soon became apparent that operating one center under a policy that differed sharply from that of the others was not going to work very well. Yet this was what Collier, motivated by his belief in the values of a pluralistic society, apparently expected. McNickle's tentative statement of policy for the Bureau's operation, drawn up while Eisenhower was director, reflected Collier's approach. When Myer became director, he was immediately aware of the contradictions implicit in this arrangement.[33]

Underlying the conflict between Collier and Myer was a basic philosophical difference. Myer was convinced that communities that differed culturally from mainstream society were inherently "un-American," and that their existence weakened the fabric of American life. Initially, he and Collier had agreed that most of the evacuees, especially those born in America, were loyal to the United States. They had also agreed, at least theoretically, that the nation would be best served by releasing these loyal citizens from the relocation centers as quickly as possible, not, of course, back to the coastal areas, but to scattered locations throughout the country. Families could be moved to cities and farms throughout the nation's interior, where they would be free to find jobs and become part of the local population. In a memo he sent to Ickes dated September 13, 1942, Collier wrote, "[Myer's thinking] is entirely in line with our own."[34] Between then and the end of the year, however, Collier had changed his mind. Theory was one thing; implementing that theory was another. From that time on, tension between the two men escalated rapidly.

According to Collier, Myer's idea for further resettlement failed to consider the degree of trauma already suffered by the evacuees during their initial relocation. They had been moved twice, first to rude assembly points for several months, then to the hurriedly built relocation centers, and now they did not want to leave the security of the camp. Periodic news that came to Poston from "outside" gave them ample reason to believe that discrimination and hatred awaited them if they left. Myer was convinced, however, despite the obvious evidence of strong anti-Japanese feelings throughout the country, that the evacuees and their families could be successfully assimilated. The relocation centers would then be needed to detain only those of questionable loyalty. An additional benefit, in his view, was that enclaves of Japanese-Americans in the coastal cities would not reappear after the war because the evacuees would have established themselves elsewhere.

Collier, however, was sensitive to the suffering already caused by the initial evacuation. After a brief visit to Poston in June, as the first evacuees were arriving, he had written to a friend about it. "I have never had in all my life as moving an experience as I had on my last experience there. The esprit of the Japanese is superb and it is a very appealing and inspiring situation. Undoubtedly the chances for great social results are real." McNickle, who visited Poston in September, noted in his diary that the evacuees had planted gardens and that the growing things had softened some of the rawness of the stark barracks where they were living. When Collier returned in early November, he was surprised and pleased that no real problems had as yet appeared. "It looks as though a rather extraordinary psychic or spiritual adjustment has taken place," he noted. During this visit he assured the evacuees that they would be safe at Poston and that they should consider the center their home until the war was over.[35]

Myer, however, visited the camp several days later and delivered a different message. He was not impressed with the Japanese-style vegetables that had been planted, and the flower gardens that had pleased McNickle looked much too permanent. They made it appear as though the people intended to stay. Unaware of Collier's speech, Myer told the evacuees of WRA's intention to relocate them once again, to areas where they could live and work freely.

Myer had anticipated a positive response to this bit of news, but the evacuees were dismayed. The thought of yet another move was intolerable. The conflict between Collier's expressed intention and what Myer told them provided a spark that ignited all the pent-up uncertainty and fear that had been building within them for months. Shortly after Myer's departure, the evacuees mounted in front of the Poston administrative offices a nonviolent but noisy demonstration that lasted for several days, during which time they shut down the routine maintenance operations of the center. John Evans, who was in charge when the demonstration began, refused to panic. He let the uprising run its course until the trouble subsided. When it did, it was discovered that there had been very little property damage and no casualties.[36]

Although Myer admitted that Evans had handled the event admirably, he was increasingly worried about the possibility of future incidents at Poston and the other centers. Given the war-time mentality, it was generally believed that the Poston strike was the result of agitation by "disloyal" evacuees, and Myer began to consider the possibility of establishing one camp, with tighter security, for those who were "disloyal." Although the BIA people again agreed to such a separation theoretically, they were concerned about how this "loyalty" might be determined. They also remained exceedingly reluctant to impose still another "relocation" on the evacuees on the basis of some very debatable standard. Myer, however, went ahead with his plans to require that all evacuees answer a questionnaire designed to reveal "loyal" and "disloyal" sentiments.[37]

Shortly after the uprising, Myer and other WRA officials met with Collier, McNickle, and the BIA staff for what the commissioner later described as a "not very satisfactory" discussion of what had happened at Poston. The WRA people, he reported, "are showing a disposition to creep up on our administrative authority in violation of the spirit and letter of the Interdepartmental Agreement." Then he added, in a somewhat ominous tone, "It is conceivable that we may decide to withdraw, unless the WRA will live up to its end of the compact."[38]

During the first six months of 1943, while Myer increasingly asserted his administrative control over Poston, the BIA failed to insist on compliance with the original contract. Collier was afraid of appearing unpatriotic if he opposed the policy of the War Relocation Authority. Wade Head kept McNickle and the Chicago office informed as events unfolded at Poston, however, and finally, in July, McNickle wrote to Assistant Commissioner Zimmerman to examine the options available to the BIA.

Part of the responsibility for the present confrontation, McNickle acknowledged, was the Bureau's apparent acquiescence as the WRA increasingly violated the terms of the initial agreement. Perhaps it was too late now to insist on compliance. It seemed to him that the Bureau had several alternatives. It could withdraw completely from the agreement, or it could offer to take over the entire WRA program. But McNickle believed, even at this late date, that the BIA's best move was to insist that WRA live up to the agreement. Myer would undoubtedly refuse and would then be forced to ask for the agreement's cancellation. At that point the BIA would be in a position to dictate the terms of withdrawal. This was especially important, McNickle felt, as withdrawal would involve the disposition of Indian land and BIA property.[39]

At stake for the BIA were the projects Collier still considered essential for his plan to resettle the Navajos and Hopis on the Colorado River Reservation after the war. The construction of a substantial irrigation system and permanent school facilities had already been started with WRA funds, although Myer had consistently maintained that such public works at Poston should be of temporary materials, useful only for as long as the camps were occupied by the internees. Myer believed he had congressional support for his position, but Collier's view had prevailed during early budgetary hearings. Now McNickle wanted to be sure that, in the event of BIA withdrawal, construction would be completed as planned.

Meanwhile, WRA went ahead with its loyalty questionnaire. Wade Head, who was not yet aware of the discussion over the BIA's possible withdrawal, wrote again to McNickle, this time revealing his unhappiness with the loyalty test. He anticipated great resistance from the evacuees, although he promised to make every effort to reduce the tension that was sure to result. Although he realized that the BIA people at Poston had no choice but to carry through with the interrogation, he was increasingly pessimistic about the Bureau's continuing role there. "We are involved in a program that must only bring discredit on the Indian Service," he complained.[40]

When McNickle told Head of his recommendation to Zimmerman, Head wrote directly to Chicago, advocating BIA withdrawal from the Colorado River site. The Indian Bureau, he told Collier, had become nothing more than a service agency for the War Relocation Authority. Although the WRA was supposed to have consulted with the Indian Bureau on matters of policy, the consultations had been in name only. He repeated his fear that the reputation of the Bureau would in the long run suffer from its association with Poston.[41]

Collier knew what Head was talking about—he himself had spent weary and largely fruitless hours at some of those "consultation" meetings. Myer, it appeared, was willing to confer about policy implementation, but not about policy itself. This administrative technique was to become all too familiar among BIA people a few years later, when Myer became commissioner of Indian affairs.

Collier conferred with Interior Secretary Ickes about the Bureau's deteriorating position in Arizona, and they agreed that, although withdrawal was inevitable, they wanted separation on the most favorable terms possible. Finally, on August 24, Ickes sent a letter to Myer (the letter had been drafted by McNickle), outlining almost word for word the position that McNickle had recommended to Zimmerman. First, Ickes explained in very clear terms why he now demanded compliance with the original memorandum:

> I am troubled particularly by the direction which resettlement has taken at Poston. I had wanted to see the Center developed to its full capacity of food production. I had wanted to see the evacuated population rehabilitated in mind, and [Indian] Service gladly lent heavily of equipment and personnel much needed by its own agencies in order to push a food production program. We also called upon the broadest experience and skills that we had, robbing other activities, in order to develop a community atmosphere within which evacuee morale might be restored. Your approach to the problem has been different and the solution that you have offered cuts squarely across the objectives with which we set out.[42]

If Myer chose to withdraw from the agreement, Ickes told him, all the land not actually being used for relocation purposes must be restored to the Indians. Then a new settlement would be worked out to compensate the Indians for use of the remaining land for the duration of the war. This was Ickes's ultimatum; Myer could live up to the agreement or withdraw from it.

As expected, Myer rejected Ickes's proposal and chose instead to withdraw. In defending his position, Myer maintained that the WRA had consulted fully with the BIA on policy matters and that administrative efficiency demanded comparable procedures and standards in all the relocation centers. He did not seem unhappy, however, about assuming sole responsibility for Poston. McNickle received Myer's reply and sent it on to Zimmerman in Chicago, commenting, "I believe every point urged by us has been accepted."[43]

The Indian Bureau, no longer bound by its obligation to administer the center, announced its decision to withdraw from Poston by the end of the year. During the next six weeks McNickle negotiated the details for transfer of land and personnel and the Bureau completed its withdrawal on schedule. The WRA continued to lease only two thousand acres of the original twenty-five thousand—the rest was returned to the Indians—and those two thousand acres were returned to the BIA in May 1945. The War Relocation Authority was incorporated into the Interior Department the following February, but the Bureau of Indian Affairs was no longer involved.[44]

Relieved of his responsibilities with Poston and finished with the Leightons' book, McNickle now was able to give serious thought to still another project that had been on his mind for some time. His contacts with Indians throughout the country had been extensive and, of course, he knew all the Indians on the Bureau's staff. Ever since the 1939 Toronto conference, he had been meeting with Ruth Bronson, Archie Phinney, and others in the BIA to discuss the possibility of establishing a national pan-Indian organization that could provide a political voice for Indian interests affected by federal legislation.

The idea of a broadly based pan-tribal organization was not new, but earlier groups such as the Society of American Indians had been short-lived and ineffective.[45] Nevertheless, Indians who were most familiar with the country's political institutions believed that only a united front could provide a politically significant Indian voice. A renewed public demand for action on long-standing Indian claims argued for the establishment of an Indian claims commission, and the need for strong Indian representation in the settlement of those claims provided the incentive for yet another attempt to create a broadly based national Indian organization.

McNickle openly began to sound out the possibility of such an organization during a field trip to the Southwest in the early months of 1944, when he met with Hopi, Navajo, Apache, and Papago tribal leaders. At the same time, Collier was encouraging a group of BIA Indians in the Chicago office to hold meetings periodically during that spring and early summer. There were hesitant voices at first. Some people feared the failure of yet another national organization, and others were concerned that their involvement might be criticized and their jobs put in jeopardy. Despite such reservations, however, a consensus eventually developed that the time was right for the establishment of another national Indian organization.[46]

The most active founders of the National Congress of American Indians (NCAI), as the new organization called itself, were McNickle himself; Ben Dwight, a Choctaw from Oklahoma who had earlier established the Inter-Tribal Indian Council in that state; Archie Phinney, a Nez Perce anthropologist who was superintendent of the Northern Idaho Agency; Charlie Heacock, a Rosebud Sioux; and Lois Harlan, Erma Hicks, and Ruth Muskrat Bronson, all of whom were Cherokee. These people established a provisional organization and set a time and place for a constitutional convention. It was in many ways a bold move; the forebodings of some of the participants were not without justification. But, McNickle recalled later with characteristic modesty, "when it was important that a few people stick their necks out to start the organization, I had the good fortune to be able to join those few."[47]

The constitutional convention of the new group met in Denver's Cosmopolitan Hotel in November 1944 as an act of faith; the organizers had no idea how many people would attend. But they had an effective communication network and the word had gotten out. Nevertheless, all of the eighty delegates, from thirty tribes, came as individuals, not as tribal delegates. "No tribal government would risk the censure of its members by paying the expenses of an official delegation."[48] Native American identity being primarily tribal, not "Indian," there would inevitably be some tribal resistance to an pan-Indian organization. But the time seemed right for another attempt.

A number of delegates from Oklahoma reserved an entire railroad coach, and the night before the convention the hotel was "crawling with Indians." Knowing that it was illegal to serve alcohol to them, the hotel management began to have second thoughts about hosting the event. Eventually, however, it agreed to overlook the situation "unless some Indian fell off a bar stool and had to be carried out." Fortunately, this worst-case scenario never happened. Fifteen years later, McNickle recalled the convention:

> At only one moment did any of us have any misgivings. That occurred at the start of the opening session. Basil Two Bears was asked to give an invocation in Sioux, which he did. But he ended his prayer with what must have been an old Sioux warwhoop, telling us to get in there and give the Bureau hell. Well, it happened that the National Reclamation Association was meeting in the other half of the ballroom, with only sliding doors between the two meetings, not much to obstruct the sound. The Reclamation Association meeting came pouring out into the hall to find out who had been stabbed.[49]

After that they settled down to several days of hard work under the able chairmanship of Ben Dwight. They drafted a constitution, defined the organization's membership, elected an executive council of four officers and eight councilmen, and outlined a program for the future. Membership in the new group was to be restricted to people of Indian ancestry, either as individuals or collectively as chapters or tribes. Non-Indians would not be admitted as full voting members, only as associates. Judge N. B. Johnson from Oklahoma was elected president, a post he would occupy with distinction for the next ten years. McNickle and Archie Phinney were among those elected as councilmen, although their election provoked a heated discussion among some who feared that they would subvert the organization for the benefit of the Indian Bureau. Sensitive to the criticism, both men resigned from the council the following year, at which time McNickle backed a proposal that prohibited the election to office of anyone employed by the BIA.[50]

NCAI's constitution, which McNickle helped to write and later to rewrite, was modeled after the constitution of the Federal Employees Union No. 780 in Chicago, to which some of the Bureau's employees already belonged. Its preamble stated the group's broad objectives:

> We, the members of Indian Tribes of the United States of America
> in convention assembled on the 16th day of November, 1944, at
> Denver, Colorado; in order to secure the rights and benefits to
> which we are entitled under the laws of the United States, the several states thereof, and the territory of Alaska; to enlighten the public toward a better understanding of the Indian race; to preserve Indian cultural values; to seek an equitable adjustment of tribal affairs;
> to secure and to preserve rights under Indian treaties with the
> United States; and otherwise to promote the common welfare of
> the American Indians—do establish this organization and adopt
> the following Constitution and By-laws.[51]

The constitution then outlined its organization and stated NCAI's program. NCAI would represent American Indians in nonpartisan political issues and advise, recommend, teach, and promote the Indian point of view before Congress. Its program also included the potential for action in Indian education, research, and welfare.

Despite the early forebodings of some of its members, the emergence of the new national organization was opportune. Argument over passage of the Indian Claims Commission Act (McNickle participated in that argument and was present at the bill's signing by President Truman on August 13, 1946), and the subsequent establishment of the Indian Claims

Commission, provided opportunities as anticipated by the founders of the NCAI for concerted tribal action. The push toward termination in the 1950s further stimulated the growth of NCAI's political stature as it repeatedly opposed termination legislation, which would shut down various tribes. Several constitutional revisions since its founding have demonstrated the viability of its structure, and a series of very able executive directors has provided essential continuity.

McNickle himself continued to play an active role in NCAI for years, speaking, writing, and representing the organization in its various lobbying activities during the 1950s. Although the question of Indian claims may have provided the impetus for the formation of the National Congress of American Indians, as McNickle later said, "some Indians were certainly looking ahead, to a time when organized Indian opinion would be sought by members of Congress, by the press, by other citizen organizations, and even by the Bureau of Indian Affairs."[52] To a large extent, that has come to pass. Basil Two Bears' old Sioux war whoop carried the voice of the American Indian out of the halls of Denver's Cosmopolitan Hotel to the halls of Congress and beyond.

5

From Reorganization to Termination

The end of John Collier's Indian New Deal coincided with the end of World War II. The loss of momentum for Indian reform was apparent to Collier even before the onset of the war, but he waited until January 1945 to tender his resignation. His successor as commissioner was William Brophy, an attorney from Albuquerque, New Mexico, whom McNickle knew well. Brophy had had years of legal experience working with Indians in the Southwest. He soon became ill, however, and for the next several years the Indian Bureau had little effective leadership. From 1945 to 1952 McNickle worked to mitigate its drift, but gradually he came to despair of the federal government's ability to deal effectively with "the Indian problem." Budgeting constraints and the unwillingness of Congress to take a long-term view precluded lasting reform.

The Indian Office remained in Chicago during most of Brophy's three years as commissioner; it did not return to the nation's capital until late 1947. Its repatriation had relatively little effect on McNickle's family. They had not been forced to move and Toni's schooling had continued without interruption. After the Bureau returned to Washington, those involved in the final work on the personality study soon became a close-knit professional family. Joseph McCaskill, John Provinse, Allan Harper, William Zimmerman, and their wives all were part of the McNickles' circle of friends. For some reason John Collier and Laura Thompson, whom Collier had married in the summer of 1943, were not included in this socializing, although they remained in Washington until the second phase of the personality study was concluded.

McNickle had only sporadic contact—none of which was the result of his own initiative—with his Montana relatives during the war years. His niece Helen, Florence's daughter, who had been born in Canada and was serving with the Women's Auxiliary Air Force during the war, passed through Washington and visited with D'Arcy, Roma, and the girls.[1] D'Arcy saw his mother and Florence for the first time in more than twenty years when he attended his sister Ruth's funeral in St. Ignatius in 1946. That brief visit, however, did little to reestablish family ties.

D'Arcy's mother had returned to St. Ignatius to help care for Ruth's family during her daughter's final illness, but she seemed to have no real home. She drifted in and out of the lives of her Montana relatives for years, returning from Milwaukee in the early 1930s, then moving on to Spokane, Portland, and back to Montana. D'Arcy kept in touch with her by mail and contributed financially when he was able, but for the most part she supported herself by working as a domestic and a seamstress. Shortly after Ruth's funeral he invited her to Washington for a visit. Erma Hicks, from the Chicago office, met her at the station there and visited with her while she waited for the connecting train.[2] This was probably in late 1946 or early 1947. Aside from an occasional visit to Washington, however, Philomene continued to wander until 1953, when she became a permanent member of the McNickle household.

D'Arcy and Roma had moved several times during their years in Washington, mostly within the suburban areas of nearby Maryland. Although McNickle traveled a great deal, he was an avid gardener when he was home. Significantly, he recorded various plantings in his diary. He put in bulbs in the fall, flowers and vegetables in the spring—wherever they lived he transformed their "piece of earth" into the neighborhood show-place. He treasured the time he could spend at home, and he took great pride in his garden.

He seldom complained about having to travel, however, and his observations about various accommodations while on the road were detailed and often amusing. On one western tour, during which he apparently conducted a private investigation of his quarters, he reported that the hotel bed had consisted of "horsehair padding over an innerspring mattress," which, as he commented wryly, was hardly conducive to a good night's sleep. He also noted in his diary the quality of the menu and the extent of the wine list. He was no longer the naive, impressionable young man from the Montana frontier who had set sail for England twenty years earlier. All his traveling across the country had turned him into a connoisseur of restaurants and hotels, and with his knowledgeable interest in such details he was a favorite traveling companion. He may have been too busy himself to notice, but he had finally acquired the worldly self-assurance that he had wanted so desperately when he and Joran first ventured to France together.

Despite his sophistication McNickle never really enjoyed the eastern cities. He loved the mountains and the open spaces of the West. He was fortunate in that his travels, for the most part, took him to reservations located in remote western areas of the country. Sometimes he took his fishing gear along with him or borrowed a pole, but unfortunately fishing was a pleasure more often anticipated than realized. He seldom found time to indulge in what he still considered one of his favorite pastimes.

By this time, McNickle's life was far removed from anything he might have imagined for himself as a young man. He had traveled widely, and he counted as his personal friends many well-known and powerful people in government and the academic world. Still, however, he harbored his early dream of becoming a writer of the western frontier. Although the demands of his work continually frustrated his attempts to find time to write, he refused to give up that dream. The Guggenheim Fellowship that he applied for in 1937 would have financed research in New Mexico for a story about Pope, the Indian leader of the 1680 Pueblo Revolt. Although he did not receive a fellowship at that time and never wrote that particular story, he began work on still another novel, a short sketch from which was published as "Snowfall."[3] By 1944, "The Flight of Feather Boy" was ready to send to Dodd, Mead, which had first refusal rights on his second novel.

The story of "Feather Boy" was to haunt him for years. The idea for the novel had originated in a series of events that began in 1907, when a Presbyterian missionary had persuaded members of the Water Buster Clan of the Hidatsa tribe (sometimes known as Gros Ventre, but not to be confused with the better known Gros Ventre, or Atsina, people of Montana) in North Dakota to get rid of its sacred medicine bundle.[4] Tribal ceremonials involving the use of the medicine bundle were no longer practiced because of Christian missionary efforts in the area, and the cleric had wanted to remove the artifact from tribal possession. The bundle eventually became the property of the Heye Foundation's Museum of the American Indian in New York City.

In the 1930s, however, Collier's policy of religious toleration encouraged the Hidatsa Indians to attempt to recover their medicine bundle. McNickle had learned of it during his work with the tribes of Montana and North Dakota, and he became the agent for its restoration. After months of negotiation, the museum agreed to return the bundle to the Indians, and two tribal elders journeyed to Washington and New York in January 1938 to retrieve their precious relic. Its restoration was cause for a celebration. The following year, however, a series of destructive floods plagued the tribe, and a BIA employee in Wisconsin suggested that the Indians give the bundle back to the museum "and let the white man control the weather," because ever since its return to the Indians, the medicine bundle had brought too much of a good thing.[5]

McNickle used the loss of the sacred bundle, which he named "Feather Boy," as the focus for his new work. The early drafts of the novel, like those of "The Hungry Generations," revolved around a romantic fantasy that was far removed from the reality of Indian life as McNickle knew it. As with "The Hungry Generations," he wrote of a utopian world where love and good will eventually triumphed, where men of different races learned to communicate with mutual understanding, and where the damage inflicted by a century of insensitivity and greed was undone and forgotten. Not surprisingly, Dodd, Mead rejected the novel, explaining to the author that the story "lacked interest for a broad reading public."[6] But, as with "The Hungry Generations," McNickle felt that the story of the sacred bundle had dramatic potential, and he would not give it up. He worked on it periodically for the next thirty years, until Harper and Row accepted it in 1976 and published it as *Wind From an Enemy Sky.* The final version reflected his mature thinking—he could not have written it in 1944.

The editors of Dodd, Mead may have felt that, with the war still going on, there was little interest in Indian material, but they were not entirely correct in their assessment of the market. In 1940, Oliver La Farge had published a photo essay on Indians, *As Long as the Grass Shall Grow,* that was selling reasonably well, and Collier was working on *The Indians of the Americas,* which was published by W. W. Norton and Company, in 1947.[7] Also looking ahead to the post-war years, Louis Adamic, an editor at J. P. Lippincott Company in New York, was planning a new series entitled "The Peoples of America." Adamic invited Collier to write the first volume, which was to be about American Indians. Collier was unable to take on the assignment, but he suggested that McNickle, who had just completed work on the Leighton book, might be interested.[8] McNickle was, indeed. In November 1944 he signed a contract with Lippincott for his first historical monograph, *They Came Here First.*

During the Collier years, of course, McNickle had been writing extensively about Indian matters for *Indians at Work* and other magazines and newspapers, as well as working on his Feather Boy story, and he had published an occasional short story.[9] He even served briefly as the Bureau's acting director of information, in Floyd LaRouche's old job. After editing *The Navajo Door,* he was ready for the challenge of this new literary venture. Unfortunately, he was forced to postpone it for some months. Collier's resignation in January 1945, followed by William Brophy's appointment as commissioner, brought inevitable changes to the Indian Bureau. Although McNickle was pleased with Brophy's appointment, he could not anticipate that he himself would become virtually an acting commissioner, at least on Alaskan affairs, for several months in 1945 and 1946. When Brophy became ill, McNickle assumed responsibility for working on the reservation status of Alaskan Indians and Inuits. Once again he had to put his own work aside temporarily.

Although McNickle himself did not go to Alaska, he was fully engaged in the problems faced by native peoples as they sought to protect their land and their way of life. He processed all incoming information and was soon making important policy decisions, especially as they pertained to Senate Joint Resolution 162 and Senate Bill 2037 of the Eightieth Congress.[10] These two documents, supported by those who favored economic development of Alaskan natural resources, challenged the Alaskan natives' claims of aboriginal rights to their territory. McNickle proved so competent in these matters that he received a citation from the Interior Department, which read, in part,

[McNickle] rendered outstanding service in determining issues concerning programs to be worked out in Alaska. He submitted creative ideas that were adopted and which inured to the benefits of the Indians and the Indian Service. . . . Mr. McNickle was also of unusual assistance to the Commissioner of Indian Affairs in giving testimony before committees of Congress. Also he rendered outstanding service in meeting with tribal delegations and assisting them in presenting their programs before the Commissioner and the various departments of Government. Because of his diplomacy he has rendered outstanding service in liaison work with the Veterans Administration, Public Housing Authority, the Federal Board of Hospitalization, and other branches of Government.[11]

The citation then listed the duties required of a field representative and explained how McNickle had performed above and beyond those duties. Normally a field representative worked under the general review and supervision of the commissioner, but, as the citation explained, "in recent months the work load of the Commissioner has been such that he was forced to depend upon McNickle's judgment, tact, and knowledge with very limited opportunity to study his reports and recommendations." Acting Secretary of the Interior Oscar Chapman, who transmitted the citation to McNickle, added his own personal note of appreciation. "We are indeed fortunate to have in our employ one of your superior judgment, tact, and knowledge, and I am glad that we can reward you in this way."[12] McNickle was totally occupied with his increased office responsibilities and his work on the personality study until the end of 1946.

Then, although time and money for research were difficult to come by, he turned his attention to the Lippincott project. Once again, with estimated expenses of almost three thousand dollars, he applied for a Guggenheim Fellowship and also sent proposals to the Field Foundation and the Julius Rosenwald Fund. Then he took a six-month leave of absence so he could devote his time to research. Although none of his applications brought the hoped-for financial support, he did obtain study facilities at the Library of Congress. Help also came from Alexander and Dorothea Leighton, who loaned him their summer home in Nova Scotia for the actual writing. He and Roma spent part of the summer there in 1948 as he worked on the final manuscript and she finished her editing chores for the personality study. Supported financially by Roma's income and an advance from the publisher, he finished the book on schedule.

They Came Here First: The Epic of the American Indian, published in 1949, was the first historical survey of Indian-white relations to be written by a Native American. McNickle organized it into three parts. The first consisted of an ethnological account of the Indians' Old World origins, their long migration into the New World, and the adaptation they made to new environments as they spread out across the Americas. In part two the sequence followed European exploration and colonization until the Atlantic colonies won their independence from England. Part three, the most original section, contained McNickle's analysis of United States–Indian relations from the earliest Federal period, ending with a summary of the Indian New Deal. McNickle's work thus became one of the earliest attempts to provide some perspective on the Collier years by one who had been a participant, although it was hardly without bias.

In the short preface to *They Came Here First,* McNickle stated the book's rationale. He told of a conversation that had taken place when he and Collier had visited a Hopi village a few years earlier. One of the Hopi men had raised questions about how and why the white man, who had come as a stranger into a strange country, felt that it was proper to impose his own rules and customs on the people he found living there. McNickle had been disturbed by the man's questions and felt that they deserved answers. "I was present at that conversation on the mesa," he recalled. "I tried to frame answers to the questions. As it turned out, there were hundreds of questions; one led into another and gave the mind no rest."[13]

In the work that followed, McNickle attempted to answer some of those questions, not only for the Hopis but for himself. The narrative structure had followed logically: "To explain [the white man's works], I discovered, one had to start way back and explain the Indians. Where did they come from? and when? and how? What was it like when they first came into the land? Where did they make their homes?" Then perhaps, McNickle admonished his readers, "if one really tried, one could visualize something of what it was like. One ought to try. It was important."[14]

McNickle's word "ought" is the key to this book. As Constance Skinner had perceived years earlier, McNickle did have a message, almost a moral imperative, for his readers. All Americans, he believed, should address themselves to the questions the Hopi man had raised. Europeans had come as uninvited intruders, and the Indians, though hospitable at first, did not ask the strangers to stay. But they did stay, and because of their superior technology they were able to impose their will on those who were there first. Despite that imposition the Indians had survived and now they were asking troubling questions that ought to be addressed.

McNickle's ability to examine the historical data objectively as he searched for answers was evident in the development of his theme. Its narrative style was essentially romantic, reflecting McNickle's debt to Vernon

Parrington, whose work he had admired while a student at Columbia University in 1931. Parrington's influence was obvious in McNickle's energetic prose and in his idealized vision of America's past. Both Indians and Europeans were tragically portrayed as judging each other by the accepted values of their respective worlds, and he made an impassioned plea for understanding on the part of all participants, Indian and white, in the ongoing historic confrontation. The book was an eloquent evocation of the Indian spirit, and, appropriately, was dedicated "To John Collier, who believed in Indians."

They Came Here First was published in 1949. Lippincott had promoted the new series heavily and the book was well received. By 1955 it had gone through two printings and had sold almost five thousand copies. Initial reviews were enthusiastic. Critics described the book as "sensitive and fresh," "scholarly and informative," "a tremendous story [covered] with surprising comprehensiveness," and "well styled [as] 'The Epic of the American Indian.'" As one reviewer noted, McNickle had provided an "understanding explanation of the feelings of hatred and friendship that existed between white and Indian civilizations." Another reviewer, however, who obviously knew little about Indians, informed his readers that the book's Indian author was born on the Flatbush Reservation.[15] McNickle, who loved baseball, would get good mileage out of that reviewer's error.

Other responses to McNickle's latest effort, both unexpected, were equally gratifying. One came from a Jesuit priest, Gabriel Menager, who had been a young prefect at the mission school in St. Ignatius when McNickle was a student there. Father Menager, who was currently teaching at Loyola University in Los Angeles, had read a review of *They Came Here First,* and he asked McNickle for an autographed copy, "for old time's sake." Another letter came from someone named Ruth Dishrow in New York City. It took a minute for McNickle to realize that Ruth Dishrow was Ruth Rae, his old friend and agent who had worked so hard to find a publisher for his and Joran's early work. The tone of her letter was

much subdued compared to her earlier ebullience, but she obviously remembered D'Arcy fondly and was pleased to hear of his latest success.[16]

McNickle received a letter somewhat later from Earl Pierce, a Washington attorney who was lending his expertise to NCAI in its early fights
against termination. Pierce was close to the action in Congress and had
become convinced that most anti-Indian legislation was the result of ignorance or indifference. If congressmen could be persuaded to read only
the final eighty-nine pages of *They Came Here First,* he told McNickle,
they would possess "a sufficiently working knowledge of the Indian problem so as to enable each member intelligently to perform the duties of
trusteeship." This was, after all, the reason McNickle had written the
book—to inform and enlighten those who were, or should be, concerned
with Indian affairs. McNickle had provided the information; Pierce wondered how the legislators might be persuaded to read it.[17]

McNickle especially valued two reviews of the book that were written
by well-known anthropologists. The first, by Clyde Kluckhohn, appeared
in the *New York Herald Tribune* book review section. Kluckhohn praised
the whole book (with a few "minor exceptions"), but he was especially impressed with the third section. That part, he observed, "is devoted to a
candid examination . . . of the dealings of the United States government
with its Indian population. This part of the book is juicy reading." This
was high praise, coming as it did from such a well-known and respected
authority in the field of Native American anthropology.[18]

The other reviewer was William N. Fenton, who was then working for
the Bureau of American Ethnology. In a review published in the *American
Anthropologist,* Fenton agreed with Kluckhohn that McNickle's greatest
contribution was in part three. Although he assumed that most readers
would be more interested in the first two parts, Fenton noted,

> McNickle makes his greatest contribution at the point where the in-
> terest of other readers may flag. He has been himself concerned for a
> number of years with Indian reorganization, and has given a good
> deal of thought to the history and development of a national Indian

policy. This is his own field. He knows the history and growth of
United States Indian policy well enough so that he is able to point
up significant problems on which historical or actional research is
needed.

Fenton concluded, "We are all very much in McNickle's debt for his read-
able survey of the problem."[19]

Following Kluckhohn's and Fenton's favorable reviews, and in part
because of them, the American Anthropological Association honored
McNickle by nominating him as a fellow. This unexpected honor meant a
great deal to him. Fellowship was generally reserved for those who had
published in the field or, as the Association explained to McNickle, those
"who possess a bachelor's or master's degree in anthropology or a doctorate in an allied field and are actively engaged in anthropology."[20] Despite
McNickle's lack of a degree, the approval of his work by two well-known
anthropologists had established his professional credentials. His many
friends in the association recognized his contribution, and his nomination
as a fellow reflected their esteem. His nomination as a fellow of the Society
for Applied Anthropology at about this same time also reflected the growing recognition of his work.

During those years McNickle continued to write about the need to incorporate the insights of anthropology and the other social sciences into
Indian policy. He was especially hopeful that anthropologists and other
social scientists could contribute to the resolution of long-standing Indian claims through the Indian Claims Commission (ICC). Indian claims
stemming from the government's violation of treaties made with Indians
in the eighteenth and nineteenth centuries had drawn the attention of legislators and administrators since the turn of the century. As early as 1903,
Indian Commissioner Frances E. Leupp had recognized the legitimacy of
such claims and had recommended the creation of a judicial process for
adjudication. Sporadic debate during the next twenty-five years had kept
Indian hopes alive, but it failed to produce any effective resolution of the
claims. The Meriam Report of 1928 had endorsed the idea, and Collier

had included a provision for an Indian Claims Court in the Reorganization Act of 1934. Congress was not yet ready to accept the idea, however,
and the provision was omitted from the final bill.[21]

Effective debate on the question of Indian claims finally began in 1944,
fueled in part by growing congressional interest in terminating tribal relationships with the BIA. Settling old claims would be an essential part of
that process, so Congress was more open to the idea than it had been previously.[22] Some of the impetus for organizing the National Congress of
American Indians had come from the fact that Indians would need a collective voice to present their cause should such a hearing body be created.

The Indian Claims Commission Act was signed by President Truman
on August 13, 1946. For McNickle the Act's most significant feature provided for the creation of an Investigation Division that would function as
a nonpartisan information-gathering body. He anticipated that such a
body, over time, would become the repository for all the information
about Indian tribes that had been gathered over the years by the Bureau of
American Ethnology, various research organizations and universities, and
the professional anthropological societies. An Investigation Division
could eventually create what anthropologist Nancy O. Lurie described as
an "institutional collective memory."[23] Such a data bank would not only
prove invaluable in determining the just settlement of Indian claims, it
would also serve as a primary resource for aiding in the establishment of
future Indian policy. It would provide the Indians with essential elements
of a "usable past." It seemed incredible to him that for all the years of its
existence the Indian Bureau had been unable, and to a large extent unwilling, to utilize any scientific, objective information-gathering system in developing its policies. A change in this practice was long overdue, and the
existence of an Investigation Division under the auspices of the Indian
Claims Commission might finally persuade policymakers to draw on
available resources for greater understanding of the Indian people they
served.

Unfortunately, believing that it would be too costly, the Indian Claims
Commission never established such an investigative body. Instead, it left

the task of generating evidence for Indian claims to the parties involved. This decision created an adversarial climate in which the commission functioned more as a trial court than as a claims referee. Anthropologists were hired as expert witnesses for opposing sides, thus lending themselves to a situation that proved confusing to many of those involved. As McNickle pointed out years later,

> Anthropologists have argued on both sides. They've been expert witnesses for the tribes; they've been expert witnesses for the government. In the latter role, of course, the goal has been to knock down the argument for the tribes. Ethnology presumes objectivity and its data can be interpreted objectively in one argument or another; but from the point of view of the Indians there is at least a question mark: How is it that anthropologists can argue against me as well as for me? I wouldn't attempt to say, but from the standpoint of the pro-Indian, there is a question as to how ethical and how objective this is.[24]

The confusion brought on by such a policy became obvious as Indian claims were presented to the ICC. Not infrequently, the Indian Bureau became the adversary of the very people it was mandated to protect.

Indians and their attorneys were not the only ones who were unhappy with this situation. Anthropologists who were involved in the various claims often felt that truth was not being well served. Nuances of interpretation rather than objective fact often became the determining element in deciding many of the cases brought before the Claims Commission. Nevertheless, some long-standing claims were resolved, and McNickle felt at the time that his labors in affecting passage of the Indian Claims Commission Act had not been wasted.[25]

Ultimately, however, the ICC fell far short of its proponents' early expectations. Indian claimants were forced into adversarial positions they did not always understand, and in a few isolated cases they were victimized by their attorneys. The Investigation Division never took effective shape, and the background information gathered for the various suits remained in the files of the litigants and their attorneys. The data bank became only a dream. Symptomatic of the times, perhaps, was that the three mandated commissioners were selected because of, not in spite of, their scant knowledge of Indian affairs. The assumption apparently was that prior knowledge of any specific case might prejudice the outcome of the hearings. Only complete ignorance of any facts except those presented by the litigants could, apparently, ensure justice. It is no wonder that McNickle and many others eventually viewed the Indian Claims Commission as a lost opportunity.[26]

It was not yet clear to McNickle, but 1950 would mark the beginning of a change in the direction of his life. By that time he could look back at a rather extraordinary government career in which he was approaching the top of the Indian Office bureaucracy. Hired in 1936 as an administrative assistant under the so-called Indian civil service, his job had been brought under regular civil service in 1944, when he was reclassified as a field representative. His salary, which had risen periodically, was augmented in 1946 by another increase accompanying his citation for superior accomplishment. In 1950 he was appointed chief of the tribal relations branch, with a grade of GS twelve and an annual salary of seventy-two hundred dollars. He was forty-six years old.[27]

The nature of the bureaucratic structure had changed, however, from the prewar years when McNickle had worked under Tribal Relations directors Allan Harper and Joe Jennings. In the late 1940s, as a result of the Hoover Commission's report, the entire executive branch of the federal government had been reorganized, resulting in major changes in the Bureau of Indian Affairs in 1950 and 1951. Most significant of those changes was the creation of eleven area offices as the operational links between field personnel and the commissioner and his staff in Washington. These area offices replaced the direct contact the various branch chiefs had previously had with agency personnel. They provided more efficient management through an intermediate level of bureaucratic control, but those who had worked with Collier, who were accustomed to hands-on administration of the field programs, became increasingly restless. It seemed to them that the Indian Bureau in Washington had lost its sense of direction as well as its contact with Indian people, and to some extent this was true. Brophy's illness and subsequent resignation, followed by the brief tenure of commissioner John Nichols, had provided little real leadership and Congress was quick to take advantage of the situation. It began a concerted effort to define a new Indian policy, implemented as usual through the budget process.[28] Funding for the B I A was cut drastically in the years after World War II.

Collier's Indian New Deal, however, had been under attack almost from its inception. Much of the opposition in Congress had come from those who continued to believe in the policy of assimilation that had characterized the pre-Collier years. In the past, Indian commissioners had enjoyed legislative support because they and Congress more or less shared a common goal. By setting his policy in a new direction, Collier had made himself the target of repeated attacks by members of Congress, and with the onset of World War II, his Indian reorganization program was progressively underfunded and weakened. Other communal aspects of President Roosevelt's New Deal administration were also increasingly attacked.[29]

Some of Collier's programs, such as the Colorado River resettlement project, ultimately failed because they were ill conceived. The irrigation systems built there during the war were never as extensive as he had hoped, and few Navaho and Hopi families were interested in leaving their homeland and moving south into the desert. Other programs, however, failed because Congress was indifferent or was actively opposed. The Applied Anthropology Unit had died an early death, in part because, as McNickle put it, "certain cave-dwellers in Congress were irrationally opposed to enlisting social scientists in the service of the Indian Bureau."[30] The personality study produced only one volume beyond the tribal monographs; when Collier resigned, no one else was able to enlist legislative support for the project. The National Indian Institute became nobody's child. The Indian Claims Commission was overwhelmed by its case load, and it failed to create the Investigation Division that Collier and

McNickle had considered essential. All of these programs had fallen short of Collier's expectations because, for one reason or another, Congress had failed to support them.

Despite continued criticism, however, the Indian Bureau had won some major victories. Collier's determination to return cultural and political autonomy to the tribes had reversed, at least temporarily, a seventy-five-year-old demand for assimilation. The allotment and further alienation of Indian land had ended with the passage of the Wheeler-Howard Act in 1934, through which Collier mounted a concerted effort to increase, rather than decrease, the Indian land base. That program, too, however, was only partially funded by Congress, and the decade of the 1950s would see a resumption of tribal lands moving into private ownership.

Perhaps the most significant change under Collier had been the establishment of the tribes as corporate legal entities, which provided them with political leverage. Those incorporated tribes, all Indian people, in fact, had discovered a new collective voice in the National Congress of American Indians. They were demanding to be heard. Collier had not, as some of his critics claimed, returned the tribes to an earlier condition of dependency, nor had he forced their termination. "The policy underlying the Indian Reorganization Act," McNickle wrote in *They Came Here First*, "is not a policy of reverting to a prior condition of things. To assert the right of self-government [for the tribes] is to assert the future."[31] Collier had provided the Indians with hope.

Within this context of hope, McNickle in 1950 predicted gradual acculturation and a lessening of the B I A's control over Indian lives. Arguing from the obvious premise of his own success as a fully acculturated Indian, he predicted that eventually all Indians would learn to live with, although not necessarily within, white society. As corporate legal entities the tribes had the same right to protection under the law as any other community, regardless of the way they organized themselves and their property internally.[32]

McNickle increasingly referred to "adaptation" as the operative principle in developing tribal autonomy. Adaptation did not require the destruction of the tribe as a legitimate form of community. In *They Came Here First,* he described how Indians had always adapted in creative ways to their physical environment; he believed that they would continue to modify their tribal institutions if given the time and opportunity to do so. The motivation for adaptation and change, however, had to come from within; it could not be decreed or legislated. Bureaucratic regulations and programs had not been and never would be able to impose the desire to change. Prior attempts from outside the Indian community constituted the basic problem in the formation of Indian policy.

"Gradualism" was the other key word in McNickle's understanding of the "Indian problem." In one of his more important position papers, written in 1949, he insisted that the federal government had a moral obligation not to withdraw arbitrarily and unilaterally from its treaty commitments. The process of establishing tribal autonomy must proceed slowly but steadily, with full collaboration between the tribes and the government, until the tribes themselves moved to take up the slack in education, health and welfare, and law enforcement. The federal government must also draw on all the resources available to it to further the cause of justice in its own eyes and in the eyes of the nations of the world. Once more he came back to the social sciences. "Indian administration," he stated, "must make increasing use of methods of the social sciences in resolving the basic problem of assisting the Indians to adjust their lives to a dominant culture."[33]

However, when Dillon Myer was appointed Indian commissioner, McNickle had grave doubts that there would be much sympathy for allowing the adaptive process to proceed in accordance with its own momentum. Myer had twice been offered the job as Indian commissioner before he finally accepted it in the spring of 1950. In view of his clashes with the BIA during World War II, his appointment by Interior Secretary Oscar Chapman remains something of an enigma. Chapman had been assistant secretary of the interior under Harold Ickes in the 1930s and 1940s, and in that position he had been a staunch supporter of the Indian New

Deal. After Ickes resigned in 1946, however, Chapman's thinking began to shift. In the face of a growing national consensus that looked askance at cultural diversity, Chapman gravitated toward Myer's position that Indian reservations, like Japanese relocation centers, served only to isolate those who lived there. He had observed Myer's management of the War Relocation Authority and his efficient (some called it ruthless) dismantling of the relocation centers after the war, and he believed that under Myer's guidance Indian reservations could be terminated as well. Chapman was convinced that the B I A, after several years of drifting, needed the kind of firm administrative leadership Myer would bring to the position, and he finally persuaded Myer to accept the nomination in March 1950.[34]

By this time Congress, in the persons most notably of senators Pat McCarran of Nevada, Clinton P. Anderson of New Mexico, and Arthur V. Watkins of Utah, had taken the lead in changing the direction of Indian policy. During Myer's confirmation hearing before the Senate Committee on Interior and Insular Affairs the senators focused on Myer's understanding that it was the legislature, not the commissioner, that determined Indian policy. The committee made it very clear that the commissioner was expected to implement the will of Congress. With policy originating in Congress, the new commissioner's philosophy, or even his admitted lack of knowledge about Indians and Indian affairs, was irrelevant.[35]

Myer had no quarrel with the prevailing congressional view of Indian policy, and he happily agreed that Congress should call the shots. Because he knew that the Collier holdovers would continue to oppose further tightening of the bureaucratic structure, he brought new people into key positions. One of his first official acts, the very day he took office, was to replace assistant commissioner William Zimmerman, who had had seventeen years of service with the Indian Bureau, with Ervin J. Utz, who had worked under Myer in the War Relocation Authority. With this appointment he set the pattern for the next eighteen months. Theodore Haas, Joseph McCaskill, Walter Woehlke, Allan Harper, and many others who had years of experience in the Bureau either were asked to resign or were transferred out of the Washington office.[36]

Like Ervin Utz, most of those who came into the Indian Bureau at this time had previously served under Myer in the War Relocation Authority, and like him they knew little or nothing about Indians. McNickle later made some pointed comments in an article for *Christian Century* about Myer's reorganization of the Indian Bureau:

> When Dillon S. Myer became commissioner of Indian Affairs a few years ago, he removed from immediate contact with his office civil servants who had prolonged familiarity with Indian problems and replaced them by young men with a reputation for "getting things done." . . . Such actions made some people uneasy. It seemed to them that neither an ability to get things done nor impeccable honesty were adequate substitutes for knowledge and experience in this difficult field.[37]

Myer, of course, was within his rights as the new commissioner to select his own people for key positions. Nevertheless, by replacing the experienced Bureau staff with people who admittedly knew nothing about Indians and who, once in office, would have no direct contact with them, he made sure that he, and they, would be insulated from the complicated reality of Indian administration.

McNickle stayed on as chief of tribal relations under Myer for almost two years. During that time he tried to ease the impact of new policies and to provide a moderating voice in staff meetings, although he found his responsibilities increasingly circumscribed and emasculated. When he wrote to Collier about the difficulty of being effective within the new administrative structure, Collier was sympathetic. "It's a hell of a job," he agreed, "to surmise what any Indian Bureau official under Myer et al ought to say for any record now."[38]

Myer did not turn his attention to policy matters until he was assured that the reordered administrative machinery in the new area offices was operating smoothly. But it was only a matter of time before his leadership extended beyond the internal reorganization of the Bureau's staff. After his appointees had settled into their jobs, his focus broadened to include ventures in policymaking and, confident of Congressional support, he began to move aggressively beyond his official mandate. Collier described Myer as "morally impeccable yet socially lethal," and in many ways this was quite accurate. Myer was "a man of character," but under his cultural myopia and tight administrative rein the "gradualist" approach advocated by McNickle was abandoned.[39] Indian tribes were presented with a choice. They could either take over their own affairs completely, with no further assistance or protection from the Bureau of Indian Affairs (i.e., have their relationship with the federal government terminated) or they could submit to increasingly rigid bureaucratic control.[40] Myer's new position, supported by Congress, would essentially reverse the Collier administration's efforts to preserve tribal land, culture, and political autonomy. Unprotected in their present state, tribes would literally be "thrown to the wolves" that were waiting to exploit their resources.

Myer's desire to distance himself and his staff from direct contact with tribal Indians once again reflected his deep-seated ethnocentrism. In the 1920s, as an agricultural agent in Ohio, he had worked successfully with people who shared his own "yankee" goals and values. While director of the WRA, he had related well to those younger evacuees in the relocation centers who most completely conformed to his version of the American ethos. Myer liked and trusted them and several of the Japanese-Americans who had supported his WRA policies became his close friends after the war.[41] Myer's opposition to Japanese gardens and cultural activities at Poston, however, revealed his fundamental mindset. Myer discriminated on the basis of culture, not race; during the war this had easily translated into patriotism.

Myer's antipathy toward cultural pluralism was revealed once again in his attitude toward the Indians. His support of efforts to relocate them into urban areas reflected this kind of thinking. He wanted to break up the tribal enclaves of the reservations by forcing the Indians into mainstream society. As with the wartime evacuees, he was oblivious to the cultural differences that stood in the way of such assimilation.[42]

By isolating his Washington staff from the Indians on the reservations, Myer was able to filter out and ignore the destructive cultural implications of his relocation and termination policies. His only conceivable solution to the Indians' dilemma, which he defined exclusively in terms of overpopulation relative to tribal economic resources, was to relocate them into the mainstream labor force. He was not interested in helping them develop the reservations' economic resources to make them more self-sufficient or preserve the tribal way of life. He was convinced that reservations were detrimental to the Indians' welfare and that economic development of tribal resources could be better accomplished by private enterprise, meaning, by definition, nontribal enterprise. He framed his policy within those parameters.[43]

Myer's philosophy of melting-pot assimilation was exploited by several western congressmen who were eager to get tribal lands onto state tax rolls and tribal resources into the hands of corporate developers. Senators McCarran, Anderson, and Watkins represented states that had undergone considerable economic expansion during the war, and they were seeking ways to increase their states' tax revenues. Untaxed Indian land was considered an affront to economically productive and taxable business enterprise. Myer's dedication to cultural homogeneity played into the hands of these senators and their cohorts, who were only too eager to provide congressional leadership in support of Myer's drive toward termination.

The commissioner's philosophy and his management style must have been difficult for McNickle to work with, although he said almost nothing for the record about their personal relationship. In some ways Myer resembled Collier. He shared Collier's appetite for battle, relishing those occasions when he was called upon to discuss Indian affairs before congressional committees or interest groups such as the NCAI. Myer was also forceful and articulate; like Collier, he could be very persuasive. In his autobiography he proudly recalled a conversation with an Indian from Oklahoma who was vice president of a large oil company. Myer was promoting a plan to sell marginally productive Indian land and use the proceeds from the sale to buy better land. "I convinced him," he recalled proudly. "I found out later, however, that the pressures were so great on him that he reversed himself again, but at the time I convinced him."[44]

Myer's comment is revealing in several respects. First, it shows how oblivious he was to the Indian land in question being ancestral land, with a noneconomic but very real value to the people who owned it. The oil man agreed with Myer's economic argument, but the land under consideration represented tribal values that were not subject to economic rationalization.

On another level, Myer always maintained that those who disagreed with him did so for unprincipled reasons. They had a hidden agenda for personal gain, or they were subject to pressures from misguided groups that passed themselves off as "friends" of the Indians. Some, he believed, opposed him as a private vendetta. The oil tycoon had submitted to unnamed "pressures." Myer seemed unable to conceive of the possibility that he might be mistaken. His forceful speech, combined with his absolute self-righteousness, made him an intimidating adversary.

In many respects, McNickle was Myer's diametrical opposite. He had never been comfortable when faced with the necessity for verbal jousting. He confessed more than once in his diary that he was unable to think fast enough on his feet to be effective in such circumstances.[45] Although he had admired Collier's talents in parrying with Congress, confrontation was not his style. He was not seriously offended by Collier's sometimes bellicose tactics because he and Collier were in general agreement on the issues in question. But given McNickle's and Myer's basic philosophical differences, the new commissioner's assertiveness was decidedly distasteful. Myer reminded him of those automobile salesmen whose high-pressure tactics had made him so uncomfortable years before. He had always disliked "pushy" people, and Myer was "pushy."

McNickle's management style also differed from Myer's. Although he expected a high level of performance and did not suffer fools gladly, McNickle was a nondirective manager, giving much breathing space to those who worked for him. He resisted what appeared to be arbitrary rules and senseless bureaucratic procedures and he sometimes preferred to operate on "Indian time," with a disconcerting disregard for the clock. He was always both accessible and flexible. In contrast, Myer ran a "tight ship," with clearly defined areas of responsibility and lines of command and a high regard for calendar and clock.

Given the differences in the two men's philosophies and personalities, as well as the general mind-set of Congress, it is difficult to understand just why McNickle decided to apply for the position of chief of tribal relations in 1950 when he knew that Myer would soon be sworn in as commissioner. The two men had been acquainted for almost ten years by that time, years marked by frequent and sometimes acrimonious contact concerning the relocation centers. After the war, when Myer briefly headed the Public Housing Authority, they had clashed over housing for Indians who were being relocated from the reservations into various urban areas. McNickle undoubtedly realized that there were deep differences between them and at first glance his willingness to work for Myer is puzzling.

There were, however, several possible reasons for his decision. First, he had been acting chief for a year; he was the logical person to apply for the full appointment. He also continued to believe that in that position he might be able to soften the impact of congressional policies on both the Indians and the Indian Bureau. The new policies had not originated with Myer; to a large extent they reflected both congressional and public opinion, and up to a point even McNickle supported them.[46] But Myer's "all or nothing" policy threatened disaster for the Indians, and McNickle, ever the peacemaker, hoped to be a moderating influence. Myer apparently never perceived McNickle as a threat and did not try to remove him as he had so many others who had supported the Indian New Deal.

McNickle kept his own counsel, however, and he had still another reason for not leaving the Bureau in 1950. Under the aegis of the National Congress of American Indians, he had been planning a community action program through an adjunct organization called American Indian Development (AID), of which he was the director. To implement the program,

he; Judge N. B. Johnson, NCAI's president; and Ruth Bronson, its executive director, had established the NCAI Fund, which was almost immediately reorganized as Arrow, Inc. This was to be a money-raising tax-exempt branch of the parent organization that would collect funds to
support the program of American Indian Development.[47] McNickle had
decided to stay with the Indian Bureau until Arrow raised sufficient funds
for at least a two-year program.

In August 1951, while still working for the Bureau, McNickle used the
occasion of a trip to New York City to solicit funds from various foundations that had supported Indian projects in the past. He met with people
from the Ford, Carnegie, Rockefeller, and Whitney foundations, the
Phelps-Stokes Fund, the national board of the YWCA, and several church
groups.[48] He was especially eager to talk with the Marshall Field Foundation, which had supported one of AID's first program efforts earlier that
summer. He had conducted a two-week community development workshop for Indians in conjunction with the BIA's in-service training program in Brigham City, Utah, and the Field Foundation had contributed
fifteen hundred dollars to it. McNickle hoped to enlist its further support.

The initial idea for AID's work in community development grew out of
the 1950 Washington Conference on Women and Children. Several NCAI
members had attended that conference. One was Elizabeth Roe Cloud, a
Chippewa who was chair of the Indian Affairs Division of the General
Federation of Women's Clubs. Mrs. Roe Cloud was the conference's hon-
oree as "American Mother of the Year." Ruth Bronson had also attended
the conference, and after it was over, she and Roe Cloud discussed with
McNickle the possibility of AID directing its action program toward the
area of community development. While local club work modeled on
women's clubs obviously was not the answer to deep-seated problems on
Indian reservations, they believed that local organizations might offer a
starting place for community revitalization. The workshop in Brigham
City and several others that followed that summer constituted McNickle's
first effort in that direction.

Though for the most part the two-week workshop in Utah was independent of the B IA, the Bureau's summer school made a conference room available and the participants had the benefit of low-cost rooms and meals. McNickle had hoped that the workshop would attract a broad representation of tribal leaders, but the number of people in attendance during the first two-week session varied. Only a few registered for the entire program. Some came for only a few days, and others dropped in occasionally from the B IA's training sessions, so continuity became a major problem. Nevertheless, the usual attendance was between thirty and forty people, indicating that there was interest in what he was trying to do.

The basic premise of the 1951 workshops was deceptively simple. As Ruth Bronson explained in a letter to Dillon Myer, "Before people can be expected to change their present living habits, they must satisfy themselves that there is a better way to live." The workshops were designed to encourage tribal leaders to look appraisingly at their own communities for opportunities to improve their physical well-being, and "at their resources of spirit and devotion that could be called upon to make that better way an actuality."[49] Once people were willing to do this they could begin to help themselves.

The first experimental workshop allowed McNickle to develop a format that he used later that summer. Participants devoted the first week to a discussion of basic problems encountered by everyone who lived on Indian reservations. They were often surprised to discover how many difficulties they shared with other Indian groups, although the details, of course, varied widely. During the second week the focus shifted to identifying the options available for dealing with some of those problems. They learned how other communities, facing similar problems, worked together to develop effective programs. The participants were then encouraged to ask, "How can *we* do it?" and to explore the kinds of expert advice and assistance that might be available as they began to help themselves.

All of this may have seemed rather mundane to the non-Indians involved, but McNickle considered it an essential first step. Decades of Indian Bureau paternalism had caused a virtual paralysis of the Indians' ability to make significant decisions about their own lives. The Indian

Bureau, in its renewed effort to assimilate the Indians and terminate government services, was making no effort to provide the Indians with real decision-making opportunities. In fact, just the opposite was occuring. Myer's policies were forcing more restrictive regulations on those tribes that resisted termination. McNickle was concerned that time was running out and that the Indians had a great deal to learn before they would be ready to control their own futures.

The first workshop in Brigham City was so well received that two others followed later that summer in Tahlequah, Oklahoma, and in Phoenix, Arizona. He began planning for still another series the following year in Brigham City, and they were even more successful. Meanwhile, he came to grips with the difficult question of whether it was time for him to leave the Bureau of Indian Affairs.

McNickle knew that that decision would be crucial to his career and his life. If he stayed with the B I A, his next move up might well be as assistant commissioner. At first glance, that was an attractive possibility. But he was not at all sure that he really wanted to continue working in the Indian Bureau, which now seemed bent on destroying all that he had labored so hard to build. Most of his earlier associates had already departed, and with them had gone the excitement engendered by Collier's vision. It seemed now that the Bureau under Dillon Myer was moving the Indians toward disaster. Instead of helping them help themselves, as Myer believed, it was doing just the opposite. Indian participation in the B I A's so-called "resource planning" sessions was only a gesture. During the Collier years, and even then not consistently, the Bureau had been more willing to consult seriously with Indians and to design a policy based on the Indians' own perceptions of their needs. But that was no longer happening, and McNickle could do nothing about it.

On the other hand, A I D's action program was getting under way with the workshops, and his fund-raising efforts had been moderately successful. Mrs. Frederick E. Hyde, Jr., of New York City, had donated $10,000 toward a project in health education on the Navajo Reservation, and the Field Foundation had offered $17,500 for a less restricted program in community development. Several smaller contributions brought the total to almost $30,000. This was enough to support a modest program for two years. He began to consider the possibility of taking an extended leave of absence, which would give him time to assess the feasibility of further community development work and at the same time provide a measure of security. If additional financial support failed to materialize, he could return to the Bureau.

McNickle admitted that $30,000 was not enough to launch a large-scale, long-term program, but he was not interested in size. He had had enough of ambitious programs that promised much but delivered little. What he wanted was an opportunity to work directly with Indian people, to become a bridge, or a catalyst, and to contribute to the restoration of a tribal people's decision-making capacities. He wanted a program that would let him work more intimately within a particular tribal community.

The final push toward his decision to leave the Bureau came with the resignation of his friend Willard Beatty in September of 1951.[50] Beatty had served as the BIA's director of education since the 1930s, and he and McNickle were among the last Collier people remaining in the upper echelons of the Indian Bureau. With Beatty gone, it seemed to McNickle that the time was right for him, too, to make the break. As he later explained to members of NCAI, "the time had come to try, if only in a small way, to stir up in the Indians some concern for the fix in which they [found] themselves and maybe get them to do something about it, by themselves."[51] In March 1952 he decided to take a year's leave to see what he might be able to accomplish through American Indian Development.

1. William McNickle, D'Arcy's father, probably taken ca. 1905. William's parents had fled the Irish potato famine in the 1840s and settled in Pennsylvania, where William was born around 1870. He died in 1929. D'Arcy's resemblance to his father was striking. Courtesy of O. J. Currie.

2. Philomene Parenteau McNickle, D'Arcy's mother, was born in St. Laurent, Saskatchewan, in 1882. Her father, Isidore Parenteau, was sympathetic to the Riel Rebellion in 1885, and after it was over he relocated his family among the Flathead Indians in western Montana. Philomene, obviously stylish and attractive, remained a handsome woman until her death in 1964. Ca. 1905. Courtesy of O. J. Currie.

3. The McNickle children, l. to r., D'Arcy, Florence, and Ruth, probably taken in early 1905. Although the three children were raised in an environment that was largely culturally white, they attended Indian schools and many of their playmates were Indian. Courtesy of O. J. Currie.

4. D'Arcy McNickle and his mother, Philomene, taken when he was sixteen years old, in 1920. D'Arcy and his mother were very close throughout his childhood, and she spent the last years of her life as part of his household. Courtesy of O. J. Currie.

5. The Sisters of Providence and Jesuit Brothers ran the mission schools for girls and boys at St. Ignatius, Montana, where D'Arcy and his sisters were enrolled for their first few years of schooling. McNickle describes this school and the nearby church, where he served as an acolyte, in his novel *The Surrounded*. Undated photo, around 1900. Courtesy of the Oregon Province Archives of the Society of Jesus, Gonzaga University, Spokane, Washington.

6. This photograph of
D'Arcy McNickle appeared
on the dust jacket of *They
Came Here First* (1949), but
seems to have been taken
some years earlier, probably
in the late 1930s. Courtesy
of the Newberry Library,
Chicago.

7. D'Arcy and his first child,
Antoinette Parenteau
McNickle (b. 1934), when
Toni was about five years
old. Courtesy of O. J. Cur-
rie.

8. D'Arcy McNickle and
unidentified tribal leaders at
Crownpoint, New Mexico,
in 1953, as his community
development work among
the Navajos was gathering
momentum. Photo by Mil-
ton Snow, courtesy of the
Newberry Library, Chicago.

6

The Crownpoint
Project

McNickle knew that the project he was proposing through American Indian Development would require patience and wisdom. Collier's plans for tribal reorganization, well intentioned as they were, had done little to restore the Indians' self-image and confidence in their own decision-making capacity. Obviously, autonomous changes in tribal communities would take place very slowly. He wondered whether he, D'Arcy McNickle, through American Indian Development, could invest enough time within a single community to make a lasting difference. Only the experiment itself could answer that question. Even though the workshops had been well received, they did not provide long-term solutions. He decided to risk an entirely different approach.

After consulting with NCAI and BIA people following the 1952 workshop, McNickle was ready to modify AID's original program. He continued holding workshops in Oklahoma, where the community response was producing good results.[1] At the same time, however, he began to formulate a new concept for a different, more isolated, situation. Suzanne Hyde's donation was targeted specifically toward "the improve-

ment of health conditions among the Navajo Indians."² If he could find
the right location, he might incorporate health education into an overall
community development project, with the two aspects of the program
complementing each other. A recent B I A report on the plight of a group
of Navajos in New Mexico had attracted his attention, and he began to
search for a site on the Navajo Reservation where a program of this kind
might be effective.³

An obvious need for such a project in a particular area, however, was
not McNickle's sole criterion. Almost any locale on the reservation would
qualify on that basis. In his view, the desired location should also contain a
group of people who retained a residual core of traditional leadership.
Such indigenous leadership would provide a local power base on which to
begin building. He believed that a small group of recognized, accepted
leaders who had had some exposure to alternatives for living beyond their
own culture could more readily visualize options for change. Many Navajos had served with the armed forces during World War II or had been
employed in war-related industries, and others as children had attended
off-reservation boarding schools.⁴ These people were more aware of the
potential for better hygiene and health and of the need for education in a
rapidly changing world. Many of them were also approaching the age
when, in earlier times, they would have been assuming positions of leadership among their people. These men and women might provide the impetus for change.⁵

In addition, McNickle looked for an existing medical facility to augment the proposed health education program and to provide continuity
when A I D eventually withdrew. In a reversal of the objectives of previous
government services that sought to replace traditional healers with modern medical technology, he wanted the healers to learn to view the technology as a supplement to their traditional healing practices. Another part
of health education was concerned with the familiar problem of translating scientific ideas into a foreign cultural vernacular. Dorothea and Alexander Leighton, in *The Navajo Door,* had described cultural differences
that were obstacles to health education in many Navajo communities, and

they had suggested new ways of teaching to make communication possible. McNickle used their book as his basic reference in formulating his health education program.[6]

Following the 1952 summer workshops McNickle began a search for the site that would, if possible, meet all his requirements. He was somewhat familiar with the Navajo Reservation, having accompanied Collier on visits there as early as the 1930s, and he had returned several times since then in an official capacity. But on all those trips he had seldom ventured beyond the tribal headquarters. This time he traveled a less direct route from Albuquerque to the four-corners area so that he might visit the BIA hospitals at Chinle, Fort Defiance, Crownpoint, Tohatchi, Fort Wingate, and Toadlena. As he was approaching Crownpoint, New Mexico, a summer cloudburst brought his search to an abrupt if temporary halt. The downpour turned the dirt roads of the area into an impassable quagmire, forcing him and his companions, Navajo linguist Robert W. Young and another BIA man, to spend the night in their jeep. According to Young, they sustained themselves on a bottle of whiskey and a tin of mutton. The BIA man was quite unnerved by the rising water around them—it seems that he was unable to swim. Fortunately, the whiskey provided a measure of solace, and although they were temporarily marooned, they were never in any real danger.[7]

An unexpected delay of two days in Crownpoint while the roads dried was serendipitous, because it provided an additional opportunity to meet and talk with many of the local people. McNickle and his companions toured the small hospital and visited with medical personnel from New Mexico and the BIA who were serving there. When the roads were again passable, they continued north to Shiprock, Teec Nos Pos, and Kayenta, but McNickle had made up his mind.[8] What he had seen of the eastern Navajo country convinced him that Crownpoint was the right place for the project that was rapidly taking shape in his mind.

Before making a final commitment, however, McNickle wanted to discover for himself just why this particular group of Navajos felt so alienated and neglected. He knew their recent history, with its sad story of Collier's misconceived stock-reduction program, but he was not familiar with what had preceded that. He wanted to know why the local people felt so helpless in bringing about any improvement in their situation. What he learned was in many ways a microcosm of the larger "Indian problem" in the United States.

The so-called eastern Navajos who lived near Crownpoint were relative newcomers to the area; their ancestors had occupied what is now the northwest corner of New Mexico only since, perhaps, the fourteenth century. The land itself was harsh, sculptured by wind and water into bold, bare forms of dramatic grandeur. Rainfall was marginal and some areas were almost a desert. Despite its harshness, however, the Navajos saw beauty in the land and they had learned to live in harmony with it. Many of them had made their homes there for generations before Kit Carson rounded them up for the "Long Walk" across New Mexico to Fort Sumner in 1864. When the army released them four years later, they wanted only to return to the land they called "Dinetah," the land of the Dine, the people.

Unfortunately, much of the land claimed by these eastern Navajos was not included within the reservation as defined by the treaty of 1868. Although the federal government later expanded the boundaries several times to accommodate the Indians' growing herds and flocks, many eastern Navajos in New Mexico still remained outside the reservation. Some of them eventually received executive order allotments from the public domain, and a few purchased land from the railroad. A small number leased their land from the government or from private owners. This mixed pattern of land ownership gave the region its name: the "checkerboard area." Although Navajo people living in the checkerboard area were included within the jurisdiction of the BIA after 1909, their land remained outside the boundaries of the reservation.[9]

The Eastern Navajo Agency, established in 1911, was one of six agencies that together constituted the BIA's Navajo administration until 1935. Crownpoint itself was not originally an Indian community; towns and villages were foreign to traditional Navajo culture.[10] Samuel F. Stacher, the first government agent assigned there, chose the site of Crownpoint as agency headquarters because it gave promise of an adequate water supply and was centrally located, although it was not within the boundaries of the reservation. During Stacher's twenty-four years as agent at Crownpoint, the Indian Bureau built roads and bridges, a small hospital, and a boarding school, with the Navajos themselves volunteering most of the labor. By the early 1930s, more than sixty BIA employees staffed the agency, the hospital, and the school.[11]

Collier's term as Indian commissioner brought changes to the Navajo Reservation that inevitably affected the little community at Crownpoint. In an effort to reduce the range damage caused by overgrazing, the BIA under his direction had inaugurated a stock reduction program that unwittingly left many families without resources of any kind. The traumatic effect of the program, especially in the checkerboard area, created a backlash that contributed to the tribe's later rejection of Collier's reorganization plan. In a more positive move, Collier fought for an extension of the eastern boundary of the reservation to include those Navajos whose property still lay beyond its borders. They were, after all, receiving services administered by the BIA, and were considered part of the tribe. Unfortunately, New Mexico politics played a decisive role in defeating that effort.[12]

Collier also moved to consolidate Navajo administration. Effective June 30, 1935, the six Navajo agencies were combined into a single agency, with headquarters at Window Rock, eighty-five miles west of Crownpoint, and Stacher retired. Local chapters, small community centers that had been established across the reservation in the 1920s to provide local representation on a BIA-created tribal council, were weakened or disbanded, apparently because Collier felt that they were the seat of organized opposition to stock reduction. Collier even suggested to Interior Secretary Ickes that he (Ickes) send a letter to the Navajos, warning them of possible repurcussions if they continued to oppose stock reduction. The confusion over reorganization, Collier told Ickes, is confined to the checkerboard area on the extreme eastern fringe of the Reservation, but that is the very area where our authority in law hardly exists for practical purpose and where, correspondingly, we are most dependent on Indian teamwork. . . . If in this eastern area any considerable number of Navajo Indians should take the advice of these unwise men [who were opposing reorganization], all Navajos should understand that the government may have no choice except to withdraw its funds and its aid from the region, for the time being only, I hope. Yet despite our wishes, the withdrawal might prove to be permanent.[13]

Ickes refused to sign such a letter, with its implied threat, but Collier's fears were soon realized. After 1938, when he lost his battle to bring the eastern area into the reservation, the Crownpoint Navajos were increasingly cut off from tribal affairs. Stacher's prewar agency staff of thirty people was eventually reduced to two men, neither of whom spoke Navajo. The school and hospital, run from Window Rock, were neglected, poorly staffed, and only marginally useful. Health conditions were deplorable, and tuberculosis was rampant.

The ultimate blow to the eastern Navajos fell in 1946. An Interior Department solicitor ruled that, because the area was outside the reservation, it need no longer be served by tribal police and tribal courts. At the same time, New Mexico claimed that it could not afford to provide such services to the Indians in the checkerboard area. As a result, the eastern Navajos were without police protection. Even health services were affected. Between 1946 and 1955 thirty successive doctors directed services at the Crownpoint hospital.[14] The people wondered if they were still members of the tribe. They felt discarded, forgotten, and powerless.

As McNickle learned more about the history of the eastern Navajos, he realized how well he had chosen the site for his project. The checkerboard area more than met all of his criteria. Although most of it lay outside the reservation, remnants of a district council composed of local headmen still met sporadically. A few widely scattered and barely effective chapter houses provided some means of communication with those who lived in isolated hogans. The BIA personnel at the hospital in Crownpoint and the handful of New Mexico health officials he had met there appeared enthusiastic about what AID proposed to do in health education; the need was self-evident. The area appeared to offer a unique opportunity for developing new methods of teaching about health and community action to a largely nonliterate people. Crownpoint's little hospital, suffering from years of neglect, would provide a focus.[15] McNickle reported enthusiastically to NCAI in Washington that the eastern Navajo area appeared to meet all the requirements for AID's project. The organization's directors were quick to agree.

McNickle would have admitted, however, that his choice of Crownpoint as the project site was not entirely rational. He knew there were several strikes against his project even before it began. The eastern Navajos had, after all, been the center of resistance to Collier, whose stock-reduction policies were still fresh in local memory. Known as a Collier man, he would have to overcome those residual antagonisms before he could begin to be effective. And the people, after all, had not asked for his help. But the stark beauty of the Dinetah and the haunting remains of the earlier Anasazi people scattered across the landscape had created a powerful impression on him. In collecting potsherds and contemplating the remains of ancient buildings, he sensed a direct contact with people who had lived in the area before the Navajos arrived, people untouched by western civilization, whose way of life seemed totally adapted to their environment. Their artifacts were all around him at Crownpoint, drawing him almost irresistibly. Both the past and the present contributed to his decision.

Despite the pull of the land, however, he never seriously considered establishing a permanent residence in Crownpoint. He believed that his continual presence in the community would only inhibit the Indians' developing autonomy. He would provide guidance and support when needed, but he did not intend to be too available. As director of American Indian Development he had other responsibilities, such as the Oklahoma workshops, and NCAI activities were also demanding his attention. NCAI was mobilizing an all-out lobbying effort in Washington to oppose the accelerating push toward termination in Congress, and McNickle's help was sorely needed there.

The McNickle family eventually did move west, however, and the decision involved a great deal of planning. Roma, who had spent her entire adult life in Washington and knew little about the west, may not have been enthusiastic about relocating her family and her home. It was important to D'Arcy that the move be as easy for her as possible. But if he kept a diary during this crucial period it has disappeared, and his daughter Toni remembers only that there was a great deal of discussion about the move.[16]

In fact, McNickle's diaries provide little insight into the McNickles' family life, and they tell almost nothing about Toni's and Kathleen's childhood. Toni apparently was a bright and precocious child, especially close to her father. She occasionally celebrated holidays in Washington with her mother, however, because Joran had continued to live there during the 1940s. As a teenager, she had spent summer vacations in Montana with Joran's family. Joran had hoped that, as the daughter of alumni, Toni would continue her education at the University of Montana in Missoula.[17] After graduation from high school, however, Toni chose instead to get married.

Her marriage meant that she was going to stay in Washington. Her sister, Kathleen, however, would soon be ready for high school, so that was a major factor in their move. Details of Kathleen's childhood, however, are even more obscure than Toni's. Her father noted birthday parties in his diary, mentioned the games and candles on the birthday cake, but beyond that he said little. She was eleven years old when the move was planned, and D'Arcy and Roma were concerned that good schools should be available for her.[18]

D'Arcy and Roma wrestled for several months with the question about where they should live if his work were to be centered in New Mexico. If they were not going to live in Crownpoint, then where were they going to live? The final decision was primarily Roma's. She was an urban person, and she wanted to find employment commensurate with her skills and experience. Another consideration was for Philomene. She had accepted their invitation to make her home with them, yet she wanted to be as close as possible to her other grandchildren, some of whom were still living in Montana. As for McNickle himself, his primary concern was convenient access to air transportation.

The choice finally narrowed itself to Albuquerque or Denver. Albuquerque was closer to Crownpoint, but they had friends in Denver, and if they moved there, D'Arcy could share office space with an old friend, Royal Hassrick, who had recently joined the staff at the Denver Art Museum. All things considered, they chose Boulder, Colorado, thirty miles from Denver, as best accommodating their various needs. They put their household goods in storage (D'Arcy had by this time extended his leave from the BIA for one more year) and moved west, leaving Toni and her husband behind.

While D'Arcy and Roma were deciding where their living place should be, NCAI had commenced its search for a health educator. McNickle wanted to hire a full-time staff person who would reside at Crownpoint as a health educator and liaison with AID. The board of directors knew, however, that Crownpoint's isolation might make the position difficult to fill; the little settlement, which was not even a town, offered few social amenities. McNickle himself, however, had a clear idea of the kind of person who would be most effective. Professional qualifications were important, of course, but he wanted someone who was also interested in ethnology and linguistics. He hoped to find a person who had worked within another culture and was aware of the difficulties in communicating across cultural barriers. As he told the board, they should look for someone (he presumed it would be a woman) "who would combine the proper professional skill with a desire to understand and work with the cultural difference she would encounter."[19] During the fall of 1952 the board interviewed a number of candidates and by the following January they had narrowed the list to one person, Viola Pfrommer.

In education and experience, Pfrommer's qualifications were impressive. She had earned a master's degree in public health from the University of North Carolina and a doctorate in education from Columbia University. She had also had extensive administrative experience before World War II at Colby College in Maine. Since the war, she had worked for the American Friends Service Committee in Egypt, Germany, Mexico, and El Salvador, and in all of these places she had established compassionate and helpful relations with the native people. Dorothea and Alexander Leighton, who first interviewed her, considered her the most promising candidate for the Crownpoint position, if she could be persuaded to take it.[20]

Pfrommer was living temporarily with her married sister in Rochester, New York, and in February 1953 McNickle went there to meet her. Like the Leightons, he sensed almost at once that she was the right person for the job. He described their first meeting at length in his diary. "[Pfrommer was] serious, small, brunette, business-like. [I] suspect she has not had much fun except incidental to her work. . . . She seemed not to be perturbed by the prospect of working on her own, in relative isolation. Her questions had to do with access to professional personnel and the possibilities of developing team work, rather than social contacts."[21]

McNickle talked at length with her about the potential for service inherent in working as a health educator with the Navajo people in the Crownpoint community, and he would have hired her on the spot if she had been ready to make a decision. But she was also considering another overseas assignment with the World Health Organization, at a salary considerably higher than NCAI could offer. That posed some difficulty. McNickle noted in his diary, "When we discussed salary, she indicated that, while salary was not uppermost in consideration, her family was insisting that she had worked for AFSC at self-denying wages long enough."[22] However, despite the higher salary offered for the overseas position, Pfrommer was reluctant to leave the United States again, and finally in mid-May she agreed to go to Crownpoint. McNickle was delighted. Pfrommer's knowledge of the matters that concerned him most was considerable, and he was eager to introduce her to the eastern Navajo

country. When they finally arrived at Crownpoint in late June, her enthusiastic response to her new surroundings confirmed his earlier impression.
She took in good humor the desolate countryside, the heat, the bad roads,
and the dust. Those things were all part of her work, and she was eager to
begin.[23]

Living conditions at Crownpoint left much to be desired, as McNickle
well knew. He and Vi, as he soon called Pfrommer, worked out of a large
trailer that they fitted with desks and bookcases borrowed from the BIA
and the school. The trailer also provided a temporary living place for Vi,
and McNickle too, stayed there when he came to Crownpoint. There was
simply no other place to stay if one had no "official" connections. Most of
the Navajos took this arrangement in stride and were, perhaps, relieved
that Vi had someone to care for her.[24] But the local traders, missionaries,
and agency personnel saw the situation, at best, as a bad example.
McNickle and Pfrommer eventually agreed to move into living quarters
provided for them at the teacherage, a much more pleasant and acceptable
situation for all concerned.

McNickle accepted the BIA's offer of quarters at the teacherage reluctantly. He wanted to divorce himself as much as possible in the minds of
the people he was working with from any connection with the Indian Bureau. He did, however, have the tacit support of the BIA. Wade Head,
who was by this time Southwest Area director, gave blanket endorsement
to AID's project. McNickle's old friend knew how much the project's success would depend on its director and he believed in McNickle's vision.
Allan Harper, who had transferred from Washington to the Navajo Reservation in 1949, was also supportive. Only the newly appointed (1955)
subagent in Crownpoint was critical of the project. During the height of
the McCarthy era, he was convinced that McNickle and Pfrommer were
"soft on communism."[25]

McNickle knew that support from the Navajo Tribal Council rather
than the BIA was crucial to the success of his project. Before Pfrommer arrived, he had met at length with council members to explain what he
wanted to do, how the project would be funded, and how it would relate

to tribal affairs generally. He was pleased when they endorsed the project and pledged their active support, and even more pleased when a number of council members participated in various aspects of the program during the next seven years. "I feel strongly that tribal governing bodies always need the kind of encouragement that comes from recognizing them and working through them," he later wrote to a friend. "When they are ignored or relegated to a secondary role, they deteriorate and fail their people."[26] He was certainly correct in assessing the importance of council support. When that support began to erode several years later, due to circumstances entirely beyond his control, his project faced a multitude of unanticipated problems.

Once the trailer facilities were set up after her arrival, Pfrommer wasted no time getting to work. As one of her first projects, she organized a field trip in which some of the community leaders and medicine men visited the reservation hospital in Fort Defiance, near Window Rock. Many of the men who went along had never been inside a hospital, but careful preparation and the enthusiastic cooperation of hospital personnel made the daylong expedition a great success. Pfrommer knew that her future projects were dependent on the interest and support of the medicine men, and her work in this area was truly pioneering. Until this time traditional Indian medicine generally was considered inimical to scientific procedures. Change was in the wind, however, and by the late 1960s the National Institute of Health was sponsoring a successful program to train Navajo medicine men in modern health practices. Pfrommer was one of the first to initiate such a policy.[27]

Pfrommer also worked closely with the newly created Navajo Tribal Health Committee. Annie Dodge Wauneka, the committee's chair and the first woman to serve on the Navajo Tribal Council (she was elected in 1951), was just beginning her battle against tuberculosis on the reservation. Since she had expressed interest in AID's health education project, Pfrommer welcomed her participation and provided her with information and organizational assistance. Annie Wauneka's battle against TB owed much to Pfrommer's continuing support. As McNickle once commented to Pfrommer, "Annie obviously thinks of you as Elder Sister." (When asked about this remark many years later, Wauneka gave her smiling assent.) In April 1954, after months of cooperative effort, Vi Pfrommer and American Indian Development, along with the Navajo Tribal Health Committee and the BIA, sponsored in Albuquerque the first of two nationally publicized working conferences on the prevention and cure of tuberculosis among American Indians. A second, the following year, was held in Gallup.[28]

The health education project at Crownpoint supported by Suzanne Hyde lasted from 1953 to 1955. That two-year period coincided with the tenure of Dr. Fred Margolis as chief of pediatrics and director of the Navajo Tribe's Field Health Program. Also serving on the reservation at that time was Dr. Kurt Deuschle, who was in charge of the Department of Medicine at the Fort Defiance medical facilities. When Margolis first arrived, he asked Deuschle about Pfrommer, what her role was, and how effective was her work. According to Margolis, Deuschle responded, "Well she is a little woman of about 90 lbs and 5 ft tall and flits around without making much noise or without saying much but seems to be one of the most able organizers [I have] met and a person whose interest in Navajo health is great."[29] The cooperative efforts of Wauneka, Margolis, and Deuschle began with the field trip to Fort Defiance and continued for the duration of the health education project. During his two years on the reservation Margolis had ample opportunity to judge for himself just how competent Pfrommer really was. He was pleased to acknowledge that she was probably the most influential person in the success of his health education efforts on the Navajo reservation.

Pfrommer's agenda was more content-centered than McNickle's, so she was able to begin work almost immediately. On the other hand, it took him several months even to appreciate the magnitude of the challenge that faced him at Crownpoint. As he had anticipated, health problems were only a small part of a larger picture of political, social, and geographic isolation. He couldn't even begin until he found a competent interpreter. On the recommendation of others who were familiar with the area, he asked John Perry, a former member of the Navajo Tribal Council, to serve in that capacity. Perry agreed to work with AID, at least temporarily.[30]

Perry, as it turned out, was one of those leaders McNickle believed could act as agents for change. He had been raised within a traditional Navajo extended family, where his mother was the first of his father's several wives. As a teenager he had worked on some of Stacher's construction projects. When he was eighteen he decided to go to school, and with Stacher's support he enrolled at Albuquerque Indian School. There he learned to read and write in adequate, if somewhat ungrammatical, English. Returning to various odd jobs at Crownpoint, he became Stacher's assistant and, eventually, chief of police for the Eastern Agency. When tribal police were consolidated at Window Rock in 1935, Perry continued to serve as regional police chief until 1950. During that time he was elected to several terms on the Tribal Council. Almost sixty years of age when McNickle arrived, Perry had achieved that degree of maturity the Navajo people traditionally considered necessary for effective leadership.

McNickle and Pfrommer relied heavily on Perry. His skills as an interpreter were more than adequate and he soon became one of the leaders of the self-styled Navajo Development Committee (NDC). This group of twelve or fourteen men, which emerged from several preliminary workshops McNickle had organized in early 1953, eventually expanded to eighteen, and it functioned as the operational arm of the community development project. The Navajo Development Committee really started from scratch; it even had difficulty at first identifying the precise meaning of the word "development." The traditional Navajo language contained no reasonable equivalent to express the inherent dynamics of that term.[31]

The meetings of the Navajo Development Committee provided an ad hoc illustration of what McNickle meant when he spoke of adaptation. Its members soon discovered that "modern" procedures such as establishing an agenda and keeping minutes were essential if the group was to accomplish its stated business. Nevertheless, discussion of the matters at hand proceeded along the traditional pattern of building toward consensus.

That process was often excruciatingly painful and time consuming for McNickle, who was determined to take no active part in the group's decision-making process. Although he attended most of the scheduled meetings, he was there to advise and facilitate when asked and he made no effort to carry a project forward. The Navajos would have to do that for themselves.

Despite his seemingly passive stance, however, McNickle was far from indifferent about the matters at hand. Rather, he was experimenting with new techniques being developed by professionals in the field of applied anthropology.[32] His interest in various research techniques had begun with his participation in the BIA's personality study and his association with the Leightons, Clyde Kluckhohn, and other anthropologists. The operating premise was that a people's self-determining capacity, given enough time and the right opportunity, could be restored through a kind of negative therapy: if all impediments to action were removed, the people would develop their own momentum toward further adaptation. McNickle, therefore, refused to "get in the way"; NDC's members would have to exercise their own decision-making capacities. And they did. They learned to isolate and identify several urgent needs, then worked toward viable solutions. McNickle informed them of various resources that were available, but he offered no solutions for problems the people might solve themselves. He maintained this hands-off role for the duration of the project.

McNickle did not invent this modus operandi—it had begun to emerge from within the social sciences in the 1930s and 1940s. Collier himself had set the stage for McNickle's project when he wrote in 1947 that the Navajo people were frustrated in trying to apply their own perceptions and understandings to effective problem solving. "There exists no mechanism for translating their insights and impulses into tribal decisions and actions," Collier had written. "As for the Indian Service, it has not often dared to pause and try to think through and feel through the problem of how the service and the issues can be merged with each of the local communities, one by one."[33] At Crownpoint the Navajos, with McNickle's support, would have to learn to solve their own problems.

From 1953 through 1960, members of the Navajo Development Committee at Crownpoint successfully identified a number of objectives and completed several major projects. The most visible of these centered around two community buildings, one new and the other completely re-modeled. The new building, made of local stone, became an assembly hall that functioned as a meeting place where committee members could gather without being under the constraints of time and place that hampered them when they met in the school or the hospital. The members of the committee raised the money, hauled the rock, and donated their labor for this building, and they were immensely proud of it. When it was finished, the community dedicated it with proper solemnity. McNickle later recalled that the workers spent the entire night before the dedication finishing the plastering and sanding and varnishing the floors. "Then the next day, the Blessing Chant was performed by Manuelito [a highly regarded medicine man] and three assistants, one of whom rubbed corn meal and corn pollen on the four walls and scattered pollen over the heads of the audience. Then we had a feast of lamb roasted over glowing coals." More than three hundred people attended the festivities that followed the house blessing.[34]

The other building, a remodeled hog barn that they called the Community House, was an even more impressive facility that provided automatic laundry machines, public showers, a sewing area, a kitchen, and a supply of folding cots. These accommodations were tangible evidence of the way in which NDC was beginning to serve the entire community. They were needed because, by 1955, pressure on the Indian Office from various parts of the reservation had accomplished what had earlier seemed an impossibility: the BIA had established four subagencies within its Navajo administration, and Crownpoint had once again become headquarters for the Eastern Navajo. Once again the people had their own police officers and tribal court, and they came to Crownpoint from miles around to take care of business, to participate in a new food distribution program, and to visit children at school or patients in the hospital. But they still faced a crucial problem when they came—there were no facilities to accommodate them if they needed to stay overnight. By making the cots and kitchen facilities available, the committee had responded to community needs in a way that was congenial to the people's traditional experience. In earlier times on the reservation the local agent, or perhaps a nearby trader, had provided a hogan for people whose business required a visit of several days. Now, once again, there was a place for them to stay in Crownpoint.

Although the two buildings were the most visible evidence of the success of McNickle's program, other projects also rose from the committee's identification of local needs. NDC members invited tribal leaders and BIA personnel in Window Rock to come to Crownpoint for a series of discussions about tribal law codes and tribal membership, and the eastern Navajos were assured that they were very much members of the tribe. They tackled such tough issues as the complicated pattern of land ownership, fencing problems, and water rights. When county school district officers arrived from Gallup to explain a new school plan that the local people had not been consulted about, committee members demanded that they be heard and that their questions be answered.[35]

McNickle was admittedly surprised, and of course delighted, that the committee had focused on genuine needs and had carried through to positive solutions. He wrote to Helen Peterson (Oglala Sioux), at NCAI's Washington office,

> I am constantly astonished at the progress we are making in winning the friendship of the people in this area, and even more astonishing is the speed at which these leaders are moving into action. For years the so-called checkerboard area . . . has been regarded as hopelessly divided and hostile. I am beginning to realize that the divisions within the group resulted from government policies and that the hostility, if there was such, was directed at the government. We have found from the beginning a great eagerness on the part of the leaders to be recognized and to be used in a responsible way.[36]

It was not surprising that tribal leaders who visited from Window Rock watched the community development project in Crownpoint with considerable interest. They sometimes used the Navajo Development Committee and its various successes as an example of what people in other areas of the reservation might accomplish by working together.[37] McNickle's project had begun to make a significant contribution toward helping the Navajo people help themselves. Pfrommer's work with Annie Wauneka illustrated what he had first envisioned when he decided to incorporate health education into the broader community development project. As he had written to Pfrommer when she began her work, "Neither the tribal council nor Window Rock has made any effort to train local leaders. The concept is wholly foreign to the Indian Service and to most tribal governments." But that was beginning to change. In appealing for a renewal of funds in 1955, he reported that the community development project had been used, "at least in part, as a device to discover leaders in the extended community, to ascertain their interests, and to bring them together in support of action programs, in which health is included." McNickle's and Pfrommer's support for Annie Wauneka as chair of the Tribal Health Committee, and for the Navajo Development Committee, exemplified this commitment.[38]

Nevertheless, the health education work had been funded for only two years, and at the end of that time, Suzanne Hyde, the project's financial backer, decided not to continue her support. Although she agreed that Pfrommer's work was productive, she was apparently unhappy because McNickle had entitled the project report "The Crownpoint Project in Health Education" rather than "The Hyde Health Education Project."[39] Her withdrawal precipitated an immediate financial crisis. McNickle had resigned from the BIA when his second year of leave ended in 1954, because he was confident that he could raise funds to continue his work in community development. Pfrommer's situation, however, was more precarious. As a health educator she considered herself unqualified to assist McNickle in community development work, although her activities were contributing directly to the larger program and they were increasingly productive. McNickle was determined that they should continue, and he included them in a new proposal he was writing. He hoped that she would stay if he could develop additional funding.[40]

By 1955, however, Pfrommer's work was to some extent superseded by the Cornell-Navajo Field Health Research Program at Many Farms, Arizona.[41] The Cornell program had institutional support from that university, as well as from the Public Health Service and the Navajo Tribal Council, and with a trained medical staff it had a much larger outreach than AID's limited budget permitted. Initially, the Cornell people had considered establishing their program at Crownpoint, and they had invited Pfrommer to join their staff. Cornell even provided financial support for her efforts for several months when the Hyde funding expired. But Cornell eventually decided to locate at Many Farms rather than at Crownpoint, and Pfrommer faced a crucial decision. If McNickle's new proposal could be funded as he had written it, she wanted to stay with him at Crownpoint. If not, she might accept Cornell's offer.

McNickle was well aware that Pfrommer's contributions to the project had extended far beyond her work in health education. As a Quaker, she had access to a network of resources that McNickle was able to exploit as his project expanded. Her contact with Friends in Albuquerque, for instance, had led to an acquaintance with Bainbridge Bunting, the noted architectural historian, who donated his expertise as well as several weekends to help remodel the old building as a community center. In addition, the American Friends Service Committee arranged for three summer work camps of high school and college students to come to Crownpoint and assist with NDC's building projects in 1954, 1955, and 1956. In welcoming the young people, who came primarily from upper middle-class backgrounds, Pfrommer arranged for several days of orientation in Santa Fe to help bridge the gap between their own and Navajo cultures, and this orientation proved very effective. Dr. Arthur Warner, chief medical officer at the Crownpoint Hospital from 1955 to 1957, was also a Friend, and he provided invaluable support for Pfrommer's projects and for the work-camp students as well. He later reported, "Vi's commitment to cultural sensitivity had a deep effect on me," as it did on everyone else involved in the work camps.[42]

The pictures that emerge of Viola Pfrommer at Crownpoint seem strangely contradictory. On one hand she was physically small, quiet, unassuming, and quite proper, perhaps even a bit prissy. She insisted that the girls in the work contingent wear skirts rather than slacks, without realizing that her own dresses, which were often made of easy-care synthetic fabrics, were more revealing than slacks would have been. Yet she was comfortable sharing the trailer accommodations with McNickle, was able to ignore the ensuing gossip, and accepted the primitive living conditions at Crownpoint without a murmur. She knew how to communicate effectively as a health educator, and won the trust of the Indians as well as the respect of her professional colleagues.[43]

Pfrommer also possessed resources of spirit that helped AID's program survive its periodic crises. As a Quaker, she appreciated McNickle's nondirective approach; she, too, knew how to wait for "openings" that would lead to new opportunities. She and McNickle soon established a close working relationship, and in their correspondence she did not hesitate to express her admiration of him. Her encouragement reflected the depths of her Quaker faith. During one particularly difficult time she wrote, characteristically,

> It is a lonely period, D'Arcy; one that every artist experiences when he labors to give form to his vision so that it may live on in others. . . . [You see] my deep faith in what you are envisioning for Crownpoint and what we are doing here today. You have that quiet flame that kindles sparks in others; as Rufus Jones [a Quaker author and teacher] writes, "When we are on the right lines of advance, doors open before us." Be of good patience and good courage.[44]

Given Pfrommer's background, it was not surprising that, whereas McNickle, on the surface at least, maintained a scholarly, objective view of the Crownpoint project, she viewed it with a sense of mission consistent with her religious faith.

Nevertheless, problems derived from Pfrommer's presence, for reasons that are not entirely clear. There is some indication that she had a personality conflict with Suzanne Hyde that contributed to Hyde's decision to withdraw her support from the health education program. In Pfrommer's defense, it must be said that Hyde had created difficulties with most of NCAI's people during the years that she supported the work at Crownpoint. From time to time, however, Pfrommer had problems with others in Crownpoint and with NCAI's staff, as well.[45]

Problems, of course, were inevitable in circumstances such as those McNickle and Pfrommer encountered on the reservation. Few of the non-Indian people who were at Crownpoint when they arrived were genuinely enthusiastic about their presence. Dr. Warner, who came to the hospital when the health education project was about to expire, was the outstanding exception among the hospital personnel who felt threatened by Pfrommer's work. The various mission people used the housing situation in the trailer as a basis for their early complaints, and later they were unhappy because, after a long discussion, NDC refused to allow them to use the new community facilities for church activities. Pfrommer also incurred the wrath of the local traders when she attempted to organize women from the surrounding area into a marketing cooperative so they could shop in Gallup or Albuquerque.[46]

Tension between Crownpoint and the NCAI office in Washington was perhaps aggravated by Pfrommer's change in status when McNickle's proposal was accepted and he was able to offer her the position of project field worker. At one point, she apologized to him for what she called her "discourtesy and alienation of friends" at an AID Advisory Committee meeting they had attended in New York. She described herself as "an independent, unbridled oldish colt," who was finding it difficult to adapt. Cliques and professional jealousies obviously accounted for at least some of the friction, but on more than one occasion Pfrommer felt that she was doing more harm than good and offered to resign. McNickle refused to consider the possibility.[47]

McNickle was accustomed to such in-house bickering and he largely ignored it. Funding was another matter. In 1955 he received a renewal of the Field Foundation grant, which provided a temporary respite from the financial emergency and ensured the continuation of Pfrommer's work. At the same time he applied for and eventually received substantial long-term funding from the recently established Emil Schwartzhaupt Foundation (ESF) of New York and Chicago.[48] The Crownpoint Project received more than one hundred thousand dollars from the Schwartzhaupt Foundation over the next five years.

By 1957, however, other funding and administrative problems were beginning to plague the project. In Washington, Arrow, Incorporated, which had been organized as NCAI's funding agency, was taking on a life of its own. Until that time, all contributions to American Indian Development had been funneled through Arrow, whose directors were now accused of misallocating some of those funds.[49] While tempers flared at NCAI headquarters, McNickle considered various alternatives. Finally, he and AID's board of directors decided to separate completely from both NCAI and Arrow. They applied for incorporation in the State of Colorado, at the same time filing for tax-exempt status with the Internal Revenue Service. Both were granted in 1957, and American Indian Development remained incorporated in Colorado until 1985. NCAI also separated from Arrow in 1957 and established its own tax-exempt fundraising branch, once again called the NCAI Fund, to administer contributions to its various programs.[50]

The grant that McNickle obtained from the Emil Schwartzhaupt Foundation in late 1955 necessitated a change of focus for AID, although in reality the change proved to be more cosmetic than substantive. Although ESF called its overall program "education for citizenship," it essentially reflected McNickle's approach. The foundation believed that "programs were needed to encourage and assist Indians to learn how to cope with those expectations of the dominant society which were more or less inescapable." At the same time, such coping mechanisms must enable the Indians to save "those elements of their heritage which were indispensable to their sense of Indianness."[51] McNickle's goal at Crownpoint had been to bring just such adaptive skills as these into the immediate world of the eastern Navajos. To comply with the conditions of the E S F grant he agreed to write a report when the project terminated that would outline its goals, describe its methodology, and evaluate its findings. Although the program at Crownpoint actually changed very little, McNickle's perception of its various phases was shaped to some extent by E S F's reporting requirements.

McNickle had every reason to be pleased with the progress of community development at Crownpoint. The original twelve members of N D C's steering committee, representing seven local chapters, had increased to eighteen, and some general meetings were attended by more than 250 people. By 1959, twenty-one chapters, all of those in the Eastern Navajo subagency, were represented, with people traveling up to seventy-five miles for meetings at Crownpoint. Issues had been met and problems solved. Net income from services at the Community House would rise from $170 during the first year to $6,190 in 1960. Other N D C assets amounted to over $5,000.[52]

In his early enthusiasm McNickle had chosen to ignore divisive undercurrents in the community, although he had recognized in his original proposal that there were "contrary drifts, aimlessness, futility, even destructiveness," in certain elements of Navajo culture.[53] But by 1957 some of those elements began to affect his project. One problem arose from the tribe's suddenly realizing a tremendous increase in income from mineral leases and production royalties. Oil royalties alone increased from $50,000 in 1955 to almost $10 million by 1959.[54] The Navajo Tribal Council had trouble maintaining its equilibrium in the face of such sudden wealth. It did decide, however, to spend some of its new money rebuilding chapter houses across the reservation. The project at Crownpoint served as one of its models.

Unfortunately, this new tribal interest in chapter houses resurrected one of the problems McNickle and N D C had faced when they began their building program in 1953. Crownpoint was not on the reservation and the land where the project's two new buildings stood was within the B I A's subagency compound. Permission to build on the site had been given by the federal government in 1954, and the arrangement subsequently had been approved by the Tribal Council. But a more recent tribal regulation stipulated, "In off-reservation areas, the buildings [for tribal use] shall be built on tribally owned or tribally controlled land."[55]

This problem became critical in October 1957, when NDC applied for the financial aid it had been promised by the tribe for expanding its Community House program. The Navajo Development Committee responded to every request by the council for information and met every deadline, but contradictory orders were given at the tribal level, personnel changed, papers were lost. The final blow came in July 1959, when a tribal delegation from Window Rock suggested that NDC abandon its project and support the tribe's offer to build a new chapter house on Navajo-owned land outside the agency compound.[56] The Navajo Development Committee was dismayed; all its efforts had been betrayed. Although a new chapter house eventually was built after AID withdrew from Crownpoint, it did not represent the same kind of investment that had built the first Community House.

The NDC had developed real unity in fighting for its position within the community and the tribe. But it, too, encountered internal problems that would eventually undermine its position and make it increasingly divisive. The most serious problem was a defection in its membership. In 1959, John Perry, who had used his position with NDC to strengthen his political base, lost a bid for reelection to the Tribal Council to his half-brother, thus beginning a long period of family quarrels. Many of these quarrels grew out of disputed property settlements within the family, but other factors were also involved. John's brother had recently become affiliated with a growing number of peyote users among the eastern Navajos. Although peyote had been illegal on the reservation since 1940, the issue of its use for ceremonial purposes surfaced periodically, and during the late 1950s a number of arrests were made in a renewed attempt to enforce tribal law. According to McNickle, who for years had considered peyote a stabilizing element in Indian culture, Perry "had acquired a bitter, unreasoning opposition" to its use. He feared that his brother would destroy not only himself but the entire family.[57]

The family turmoil soon extended through local kinship networks, and those who had voted against John stopped coming to the regular meetings. Because McNickle had maintained such a low profile, many local people had come to think of N D C as John Perry's project, a view that Perry himself seemed at times to share and did little to correct. Although some people later regretted the outcome of the 1959 election, the damage to N D C's position was irreversible. Several of its most influential members had stopped supporting it.

Still another major problem surfaced when N D C tried to select a competent person to train as on-site manager of the Community House. McNickle had hoped that a Navajo manager would be in full charge by the end of 1960, when A I D anticipated withdrawing from Crownpoint, and the Schwartzhaupt Foundation had provided additional funding to train such a person. But a pervasive cultural distrust of anyone who would control the committee's finances precluded a rational decision. The committee hired a man because of his kin relationship with some of the members, and he proved to be woefully inadequate.[58] Finding a competent manager was a problem for which there seemed no satisfactory solution.

Then, like ripples in a pond, the committee's troubles spread. Help from the tribe became increasingly mired in the bureaucracy at Window Rock. Tribal elections brought changes in leadership that further eroded N D C's influence in the Tribal Council. The older, traditional leaders were being replaced by younger men who, it seemed to McNickle, were concerned only with their own political destiny. As tribal bureaucrats, they disregarded the previous council's commitments of support and ignored or overrode N D C's repeated petitions. "Navajo leaders for generations had been critical of bureaucracy," McNickle wrote, noting the irony of the situation. "The term Waashingdoon (meaning the federal government) had been a term of contempt, for at Waashingdoon all power resided, and the voices of the people were never heard. And now, the new leaders, pushing hard to assert their individual ambitions, had created their own

Waashingdoon, and it was called Window Rock."[59] In one way or another, all of these events impinged on the Crownpoint Project, and by 1960 its future was very much in doubt.

McNickle was worried about other events in the Indian world as well, events that scarcely touched the Navajo Reservation. At the same time that he was trying to cope with financial problems at Crownpoint, congressional attacks on Indian tribes were gathering momentum in Washington. Although Dillon Myer was no longer commissioner—he was succeeded in early 1953 by Glenn Emmons—the determination of the administration to "get the government out of the Indian business" had became official congressional policy. In 1953 the federal legislature had passed two measures that stated its position clearly. House Concurrent Resolution No. 108 declared its intent to release from federal supervision and control "at the earliest possible time" those tribes considered most ready for self-government. Public Law 280 allowed for the transfer of responsibility for reservation law and order from the federal government to state governments without prior approval of the tribes themselves. During Myer's term as commissioner termination had been primarily an administrative concern within the BIA, although it had reflected the view of a number of powerful congressmen. With the passage of these two measures, however, the push toward termination officially moved from the Indian Bureau to the halls of Congress. Concurrent Resolution 108 specifically expressed the intent of Congress as supporting unilateral withdrawal from its treaty obligations to Native Americans as soon as possible.[60]

The National Congress of American Indians, founded as it was in 1944 to support the work of the Indian Claims Commission, would eventually lead the battle against congressional termination, but its position was not arrived at without pain. The federal legislation of 1953 marked a crucial period for the organization, which came close to disbanding by the end of that year. NCAI faced a real dilemma: how to respond to those member tribes that favored termination, and a few of them did, when the organization opposed that policy.[61] Arguably, if NCAI truly believed in tribal self-determination, it should not take any position on this vital issue. Each tribe should respond to its own particular situation. Although NCAI was unable to formulate any clear resolution, it remained generally opposed to termination, since it felt that few tribes would be able to protect their resources without federal assistance. It reorganized for its 1953 annual meeting and gathered its forces together to face what it saw as a major crisis in Indian affairs. When its leaders called an emergency session in February 1954 to develop an offensive strategy against Congress, McNickle was off to Washington.

NCAI's specific target that year was House Report No. 2680, which was concerned with a drastic measure that threatened to repeal the 1934 Indian Reorganization Act and revoke all tribal constitutions that had been adopted under it. Three members of NCAI's Resolutions Committee—McNickle, Frank Parker (Seneca), and Frank George (Colville)—prepared a brilliant statement that refuted the House Report point by point. NCAI's 1954 convention, which met shortly thereafter in Omaha, passed the Resolutions Committee's statement, along with an accompanying resolution, and sent both documents to Congress. The logic of NCAI's rebuttal was irrefutable, and Congress, much to the collective relief of NCAI, refused to pass the offending legislation, although Concurrent Resolution 108 and Public Law 280 remained on the books.

Vine Deloria, Jr. (Sioux), who became executive director of the NCAI in the 1960s, has stated that NCAI's united stand and the courage and wisdom of the Resolutions Committee "broke the impetus of the movement" to destroy the tribes."[62] His assessment of the end of termination was somewhat premature, however. McNickle and other representatives from Montana in the following months successfully headed off another bill that would have terminated the Confederated Tribes on the Flathead Reservation, but the Klamaths and Menominees were less fortunate, although the Menominees later succeeded in reversing the legislation. Congress continued to support termination legislation for several more years.[63]

The physical drain on McNickle's energy as he tried to deal with prob-

lems on these several fronts took its toll. In 1954 alone he traveled to
Washington, D.C., several times. He attended NCAI's annual convention
in Omaha, addressed two conferences in Montana, and visited Oklahoma
and Crownpoint repeatedly for American Indian Development. In the
rare weeks when he was home he wrote innumerable letters, explaining
his program, asking for money, and enlisting support for the battles with
Congress. In late 1954, Roma wrote to Helen Peterson that D'Arcy
looked "positively wretched." "If one person furnishes the ideas, does the
administration, speaks and writes endlessly, *and* has to raise the money,
he's not going to last long. . . . I don't think he can keep this up much
longer."[64] McNickle, who had been a heavy smoker for years, had developed a nagging cough that suggested a potentially serious bronchial condition.[65] He was beginning to realize that there was a limit to what one
man could do. Although he continued to offer creative leadership to
NCAI, congressional actions receded somewhat from his mind as he became more concerned about what was happening in Crownpoint.

McNickle and Pfrommer's final year on the Navajo Reservation, 1960,
was disheartening for both of them. The Navajo Development Committee was unable to find a satisfactory manager for the Community House,
and McNickle increasingly questioned the wisdom of the committee's dependence on John Perry, whose local support continued to erode.[66]
McNickle and Pfrommer ended the year, and the project, with a feeling
that their efforts had had little lasting effect.

Although they had anticipated and planned for the end of their project
in 1960, leave-taking was difficult. Pfrommer had decided to settle permanently in New Mexico and had bought some property in Albuquerque.
When she began to move out of the teacherage in October, there were few
farewells. One couple who had been very much involved with activities at
the Community House gave her a traditional silver bracelet and McNickle
a remarkable old ring with a carved turquoise frog set among silver leaves,
which he wore for the rest of his life.[67] Other than that, little notice was
taken of their departure.

McNickle subjected himself to much soul-searching as he tried to evaluate the effectiveness of AID's program among the Navajos at Crownpoint. Obviously there had been some successes. Health education was now a concern of the entire tribe, thanks to Annie Wauneka's growing influence, and the two new buildings, not yet displaced, were evidence of a renewed spirit of self-determination among the eastern Navajos, because the people themselves had built them.

The Crownpoint project, however, had been conceived as more than a search for tangible results. It was designed primarily as an attempt to discover a process whereby self-realization could be restored to a traditional society, and McNickle was unable to see that that had happened in any lasting way. The eastern Navajo still seemed to be at the mercy of an outside bureaucracy, whether in "Waashingdoon" or in Window Rock. He had consistently avoided taking an active position while working with NDC, but he began to wonder if he had been right to do so. He asked himself what might have happened had he intervened in the decision-making processes. Perhaps his direct participation in helping choose a Community House manager, or as an advocate before the Navajo Tribal Council, would have made a difference. But if he had intervened and acted more directly on their behalf, he would have compromised the credibility of the whole enterprise. Its apparent failure, as well as its obvious successes, emerged from the community itself. The Navajo Development Committee might not be able to sustain itself without, or even with, AID's continued presence, but that was ultimately beside the point. He was unable to say with any certainty that the people's decision-making capacity had been enhanced in any lasting sense. After seven long years, he felt that he still had no definitive answers.[68]

In his final report to the Schwartzhaupt Foundation, written several years later, McNickle admitted that one of the premises of the project had been too narrowly conceived. In his original proposal he had asserted, "Decision-making in a society is as good as the information with which the people have to work. . . . To widen the scope of action, it is only necessary to increase the fund of useful information."[69] This was a truly extraordinary statement coming from someone who had maintained for years that men and women of different cultural backgrounds make apparently irrational decisions on the basis of varying cultural interpretations of what appears to be identical data. He had said repeatedly that information alone, uninformed by cultural awareness, could not solve problems arising from different cultural values. The only justification for the statement in his proposal, and it is a self-serving one, is found in the context of his own proposed role in the project. He viewed himself as the expediter, whose function would be to provide and interpret all the information needed. His effectiveness in this role, however, had clearly been limited by external circumstances and by his self-imposed nondirective leadership.

In his final appraisal of the project, McNickle admitted that his premise had been valid only to a point.[70] The crucial choice of a Community House manager, for instance, was determined not by any objective information as to whether the man in question was truly qualified, but by cultural factors such as kinship networks and traditional Navajo distrust of those who controlled large amounts of money. Cultural elements that were of positive value in one society became counterproductive in another social context. Obviously, the possession of information did not in itself ensure "rational" behavior. He also had to remind himself that some of the events that had determined the outcome of the project were totally beyond the control of the local people.

In another area, too, McNickle began to wonder if perhaps he had been mistaken. He had acted on the premise that change would be most effectively implemented through the traditional leadership of older people. His experience at Crownpoint, however, revealed emerging patterns of leadership among the Navajos that were rapidly overriding the leadership positions of traditional older medicine men and headmen. "Tradition was not the force it once was," he observed ruefully.

Younger men were coming along and, for reasons that had nothing to do with age and experience, people were following their leadership as well. Some of these young men could not speak the language of the people properly—they had to use an interpreter! Still the people followed, because the young men understood how to get a job for a kinsman, how to obtain tribal funds for local projects.[71]

He noted that these new officeholders were younger men "who were marginal to Navajo society and who therefore were not responsive to tribal consensus. They had no stake in the perpetuation of the society, only in their own personal fortune. They wore city clothes and had college haircuts."[72]

McNickle was not entirely critical of this new young leadership, however. He appreciated the dilemma that had settled on their shoulders. Acculturation was taking place rapidly, and the young people were loosening or losing their ties to the traditional culture at an alarming rate. Nevertheless, he knew that the older people would soon be gone, and unless the young leaders developed and valued a sense of who they were as Navajos, the traditional culture would indeed be lost. That would be a tragedy unless all the people, young and old, were able to make an informed choice, and this was not happening. Neither the young nor the old, he felt, truly perceived the options. The new leaders "with city clothes and college haircuts" had been educated away from their culture in BIA or mission schools that did not teach them to be proud of their Indian heritage. They knew little of their own tribal history and even less of the broader history of Indian people or Indian-white relationships. Yet these young people were moving into leadership positions within the tribes, and, without realizing what was at stake, the older people were following their lead. He wondered how any of them, young or old, could make a truly intelligent choice about what was most valuable among the old ways and the new.[73]

In response to that question, even while he was fully engaged at Crownpoint, McNickle began to reach out to young Indian leadership across the country. He gradually accepted the fact that the future of the tribes depended on the young people rather than on those who in the past would have been the traditional leaders. The next decade would reveal his new direction.

7

Education for Citizenship

Perhaps as an occasional escape from the momentous decisions he had faced in the early 1950s, McNickle had worked occasionally on the "Feather Boy" story, and by the time he started the project at Crownpoint, he had even found time to write another novel. Titled *Runner in the Sun: A Story of Indian Maize,* it was published in 1954 by Holt, Rinehart and Winston as part of their Land of the Free series for young adults.

Although *Runner in the Sun* is less well known than *The Surrounded* and its sources in McNickle's creative psyche are more obscure, it fits logically within the larger body of his writing.[1] It emerged from the ethnographic and historical material he had unearthed while doing research for *They Came Here First* and for a long article, also published in 1954, that he wrote on North American Indians for the fourteenth edition of the *Encyclopaedia Britannica.* When Holt, Rinehart and Winston asked him to contribute an Indian story to its young adult series, the research was essentially finished. What he needed was a hero and a plot.

While working on his narrative history for Lippincott in the late 1940s, McNickle had been impressed by the fact that archeologists had found no evidence of warfare for almost six hundred years between the Anasazi people in present Arizona and their neighbors to the south. "No defense works were built along that international boundary," he had observed. "The archaeologists have uncovered no fire-blackened walls, no arrow-pierced skulls." He had been intrigued with that long period of apparently peaceful coexistence, and he decided to develop fictionally the theme of the ancient pueblos inhabited by the peaceful people he had described in the historical account. In the foreword of the new novel he repeated what he had written earlier, that "scientists digging into old village sites tell us of tribes living side by side for hundreds of years without warfare." Then he added, "The myths and legends of the many tribes are not battle stories, but convey instead a feeling for the dignity of man and reverence for all of nature. . . . Corn was, indeed, a great gift to the world, but a greater gift was one that the world let lie and never gathered up for its own. That was the gift of peace on earth."[2]

The plot that he worked out was relatively simple. The hero, a teen-age boy named Salt who lives in a cliff dwelling loosely identified as Chaco Canyon, wears a turquoise amulet that betokens his initiation as a man into his village's dominant Turquoise clan. As the story begins, however, Salt is in trouble. For many years the villagers have grown their crops on the top of the mesa, where they are entirely dependent on rainfall. A spring at the bottom of the canyon has provided water for the people's other needs. Rainfall, however, has diminished and the corn is stunted, so Salt violates village custom and plants his corn in the canyon, where it is watered by seepage from the spring.

Salt's actions are reported to the clan elders by Flute Man, a secret ally of Dark Dealer, leader of the hostile Spider clan. These two men conspire to challenge the leadership of the Turquoise people, and they use Salt's transgression to further their cause. Flute Man claims that Salt's actions are causing the water in the spring to disappear. Salt has violated the ancestral practice by planting in the canyon rather than on the top of the mesa and has thus angered the powers that provide water for the people and endangered the entire village.

The enemy's charge that Salt's actions have jeopardized the well-being of the village provides the rationale for the story that follows. Salt is both punished and protected when Eldest Woman and the other leaders of the clan remove his turquoise amulet, thus returning him temporarily to childhood status. Humiliated, Salt seeks out the Holy One, the senior person of the village, for comfort and support.

Instead of sympathizing with Salt's predicament, however, the Holy One confronts him with a challenge. Salt must complete several tasks if he would win back his amulet and be restored to manhood. First he must discover for himself a secret trail leading from the top of the mesa to the canyon floor. If he succeeds in that, he must then undertake a long journey south into the Land of Fable and bring back some unidentified "something" that will restore health and vigor to his people.

Salt's personal problems become insignificant when the Holy One explains the needs of the people, and he accepts the Holy One's challenge. In finding the hidden trail, he discovers Dark Dealer's plan to dam the village spring and frighten the people into submission. While he is unable to prevent this disaster, he acts bravely in the face of great danger. The Holy One bestows on Salt his own amulet for protection, and Salt departs for the south. After a series of adventures, he returns to the village with a lovely young woman known as Quail. Quail has brought new red, blue, and black seed corn from her own country, so the people rename her Red Corn Woman. As the people are rejoicing over Salt's safe return, however, Dark Dealer appears before them. He and his followers, anathema to the other villagers, are now powerless and have been starving, and they beg only for food. But Salt, in a final act of mercy, restores them to full participation in the tribe, which is thus made whole again. When the Holy One dies, Salt becomes head of the village, and he and Red Corn Woman lead the people away from the old village to a new and better place.

In many ways this is a violent story, seeming to contradict McNickle's explicit desire to write about "the gift of peace to the world." Salt's village is literally torn apart by conflict. At least three people, including the much-revered Eldest Woman, are killed. Although Salt ultimately restores peace to the village, it is difficult to believe that violence will never return. But the conflict is within the village and its resolution takes place there as well. McNickle did not say that violence does not exist, but rather that it can be contained and that reconciliation can eventually triumph. Thus did the villagers learn to live at peace with their neighbors.

McNickle's interest in myth and folklore had become considerably more sophisticated than it was when he first discussed such matters with William Gates. Since writing *The Surrounded*, he had read most of the recent publications in the field, as was evident from the extensive collection of such literature in his personal library.[3] Among his books were a number by Joseph Campbell, and it seems quite possible that when Campbell's *Hero With a Thousand Faces* appeared in 1949, McNickle drew some elements of Salt's story from it. Campbell illustrated aspects of the universal mythic hero by relating them in part to various Native American myths, and McNickle may have realized the possibility of using them to create a myth of his own.

Campbell outlines the monomyth this way: "A hero ventures forth from the world of common day into a region of supernatural wonder: fabulous forces are there encountered and a decisive victory is won: the hero comes back from this mysterious adventure with the power to bestow boons on his fellow man." He then elaborates on the plot by establishing a sequence of the hero's "separation, initiation, and return."[4] The hero of *Runner in the Sun* follows this model closely, and it is no coincidence that a draft of *Runner* in McNickle's papers bears such titles as "The Boy Who Stole the Sun" and "Journey into the Sky." Such titles reveal McNickle's intention of writing a myth patterned after the American Indian tradition. As John Purdy notes, "In a brief space, McNickle gives his readers a synopsis of countless stories from the Native oral literatures of this continent."[5]

To fully understand *Runner in the Sun,* the reader must view it within the context of the mythical tradition. Inconsistencies are not inappropriate to mythological narration, and unlikely occurrences become valid experiences for an Indian boy-hero on a quest that will benefit his people and reestablish his place among them. When Salt answers affirmatively the Holy One's call to adventure, he provides new hope for the future of his people and becomes a role model for young people. Non-Indian readers will find the story interesting for its native lore and the generous, brave character of Salt. Young Indian readers may find still another lesson: there are times when one must risk going beyond the traditional to find new things that can make life better for one's people.[6]

Holt, Rinehart and Winston published *Runner in the Sun* in 1954, but despite an exciting story and the delightful drawings by Apache artist Allan C. Houser, it did not sell very well. In fact, most reviewers of adult novels paid no attention to it. Those who did were mystified. Because it was set prior to European contact, there were no non-Indian adversaries, no mixed-blood controversies, no imposition of "foreign" cultural elements. The most favorable comments about the book were written by Lawrence Lindley, who reviewed it for *Indian Truth,* the official publication of the Indian Rights Association. Lindley wrote, "The superb English, enriched with Indian philosophy and word pictures, makes one want to read every line of every page. It is an unusual book well worth the reading." Learned T. Bulman, writing for the *Saturday Review of Literature,* described the story as a mixture of mystery and history, "to the detriment of neither." Another reviewer, in *Library Journal,* generously conceded that it would, at least, prove more popular than other volumes in the series.[7]

Although the novel is unlike McNickle's other works and does not fit well within the genre of literature written by Native Americans, it does shed light on the author's creative talents. As perhaps the first novel written by a Native American author to feature Indian life before the time of white contact, the book has its place in the literature. *Runner in the Sun* was reprinted in 1987 by the University of New Mexico Press.

After completing *Runner in the Sun,* McNickle was too involved at Crownpoint to write more fiction. Now that he was no longer employed by the BIA, however, he felt free to comment on contemporary Indian policy, and during the next few years he wrote a number of position papers criticizing Congress and the Indian Bureau for their termination policy. With effective leadership, termination need not mean total assimilation, but the government had failed to train Indian leaders so that the tribes might be prepared for eventual economic and political autonomy.[8] Effective Indian self-government, the long-term goal, required well-trained leaders. Termination without them spelled disaster.

McNickle's next book-length project, written in collaboration with Harold Fey, happened almost by accident. Fey, who had been managing editor of *Christian Century* magazine since 1947, was an outspoken friend of minority groups in America and a long-time admirer of McNickle's work. In late 1954 and early 1955 he had made an extensive survey of conditions on Indian reservations in ten western states. He even visited Crownpoint, where, in McNickle's absence, Pfrommer showed him what the eastern Navajo people were accomplishing for themselves. Fey then reported his findings in a series of articles in *Christian Century,* which were republished as a pamphlet and widely distributed among people concerned with Indian affairs. Fey provided a ray of hope for those who were dismayed at what was happening to Indian people under the threat of termination, and at NCAI's annual meeting in Spokane in 1956 he was recognized for his "courageous and penetrating analysis of vital issues affecting Indians."[9]

Fey then reworked the articles into a full-length manuscript that Harper and Brothers accepted for publication. When he became ill and was unable to complete the editorial revisions, McNickle was asked if he would help. He agreed to edit the manuscript and also suggested some additions to the text. He was particularly eager to discuss the changing role of the commissioner of Indian affairs, which had degenerated from one of helping establish Indian policy to an enforcer of congressional will and whim. As he explained in a letter to Collier written at about that time, "The recent batch [of commissioners], Nichols-Myer-Emmons, have all lent themselves to a conspiracy of ruination, moving against the Indians, in the mistaken notion that the role of the commissioner is to cajole and coerce."[10] He wanted to explore this idea and Fey was more than pleased to have his input.

The premise of *Indians and Other Americans* was timely and uncompromising. After tracing the meanderings of past Indian policy, the authors demanded that a new federal policy be extended to American Indians that would provide them with the same kind of aid that was being offered to Third World countries through the Point Four Program. McNickle had proposed such a domestic program for Indians as early as July 1951, in an address before NCAI's annual convention in St. Paul, Minnesota, and he had repeated the suggestion in an article in 1953.[11] Congress had not responded, and he wanted to bring his proposal to a wider audience, now that Point Four assistance programs overseas were bearing fruit.

McNickle and Fey pointed out in their work that a key element of the success of those programs was that the recipient nations themselves determined what particular projects were to be funded in their countries. No paternalistic strings were attached to the aid provided. The very least the American government could do for Indians, they argued, would be to give them the opportunity to make the same kinds of decisions about funds being spent on Indian reservations.[12] With good seed the soil of the reservations, like that of the Third World countries, would be capable of renewal. They insisted that the federal government should no longer impose its programs upon Indians without their consultation and consent. They summarized their views in the book's final paragraph:

> The unfulfilled dream of the Indians of this country is that they will be permitted at last to make the primary decisions affecting their lives and their property. Not that their decisions will be superior to those made by men possibly more skillful; but that, being their decisions, the people will be content to live with them and to change them as experience teaches the desirability of change.[13]

When the work was completed, Fey insisted that McNickle be named as coauthor. In Fey's opinion, McNickle's editing and his additional material had improved the work significantly. McNickle was reluctant to accept, because Fey obviously had done most of the writing. He eventually agreed, however, when others convinced him that the book would reach a larger audience with his name on it as well as Fey's. *Indians and Other Americans: Two Ways of Life Meet* was published by Harper and Brothers in 1959, and revised and expanded in 1970. Fey insisted throughout that the royalties be divided equally.[14]

McNickle and Fey presented such a cogent summary of the effect of Congress's vacillating Indian policy that Helen Peterson at NCAI wanted to send copies to every congressman who served on House and Senate Indian affairs committees, a plan which, unfortunately, died for lack of funds. However, Richard L. Neuberger, chairman of the Senate Indian Affairs Subcommittee, drew attention to the book in a widely read critical essay that appeared in the *Saturday Review*. Though he did not directly attack the authors' proposal for an Indian Point Four Program, Neuberger questioned whether such a program would provide the ultimate answer to America's Indian problem. "Are most Indian reservations susceptible of such development," he queried, "or was the original theft [of independence and autonomy] so thorough that the soil will not accept the seed?"[15] Fey and McNickle had maintained that, although a Point Four program would offer no ultimate answer, it would assuredly lead to greater Indian autonomy. The answer to the Indian problem must come finally from the Indians themselves. Neuberger, however, doubted that outcome.

Other readers' response to *Indians and Other Americans* was more gratifying. Although Neuberger's review probably helped sales, his comments were received less enthusiastically than was the book itself. After Angie Debo, the Oklahoma Indian historian, read his review, she wrote to Helen Peterson at NCAI. She confessed that she had only read Neuberger's review and not the book itself, but she would have liked to review it for the *New York Times*. "I have enough confidence in the integrity and scholarship of the authors to trust what they have said," she told Peterson, "I am sorry they did not rate a reviewer of greater integrity. [The authors] are two writers whom I admire very much."[16]

Other people who wrote to NCAI were also impressed with the new book. John Rainer of Taos Pueblo, who had been associated with Arrow, Incorporated, and knew McNickle well, expressed the thoughts of many when he commented, "It is rare to find a study of Indians that objectively evaluates the causes, obstacles, and results of Indian policy so clearly as this one does."[17] Rainer felt that he had been rewarded generously for having read a book that was not only informative but that took seriously the task of objectively evaluating the causes and obstacles of Indian problems. Others apparently felt as he did, and the first edition went through three printings for a total of sixty-five hundred copies.

After the intense and emotionally draining activities of the 1950s, McNickle was exhausted, and when the Crownpoint project drew to a close in December 1960 he looked forward to a much-needed rest. Boulder, Colorado, had remained "home" for D'Arcy and Roma during those hectic years, although he had been away much of the time. Roma had found adjustment to life in the West more stressful than did D'Arcy himself. As a professional woman, she had been accustomed to the sophisticated life of the nation's capital, and the relatively raw, muscular Denver provided a distinct contrast. Although Boulder, thirty miles from Denver, was the home of the University of Colorado, it, too, had many rough edges. Not knowing in 1952 whether their move would be permanent, Roma and D'Arcy were reluctant to put down roots, and their first house, which they rented, was only a living place.

McNickle officially resigned from the Bureau of Indian Affairs in 1954 and at that time he and Roma began to look for a more permanent home. Sharing office space with Royal Hassrick at the Denver Art Museum had been temporary from the beginning; Hassrick's office was small and too far from Boulder to be practical. What McNickle really wanted was an office in his home. He and Roma eventually found a substantial twelve-year-old brick house with a double garage that they converted into an office. With the records of American Indian Development more accessible, Roma assumed much of the responsibility for the routine office detail, for which, apparently, she received little if any salary. When funding from the

Emil Schwartzhaupt Foundation began in 1956, McNickle hired a part-time secretary and relieved Roma of some of the correspondence, but she continued to oversee AID's record keeping.

That was hardly full-time employment, however. With her excellent professional background, Roma soon found work as research editor for the Western Interstate Commission for Higher Education (WICHE). This was work for which she was well qualified. WICHE had been organized in 1951 to assist western colleges and universities as they responded to changing educational and social needs.[18] By 1961 Roma had became coordinator of its student exchange program, which facilitated the training of medical, dental, and veterinary students among its various cooperating universities. She also assumed an active role in the Colorado League of Women Voters, where she served as chair of the League's State Water Resources Committee and eventually became the League's state president.

Roma's steady income from WICHE during the early years of the Crownpoint Project proved to be a blessing. Arrow's increasingly erratic disbursements had resulted in frustrating delays of operating expenses for American Indian Development, as well as for D'Arcy's salary. After AID's incorporation in 1957, funding came directly to Boulder and that situation no longer pertained, but with the conclusion of the Crownpoint Project in December 1960 D'Arcy drew only a small salary as director of American Indian Development, Incorporated. Roma's income provided additional security.

Their family structure was hardly typical of the nuclear family model common in the 1950s. Roma worked full-time, and D'Arcy was frequently away from home for days at a time. But Toni remained close to her father, despite the distance between them. She corresponded with him and visited him occasionally, although she knew very little about his work. Kathleen was home until she finished high school in Boulder, then, like Toni, she married and returned to Washington. There was apparently some estrangement between Kathleen and the rest of the family, as she is never mentioned in her father's later diaries or correspondence. Years later she attended her father's funeral, but nothing is known of her life or subsequent whereabouts.

As D'Arcy and Roma had anticipated when they moved west, Philomene, in her seventies, became part of the household after they moved to Boulder. She had on at least one occasion visited the family in Washington, and D'Arcy from time to time had helped her financially. When she was no longer able to support herself, he and Roma made room for her in their home. Philomene, or Phyllis, as she now preferred to be called, had always been an attractive woman. She was also an accomplished seamstress and often sewed for Roma and her friends.[19] But her chronic heart condition gradually worsened and she needed increasing care.

Although Philomene's presence in the home gave Roma little privacy, the two women got along reasonably well. Given their respective backgrounds, it is difficult to see how they could have had much in common. As Philomene recalled when she wrote to one of her nieces in 1962, her greatest joy "was to take the childer to picnic They enjoy that. Roma don't care for any thing like that so we never go on outing."[20] Roma was afraid of ticks and Rocky Mountain spotted fever, and she was reluctant to expose her family to such dangers.

Life in Boulder, of course, offered some compensations. The area was spectacularly beautiful and it drew a large number of out-of-town houseguests to their door. In addition, the nearby University of Colorado attracted scholars in various fields, so they attended lectures and concerts. They also enjoyed good food and drink with a group of congenial friends. D'Arcy's reputation as a connoisseur by this time had become almost legendary, and in pleasant surroundings, he was a delightful companion. He had a peculiarly Indian sense of humor and frequently indulged in puns and good-natured practical joking. He took his work very seriously, but he viewed himself much less so and often enjoyed a joke at his own expense. Roma was just the opposite. She took herself and her work very seriously indeed. A college classmate has remembered her as studious and brilliant, but seldom given to laughter. Only rarely was she demonstratively affectionate.[21] Her background had provided her with no way of sharing with D'Arcy his love for the out-of-doors.

D'Arcy, of course, relished an outing of any kind, especially if he could take his fishing rod along. Fishing had retained its potency for him as a beneficent symbol of his childhood. Unencumbered by the emotional trauma of family troubles, it conveyed instead happy memories of the times he and his sister Florence had fished in the streams near the family home in Montana. Often in his diaries, and sometimes in correspondence, he would anticipate the opportunity and ask if someone might have a pole that he could borrow. No mention was ever made of his having caught any fish—it was the ritual act itself, rather than the catch, that was important to him.

Perhaps it was a lack of warmth and humor in D'Arcy's and Roma's marriage that made Vi Pfrommer increasingly attractive to him. Roma and Vi were both intelligent women; D'Arcy would not have been attracted to anyone who was not. Vi also shared many of D'Arcy's personal and professional interests. Despite her seeming seriousness that D'Arcy had noted during his first meeting with her, Vi was lively and fun. Friends described her as "very pretty, vivacious, lovely of face and figure, [with] a passion for living life to the full, . . . a lively, sparkly, fun-loving person."[22] She and D'Arcy complemented each other well.

Vi also had the ultimate advantage over Roma in working closely with D'Arcy, day by day, on the project that expressed his deepest aspirations for Indian survival and self-determination. While Roma managed the office details in Boulder, Vi held the "operative" position in Crownpoint. She understood D'Arcy's dream and their shared commitment to the task at hand. In December 1953, after their first six months in Crownpoint, he wrote to tell her what having her there had meant to him. "The year of working together has been a wonderful learning experience for me," he told her. "You will deny it, but your insights have been true every time, your planning never failed, and only your modesty exceeded your success in moving people to action."[23]

Although their relationship remained on a professional level for the duration of the project, the frustrations of its last months inevitably drew them closer together, and when the project was over, Pfrommer remained on AID's payroll as field director. She bought an old adobe structure in Albuquerque's North Valley and remodeled it into a comfortable and attractive home. Her presence on the staff of American Indian Development continued to draw criticism from various quarters (she was, after all, non-Indian), but McNickle by this time was fiercely protective. Those who disapproved of her participation in NCAI affairs did not do so in his presence.[24]

It is impossible to know specifically how the change in Vi's role affected the relationship between her and Roma. Vi had been a house guest in Boulder on several occasions and she was always solicitous about Roma and the family in her correspondence with the Boulder office. She had even provided a second mortgage for the purchase of the McNickles' house in Boulder. Both women must have been aware, however, that her relationship with D'Arcy was no longer exclusively professional. By 1962, when he wrote to tell Vi of his plans to visit Albuquerque during the Christmas holidays, his feelings were quite open. "I want only one gift," he told her, "No one else in the world has it. No other world have I, no warmer heart, no kindlier eyes to view me, no softer voice to encourage me. Is there anything more in the world besides these? Happy New Year!"[25] Roma could hardly have been unaware of the altered relationship between her husband and Vi Pfrommer.

The question remains, however, whether D'Arcy's frequent absences from Boulder in the 1950s, and his growing affection for Vi, contributed to tension between him and Roma or provided an escape from it. Their marriage had shown signs of stress even before they left Washington and perhaps it would have failed under any circumstance.[26] Vi's presence was probably not the decisive element in their eventual separation, although undoubtedly it was a contributing factor.

With completion of the Crownpoint Project in December 1960, D'Arcy and Roma discovered that they had traded roles. In her new position as director of WICHE's student exchange program, Roma traveled extensively, while D'Arcy was more often at home. More and more he was recognized as an authority on Indian affairs and received numerous requests for articles from major publications during this period, so he continued to write. He was pleased that he was able to spend more time with his increasingly frail mother, who died in 1964.

The major continuity in McNickle's life between 1960 and 1965 was a series of summer leadership training workshops that were held at the University of Colorado in Boulder. The more he thought about the Point Four concept in the context of his experience at Crownpoint, the more he realized how urgent it was that young Indian people be offered some training in the knowledge and skills they would need for leadership roles in their tribal communities. Much as he valued the older traditional headmen, times were changing too rapidly for the approach he had used at Crownpoint to have more than local effectiveness. He had seen his work there endangered by more modern institutions. It was not long before he was much more involved with the leadership training workshops in Boulder than he had been when they were first organized.

These workshops had originated over breakfast one morning in the mid-1950s at the Washington home of Ruth Bronson. After serving in the Guidance Office of the Indian Bureau's Office of Education for twelve years during the Collier administration, Bronson was still concerned with Indian education. She; Galen Weaver from the Board of Home Missions of the Congregational and Christian Churches; and Elizabeth Clark Rosenthal, who represented the National Council of the Episcopal Church, were members of a Council on Indian Affairs composed of delegates from various organizations that had traditionally supported Indian causes.[27] These organizations were disturbed about the high dropout rate among the relatively few but growing number of Indian college students across the country. That rate seemed only tangentially related to academic ability. At the urging of these three people who were backed by the Council on Indian Affairs, Sol Tax, chairman of the University of Chicago's Department of Anthropology, led the way in planning a six-week summer workshop in 1956 to explore this disturbing trend. Tax enlisted the aid of

Robert J. Havighurst and a University of Chicago graduate student, Frederick O. Gearing. Helen Peterson from NCAI, Fred Segundo from the Papago tribe, and a number of other individuals contributed their own ideas and financial support.

McNickle himself did not participate in the initial planning sessions in 1955 and 1956, because he was still occupied with the Navajo Development Committee at Crownpoint. He knew most of the people involved, however, either personally or by reputation. Sol Tax, who had originated the term "action anthropology" a few years earlier, was a fellow recipient of Schwartzhaupt Foundation grants for his work with the Fox tribe, and Robert Havighurst had been one of the consultants for the BIA's personality study in the early 1940s. Fred Gearing, who would direct the first workshop, was a new face, recommended by Tax and Havighurst. Rosalie Wax was involved from the beginning, and she would serve as workshop director in 1959 and 1960. Wax had done research among those Japanese Americans who were relocated to Tule Lake in California during World War II. She had also spent a brief but personally significant period at the American Indian Center in Chicago. So McNickle knew of her at least by name, and he may have met her at some previous time.

Although McNickle was involved in the leadership training workshops at first only as a guest speaker and occasional consultant, he observed their development with considerable interest. As Helen Peterson wrote to a friend in 1957, "I suppose that D'Arcy has given more thought to this field than anyone among us. He has kept informed of community programs virtually all over the world and he has made considerable study of how those people who are sent abroad on Point Four jobs are oriented, trained, and instructed, to work in under-developed countries."[28] With that kind of informed interest, McNickle observed as the workshop format evolved on a trial-and-error basis for several years. Gradually, the leaders developed clearer ideas about why Indian young people who had seemed well prepared for college were dropping out in such alarming numbers. Rosalie Wax, who later prepared a detailed evaluation of the first five workshops, diagnosed the problem as one of confused identity and a loss of cultural moorings. In her report she wrote, "Many young Indians, whether of tribal or detribalized background, suffer from anxieties and confusions that the sociologist has attributed to 'marginality': they are unable to see themselves as either Indians or as white people."[29] The usual Indian response to such uncomfortable ambivalence, she noted, was to withdraw from the situation until the confusion was resolved.

But perhaps that withdrawal could be prevented if the students could be helped to develop a more positive identity of themselves as Indians. Their previous education, whether in BIA, public, or mission schools, had denigrated their people's heritage, but the workshop experience might begin to change that. "Even the knowledge that other young people are in the same situation often increases their self-confidence and their ability to cope with their own problem," Wax observed.[30] Responding to the students' perceived marginality, the workshop staff focused on designing strategies for helping them rediscover and accept the value of their tribal identity while gaining skills for survival through a college education.

The problem of dealing with marginality in the workshops was complicated by the fact that the students who attended came from a variety of backgrounds. Some were conservative and traditional, whereas a lesser number were totally acculturated; by Wax's definition, most were marginal to some degree. Although they had retained many Indian attitudes, they had also adopted white middle- and lower-class ideas and mannerisms. However, their experience with whites and with urban life was limited; depending on the region of the country they called home, they had been "respected, tolerated, ignored, or despised" by their white neighbors.[31]

What was most surprising to the predominantly non-Indian staff, according to Wax, was how little the students knew of Indian history and culture. Not only were many of them ashamed of their reservation background, they were ashamed of being Indian. The staff was shocked by the students' rejection of their native communities and their past, as well as by the parochialism of the concept of white behavior they sought to emulate. The goal of most of the students was to transform their reservation communities into rural small-town America where everyone would act as whites. The students, in turn, were distressed when the workshop staff reacted negatively to these aspirations. Always before, assimilationist goals had won the approval of their white teachers. It was disconcerting to be told that their former role models had often been "ignorant, short-sighted, 'corny,' and cruel."[32] During the first workshops, painful and frustrating collisions occurred between students and staff as both groups worked toward a reassessment of their particular stereotypical misconceptions.

Wax and the other staff people soon realized the necessity for designing a program with a double focus. On one hand, Robert Thomas, a Cherokee anthropologist who was a primary staff person during most of the workshops, taught Indian history and culture from the Indian point of view. He was a gifted teacher, and the students were hungry for all that he could give them. McNickle later observed that it was Thomas

> who most influenced the shaping of the workshop as a center for discovery and understanding. The teaching faculty looked to him for intellectual challenge, while the students responded by improving academic performances—something most of them had never before aspired to. . . . [He was] a teacher who was equally capable of reaching students and encouraging them to stretch their intellectual grasp.[33]

The staff literally stumbled onto the other focus of the workshops through a technique that proved so effective it became a regular part of the curriculum. Rosalie Wax's husband, Murray, who accompanied his wife to the 1959 workshop "for the fun of it," was a sociologist with an interest in anthropology. He volunteered to lecture on EuroAmerican cultural values, and quite by accident he discovered an approach that became standard. His wife recounted what happened.

> In his presentation, Murray described casually and unemotionally the Indian style of life that the European has regarded censoriously

and then explained the moral and religious rationale that the Indian gave to those traditional ways. The conservative students were entranced and the assimilationists stunned, having never heard the ways of their elders spoken of with such respect by a white man.[34]

When a similar approach was used to explain the ways of white society, the students were intrigued almost as much. Neither group had ever heard the white people's style of life explained with equal sympathy and justice, rather than with extravagant praise or bitter criticism. Murray Wax's objective comparison of cultural differences, coupled with what Thomas was offering, led to the development of an increasingly effective core curriculum.

While some of the students complained at first about the need to concern themselves with whites' motives and rationale, they soon learned that there was good reason for understanding why white people acted as they did. "Whether [the student] wished to assimilate, accommodate, be marginal, or encapsulate himself," Rosalie Wax observed, was a matter of personal choice. But each could exercise any of these options more easily and efficiently "if he knew about the white man's ways and learned some of his techniques, if he, in short, studied the white man with the same care and patience that some of his ancestors had studied the buffalo."[35] To use another analogy, they, like Salt, would need to travel to far places before they could bring home to their people new ways of adapting to the world.

The rest of the workshop format was flexible. Native American leaders from various fields were invited to attend one or more sessions as guest lecturers and role models, and they, too, provided the students with information about white society and white-Indian interaction. In 1959 alone, guest speakers included Iliff McKay, secretary of the Blackfeet Tribal Council; Moses Two Bulls, chief judge of the Oglala Sioux Tribal Court; Ben Reifel, a Brule Sioux who was director of the BIA's Aberdeen Area Office; Clarence Wesley, chairman of the San Carlos Apache Tribal Council; Martin Vigil, secretary of the All-Indian Pueblo Council in New Mexico; Helen Peterson, executive director of NCAI; and McNickle himself.

The effect of these Indian leaders on the students was incalculable. As Rosalie Wax explained, "The idea that Indians ought to run their own affairs and plan their own futures becomes [for the students] not a theory in the social sciences but a modest reality which can be expanded. And the fact that knowledge and skill are needed for this expansion is so obvious that it need not be put into words."[36]

The orientation of the workshops obviously reflected McNickle's concern about the loss of tribal identity and personal choice and about the kind of leadership he thought he saw emerging within the Navajo tribe. At Crownpoint he had seen for himself what happened when the young 'marginalists' returned to positions of leadership. They attempted to plot the course of their people's future without an understanding of the past, a practice that, he felt, would almost surely lead to the ultimate destruction of tribal identity, whether it was intended or not. At the Boulder workshops young people could begin to acquire greater understanding of their own heritage and of the non-Indian world as well, an understanding that would enable them to make better-informed decisions about their own future and the future of their people.

From 1956 to 1959, McNickle had attended the workshops only as a visiting lecturer. However, when the Schwartzhaupt Foundation granted a total of ten thousand dollars to the workshops for 1959, 1960, and 1961, McNickle agreed to accept and disburse the funds through American Indian Development, Incorporated, much as Arrow had originally done for AID.[37] After the 1960 workshop he assumed responsibility as director for the entire program, and Pfrommer, as field director for AID, took over the administrative details.

Workshop structure and content, which had developed on an ad hoc basis, were more or less established by that time, and only minor changes were made thereafter in the basic curriculum. Each workshop began with an introduction to such social science concepts as culture, society, and personality as they applied to individual and group identities, both Indian and white. In succeeding sessions, participants learned about the nature of folk and urban societies within the specific context of Indian-white relationships. Each workshop had a specific theme, and the students designed individual research projects related to that theme. Visiting experts discussed current legislation, legal questions, and other matters that had a bearing on Indian affairs, thus exposing the students to a broad spectrum of concerns vital to Indian people.

The workshops had a tremendous impact on most of those who attended, and McNickle later regretted that he was unable to follow the subsequent careers of all the young people who had participated. Each session had been run on a shoestring budget provided by the Council on Indian Affairs, NCAI, the Schwartzhaupt Foundation, and a number of small individual donations. As director of American Indian Development, Incorporated, McNickle wanted to evaluate the workshops through follow-up studies of the participants as they returned to college and in their later careers, and he applied to several foundations for grants that would permit such studies. He also hoped to expand the workshop program to include the training of tribal leaders in a wide variety of management skills, planning procedures, and problem-solving techniques. Unfortunately, nothing came of his various proposals, and the workshops struggled along on a minimal budget until 1968.[38]

The single most notable exception to the workshops' established curriculum occurred in 1961, when McNickle arranged for the first week of the workshop to coincide with the American Indian Chicago Conference. Many Native Americans have since considered that conference to be the most significant event in recent Indian history, and McNickle's contribution was crucial to its success. The idea for such a gathering germinated in the summer of 1960, when the Schwartzhaupt Foundation, still concerned with "education for citizenship," asked Sol Tax to draw up guidelines for a new direction in Indian policy and administration. Termination was finally dying a slow death in Congress, after having wrought havoc among Indian tribes across the country for a decade, and with a new president about to be elected, the foundation believed that the time was right for new policy suggestions.[39] Responding to the Foundation's invitation, Tax suggested that a pan-Indian conference might provide a forum for the

Indians themselves to suggest an agenda for the future. Such a conference, in Tax's view, would be another project in "action anthropology." He and the University of Chicago would act as facilitators; the Indians, primarily through NCAI, would actually plan and run the conference.

Coincidentally, Helen Peterson as executive director of NCAI had issued a call that same year to a select group of colleges and universities, inviting them to attend the annual NCAI convention in November. For the most part, colleges and universities had avoided nongovernmental Indian affairs, but Tax's interest in the Boulder workshops on behalf of the University of Chicago encouraged NCAI to make an appeal for their broader involvement. In fact, NCAI invited Tax to Denver to chair the convention's opening session. He seized the opportunity to ask if NCAI was interested in cosponsoring, with the University of Chicago, a pan-Indian conference designed to suggest a new course for Indian policy and administration.

Tax's proposal was attractive for several reasons. First, the University of Chicago had offered to provide logistical and financial support from a fund set aside specifically for public policy conferences. Such support from a major university for a conference on contemporary Indian affairs marked a significant breakthrough. In addition, the Schwartzhaupt Foundation had responded to Tax's proposal by offering $14,800 for seed money. Tax himself was insistent on only one issue: Attendance must not be limited to tribal groups or enrolled Indians. The conference must be open to all Indians, affiliated or not, who wanted to participate.[40]

With committed support from the University of Chicago and the Emil Schwartzhaupt Foundation, NCAI enthusiastically endorsed Tax's plan, and a date for the conference was set for the following June. Shortly after the Denver meeting, NCAI's planning group gathered in Albuquerque and appointed McNickle chairman of the conference steering committee. He was the logical choice in terms of knowledge and experience, and with the Crownpoint Project drawing to a close, he would be available. He agreed to write a working draft for a statement of Indian goals that would then be circulated to various Indian groups for comments and revision.

NCAI organized an intensive campaign to elicit as wide a response as possible to McNickle's original draft, holding regional meetings across the country to discuss it. After collecting feedback from those meetings, McNickle incorporated the suggestions into a thirty-page document entitled "A Declaration of Indian Purpose," which he submitted to the first plenary session of the conference in Chicago as the basis for discussion by the participants. The revised document became the definitive statement of the conference, and has been quoted extensively ever since.[41]

The weekly *Navajo Times,* in an article telling its readers about the impending Chicago conference, anticipated it as "the greatest Redskin invasion of Chicago since the Ft. Dearborn invasion," and that was not too great an exaggeration. Ninety bands and tribes, recognized or not, were represented by the 467 Indians who registered as participants. In the view of all concerned, it was an outstanding success. The conference had provided a unique forum for nonaffiliated Indians who until that time had been excluded from tribal programs and conferences. Comments by Gerald Wilkinson, who later became director of the National Indian Youth Council, convey the significance of permitting all Indians to have a voice:

> For those of us at the Chicago Conference, something important happened on a personal, social, and political level. All of us were from different tribes, and although government for administrative reasons had always treated us as one people, we sitting in the conference room felt we had no relationship with each other. It was as if people from different countries in the world had been dumped into a single geographical site to discuss common national problems.
>
> By the end of the conference, something profound had happened to all the Indians there. . . . They could see that Indians were in a sense one people and were becoming more so. With the Pan-Indian Movement for Indian rights in the 1960s and 1970s, it is easy to forget the profundity of the revolution that occurred in Chicago.[42]

As chairman of the steering committee, McNickle was involved with all aspects of planning the conference. He even contributed a skit entitled "Reverse History," a role reversal of the "Bureau of White Man's Affairs" that created hilarious situations in which Indians as the dominant group tried to cope with the irrational behavior of white people. Such role play had already proven successful at some of the workshops and it did much to lighten the more serious moments in Chicago.[43] He certainly had enjoyed writing it.

Not surprisingly, preparation for the conference had become increasingly hectic as the date drew near, and the final intense, emotionally draining week of meetings left McNickle totally exhausted. His immediate reaction reflected his fatigue. When he got back to Boulder, he wrote to his old friend Bill Zimmerman,

> I had hoped to have more time with you in Chicago, but towards the end I didn't have time to talk with myself. That was about the most confused and rumor-ridden conference I ever had the misfortune to get mixed up in, and I'm surprised we came out with our shirts. There were moments when I was ready to quit and go home, and I suspect many others felt the same way.[44]

It would take a while before he developed a more realistic perspective about what had taken place in Chicago.

McNickle had planned in advance for the entire workshop contingent to attend the Chicago conference, and the young people provided assistance wherever they were needed. It was the first time that many of them had participated in a gathering of Indian people from tribes other than their own who expressed their common needs and aspirations. Like Gerald Wilkinson, they were deeply affected by that common experience. After the conference, as the entire group traveled by bus to Colorado for the remaining five weeks, it was obvious to the staff that something vital had happened to everyone. The young people were excited, exhilarated, even perhaps somewhat frightened, by their conference experience. A whole new way of relating to other Indians and to the outside world had been revealed to them. They had discovered, for the first time, that Indians could make demands on the white power structure. They realized that by acting together as Indians they had political power.[45]

To some of those workshop participants, McNickle's approach to tribal change suddenly seemed too slow and cumbersome, and a few even walked out before the workshop was over. Later that summer, the most dissatisfied among them met again in Gallup, New Mexico. Building on an earlier regional organization, they founded the National Indian Youth Council (NIYC), whose board of directors included Mel Thom (Walker River Paiute), Shirley Hill Witt (Mohawk), Bernadine Eschief (Navajo), Clyde Warrior (Ponca), Howard McKinley (Northern Ute), and Edison Real Bird (Crow).[46] NIYC, created as an activist organization, has continued its educational and advocacy roles to the present time. McNickle later was asked to serve on its advisory council.

Indians had indeed succeeded in making themslves heard nationally through the 1961 American Indian Chicago Conference, but whether the conference itself was a valid exercise in "action anthropology," as Sol Tax had asserted, was open to question. Indeed, it became part of the larger issue of whether action anthropology as such was a legitimate exercise in professional field work. Wilcomb Washburn, at the Smithsonian Institution, denied the value of the conference as objective research. He claimed that the "anthropologist-intervenors" who had organized it had failed to meet the scholarly demand that it produce an advance in knowledge. The project lacked a theoretical framework, and the organizers had provided no final evaluation of the project as a result of their "research."[47]

According to Washburn, objective evaluation of the conference was not even possible in terms of professional research, because Sol Tax and Nancy O. Lurie, who was his assistant coordinator, had interfered with the integrity of their subjects by changing the relationships among Indian tribes and between Indians and whites. Their own participation in the event had altered the conditions of the people they were presumably studying, thereby casting doubt on the validity of the enterprise as anthropological research. Washburn did not deny Tax and Lurie the right to intervene as individuals, but he did question their role in the conference as professional anthropologists.

The complementary question of whether McNickle viewed himself and the other Indian planners as the subjects of anthropological research cannot be answered. Having just concluded a project in which he himself played the role of action anthropologist, McNickle was undoubtedly sensitive to the terms of Tax's proposal. Even if he did see himself and the project as Tax had suggested, he apparently decided that the conference offered a unique opportunity for Indians to make themselves heard, and he did not hesitate to give it his full attention. It is an interesting commentary on his compound identity that he could shift roles and apparently be comfortable with both.

McNickle's ambivalence in this matter was not completely painless, however, as his diary later revealed. When Nancy Lurie published a detailed account of the conference the following December, she adhered to proper academic form by referring impersonally to the Indian participants. For the most part, individual efforts were referred to collectively under the rubric of "the NCAI."[48] McNickle was deeply hurt by what he perceived as her lack of appreciation for his considerable contribution. At that point, he obviously considered himself a colleague of Tax and Lurie's and not the subject of anthropological study. In his diary entry at year's end all his disappointment, anger, and frustration spilled out. He listed his grievances in detail:

> I went to great effort to prepare a basic document for the projected Chicago Conference. This document became exactly what was needed—and it emerged from local tribal discussions and the weeklong Chicago Conference in essentially the form in which it was cast. I chaired the Steering Committee, was centrally involved in all planning. Was Chairman of the Drafting Committee which produced the final document. When it was all over and all of us were on the point of collapse—Sol never even said Thank You. I never had a letter from him after the conference until, months later, I got his bill

for the workshop students who participated in the conference. Even in that letter he made no mention of my contribution.[49]

That entry, made on New Year's Eve, reflected all the confusion, disappointment, and frustration that had followed the conclusion of the Crownpoint Project during the past year.

With the year over and the conference come and gone, McNickle finally confronted another writing assignment that, subconsciously, he had been trying for some time to avoid. The Emil Schwartzhaupt Foundation, which had granted a total of $128,800 to the Crownpoint Project, was still waiting for McNickle's final report. Although he was committed, D'Arcy felt little enthusiasm for the job. He found it painful to recall the high hopes raised by the project's early achievements and then face its gradual decline and the apparent failure of all that had meant so much to him. Writing about it was not going to be pleasant or easy.

Contributing to his reluctance was the fact that the report would generate no income. As a solution to that particular problem, Sol Tax urged him to apply again for a Guggenheim Fellowship. Although McNickle was pleased and touched by Tax's encouragement, he was skeptical about his chances for getting it. He had been rejected twice before, when he was much younger; now he was almost sixty. "I am well beyond the age limit," he told Tax, "and my academic background is notable for its absence."[50] Nevertheless, he filled out the application, and, much to his surprise, it was accepted. He had finally been granted a Guggenheim Fellowship.

His reluctance finally overcome, McNickle went to work. He visited Albuquerque several times in 1963 and 1964 so that he and Pfrommer might sort out the voluminous field notes, progress reports, interview transcriptions, and other pertinent material they had collected. They also returned several times to Crownpoint and looked up their old friend Manuelito, the medicine man who had been such a strong supporter of their work. Unfortunately, the Community House was barely functioning, and the visits served only to rekindle their frustration.[51] The report, which was finally completed in 1964, included a definitive statement of

McNickle's purpose and methodology, along with a detailed narrative of the project itself. Greatly relieved at having fulfilled his obligation, McNickle sent it off to the Schwartzhaupt Foundation. Harper and Brothers had asked to see the manuscript and Sol Tax had agreed to write an introduction for it, but for some reason it was never published. McNickle may never have submitted it.

He also sent a copy of the report to John Collier, who, in failing health, had retired to a little mountain village near Taos Pueblo in northern New Mexico. The former commissioner was by this time quite frail and McNickle expected no response, but he wanted to share the Crownpoint experience with his old friend and mentor. Collier had, after all, contributed a great deal to it, if indirectly, and McNickle wanted to tell him about it. "I did want you to know of this experience and some of the things we learned from it," he wrote. "It was remarkable in many ways—deeply satisfying at times, but profoundly frustrating at the end. Whether the people's genius for remaining Navajo through all vicissitudes will yet assert itself is left under a cloud as our report closes. But perhaps this is only the short view—I hope so."[52] Despite his pessimism concerning the outcome of the project, McNickle's completion of the 250-page report was unexpectedly satisfying. Writing it not only fulfilled his obligation to the Schwartzhaupt Foundation, it provided excellent therapy, and by the time it was finished, he had dissipated most of his frustration over the outcome of the Crownpoint Project.

Those years from 1961 to 1965 were productive ones for McNickle, even though they were not financially remunerative and seemed without focus. He completed numerous articles and became a regular contributor of book reviews to the *Nation*. He also served as consultant for several projects directed by the American Friends Service Committee. He even sent another revision of "Feather Boy" to Harper and Brothers, with the anticipated negative results. All this activity, however, was anticlimactic, and McNickle felt that he was only marking time. In his correspondence with Vi Pfrommer his frustrations are quite evident. She urged him to be patient, assuring him that another "opening" would appear in due time.[53]

The summer workshops in Boulder provided some measure of continuity during those difficult years. So, also, did his relationship with NCAI, which had contributed toward the workshops' financial support. However, NCAI's new executive director, Vine Deloria, Jr., who succeeded Helen Peterson to that position shortly after the Chicago Conference, was not particularly impressed with the whole workshop concept. Deloria had been a guest speaker at the 1965 workshop in Boulder and may have been describing his own experience when he wrote about generic workshops in his book *Custer Died for Your Sins*. One workshop, he told his readers,

> discussed the thesis that Indians were in a terrible crisis. They were, in the words of friendly anthro guides, *between two worlds*. People between two worlds, the students were told, *drank*. For the anthropologists, it was a valid reason for drinking on the reservation. For the young Indians, it was an authoritative definition of their roles as Indians. Real Indians, they began to think, *drank*, and their task was to become real Indians, for only in that way could they recreate the glories of the past.
>
> So they *drank*.
>
> I lost some good friends who *drank* too much.[54]

Deloria obviously confused description and prescription and he failed to give his friends sufficient credit for being able to discern the difference. Those at the workshops who felt the urge to drink may have found a rationale for doing so, but the Boulder workshops' "anthro guides," especially Robert Thomas, stressed the positive values in Indian identity, not the negative ones. McNickle said later of Deloria's comments, "Some of his choler is justified, but much is leg-pulling and verbal calisthenics."[55]

He acknowledged, however, that anger sometimes erupted when the workshop experience touched too close to the nerve. In another letter to Collier at this time, he described the students' response to certain parts of the curriculum: "Some of them get so excited they want to go right out and start a war against all the teachers and administrators they have ever known who all along were telling them that as Indians they were dead."[56] Their anger was generally constructive, however, and he was convinced that the workshops were filling a real need. The summer sessions continued until 1968; by that time other resources were available for Indian students and McNickle himself was responding to new "openings."

Taking a longer view, McNickle had reason to be pleased with what those summer workshops had accomplished. He later recalled:

> That workshop experience, seen now in retrospect, was an awakening for most of the 300-odd students who took part in it. Of the young Indian leaders who have come to national attention in recent years and who contributed markedly to the development of their own communities, many came through the workshop. The thing that made the difference in their lives, I am confident, was the exposure to the social sciences, which provided insights into their own and the general society, as well as the conceptual tools for analyzing the forces around them. They became articulate and, in some cases, quite angry about the exploitation to which they and their kin had been subjected. But the anger, when it was present, was informed and usually effective.[57]

McNickle's interest in encouraging young Indians to prepare for leadership roles was not limited to those who participated in the Boulder workshops. From 1957 to 1971, he served on the Fellowship Awards Committee of the John Hay Whitney Foundation's Opportunity Fellowship Program, which screened applications from minority students of exceptional promise who, because of cultural or other barriers, did not have the opportunity to continue their education. During his years as director of the workshops he had met many promising young people and he encouraged them to apply for fellowships. As he told Vi Pfrommer, "It has [almost] come to the point that an Indian is accepted automatically unless I say no."[58] Among those who received fellowships while he served on the screening committee were Alfonso Ortiz (San Juan Pueblo/Tewa), an anthropologist who later became his close personal friend; Dave Warren

(Santa Clara Pueblo and Chippewa), whose father, Alvin Warren, had known and worked with McNickle through NCAI; and Anne Rainer, John Rainer's daughter, from Taos Pueblo. Clyde Warrior, a workshop participant and one of the founders of the National Indian Youth Council, also received a John Hay Whitney Fellowship because of McNickle's support.

Although McNickle was not able to follow the careers of all the workshop participants, he did have a continuing relationship with a number of them. For Gerald Brown (Flathead); Nancy Dumont and Robert V. Dumont, Jr. (both Sioux and Assiniboine); Gloria Emerson (Navajo); Faith Smith (Chippewa); Clyde Warrior; Dave Warren; Anne Rainer; and many others, he became a valued friend, confidant, and mentor. Robert Dumont, who attended in 1960, later described the workshop he attended as "probably the most important academic experience of my life, for it provided a framework for learning which was related to my environment."[59]

Despite the frustrations of those years in the early 1960s, McNickle later looked back and realized the significance of what had been achieved after he left the BIA. The pioneering effort in Crownpoint was in a short time reflected elsewhere on the Navajo Reservation; the operation of new chapter houses incorporated many of the features that the eastern Navajos had considered important. President Lyndon Johnson's war on poverty in the mid-1960s reached the Navajo people through the Office of Navajo Economic Opportunity (ONEO), the local arm of the Office of Economic Opportunity (OEO), and Peter McDonald, head of ONEO, drew directly from the eastern Navajos' experience with AID, Incorporated, in establishing community action committees throughout the reservation. Many of those who were involved had been active in the Crownpoint Project, and they described "community action" in words identical to those they had learned from McNickle a decade earlier.[60] By 1970, the eastern Navajo area boasted the only active community action committee on the reservation; others had come and gone. While this was positive evidence that the process he had initiated had made a lasting impact, it also revealed how difficult it was to sustain the motivation for change within the traditional Navajo community.

Although the leadership capacity of the eastern Navajo people was a direct legacy of his work at Crownpoint, McNickle himself was never involved in the OEO program. It began just a little too late for him, for by 1965 other "openings" had appeared. He may also have become somewhat embittered by the fact that there had been so little support for his program in the 1950s, when he had worked so hard to keep it going. By the mid-1960s, all kinds of financial aid was available.

Nevertheless, he watched what was happening with considerable interest, and he later explained why the OEO had been relatively successful among the nation's Indian population. Essentially, he felt, it was because the OEO operated independently of the BIA and did not inherit the Bureau's paternalistic approach to Indian administration. Instead, OEO operated as McNickle had suggested years earlier, as a Point Four Program for Indians. It invited genuine tribal consultation on local projects and whenever possible it contracted for tribal management and resources. It was a real revolution. "This transferal of authority and responsibility for decision-making to the local community was an administrative feat which the Bureau of Indian Affairs, after more than one hundred years of stewardship, had never managed to carry out," he observed somewhat sardonically.[61]

As for the independent efforts of the Indians themselves, there was little doubt about the importance of the American Indian Chicago Conference. Even Wilcomb Washburn, who had been critical of it as an exercise in applied anthropology, conceded that it had had a permanent impact on Indian life. "In a subtle but effective way," he admitted, "Tax and his associates can be said to have laid the basis for a reform of the Indian/white relationship that can justly be compared with the political reforms of Indian affairs of the 1880s and of the 1930s."[62] In addition, the National Indian Youth Council, a direct offspring of the Chicago conference, continued to provide some of the active leadership McNickle had been seeking. Within a few years, members of NIYC, adopting the slogan "red power," were making their presence felt, from the "fish-ins" in Washington state to the "sit-ins" in Washington, D.C.

For McNickle, who was the only one of NCAI's founders to attend the Chicago conference (few of the others were still living), the conference and NIYC became the culmination of what he and the others had begun through the National Congress of American Indians in 1944. Indians were learning that there was political strength in unity of numbers, and that there was a bond among themselves as Indians that was, in some ways, as strong as kin or tribe. By speaking with one voice, they made their demands for self-determination increasingly difficult for the government to ignore.

McNickle wrote one other book that belongs to this period of his life. After publication of *Indians and Other Americans* in 1959, the Institute of Race Relations in London, which had been established the year before, had invited him to write about American Indians for its English readers. He obliged with a compact narrative of American Indian history entitled *The Indian Tribes of the United States: Ethnic and Cultural Survival*, which was published by Oxford University Press in 1962. *Indian Tribes of the United States* was a brief, authoritative handbook on Native Americans that contained, in addition to the text, two maps and a concise listing of tribes that included their geographical areas, their populations, and their linguistic families. Using comparative statistics, McNickle proved, once and for all, the fallacy of the vanishing red man. He was pleased to tell his readers that the Indian population, estimated at 220,000 in 1850, had almost doubled in the hundred years since then. He explained how Indian cultural identity had persisted despite the dramatic environmental changes that had occurred in North America since the advent of the Europeans, and he concluded with an extended quotation from the "Declaration of Indian Purpose" issued at the American Indian Chicago Conference. Although the conference was still too recent for him to have developed much perspective on it, he obviously felt that the Indians who gathered there had taken another important step toward ethnic and cultural survival. The "Declaration of Indian Purpose" was only the latest evidence of the Indians' ability to adapt to constantly changing conditions.

8

In the Fullness
of Years

Despite various projects that occupied his time during the early 1960s,
McNickle's frustration with the lack of focus for his work led him briefly
to consider returning to the Bureau of Indian Affairs. In 1961 and again in
1963, Dorothy Van de Mark, president of the General Federation of
Women's Clubs, who had corresponded with him for years concerning
various Indian issues, urged him to make himself available as a candidate
for Indian commissioner in the new administration.[1] But McNickle knew
too much about that job to want it. He also knew that even if he were
nominated the chances of his being confirmed were miniscule. As a "Collier man," he still had enemies on the Senate Indian Affairs Subcommittee, which would have to approve his nomination.

He might have accepted some lesser job, however, and even went to
Washington to explore that possibility. He met with Philleo Nash, the
newly-appointed Indian commissioner and an old friend, who offered
him nothing. He later recorded a bit of gossip from Helen Peterson.
"Philleo told her in confidence, which she was not to repeat even to me,
that he could not offer me a Bureau appointment. [New Mexico Senator]

Clinton Anderson had said in no uncertain terms that neither Bill Zimmerman nor I were to have any part in the new administration." Anderson, an avowed assimilationist, had previously tangled with McNickle and Pfrommer over the efforts of the Taos Pueblo people to regain control of their sacred Blue Lake in New Mexico's Carson National Forest. As chairman of the Senate Interior and Insular Affairs Committee, Anderson would have blocked McNickle's appointment at any level of administration. McNickle might have considered the possibility of another position with the Indian Bureau had it been offered to him, but it never was.[2]

His long wait for a new direction ended finally in 1965, when possibilities for larger involvement began to appear once more. The first came early that year, when Indiana University Press asked him to write a biography of Oliver La Farge, who had died in 1963. Indiana had first approached Alvin Josephy, Jr., a well-known author of Indian history, but Josephy was unable at that time to take on an additional assignment. He had met McNickle at a conference in the 1950s and suggested to Indiana that they contact him. After hesitating briefly, McNickle agreed.[3] He signed a contract, with the end of 1966 as his deadline.

His research on the La Farge biography began in Santa Fe, New Mexico, where La Farge had lived for twenty-five years prior to his death. Most of the records McNickle needed were in the East, however, so he spent several months in late 1965 in Rhode Island and New York, sorting through the extensive collection of papers and memorabilia that had been accumulated by various members of the La Farge family. He commuted for several weeks between Greenwich, Connecticut, which provided access to the La Farge family material in Saunderstown, Rhode Island, and New York City, where he dug into the files of the Association on American Indian Affairs (AAIA). After one particularly harried day, he described what the daily trip was like: "The morning commute scene, with all the able-bodied male population rushing puppet-like to the demands of the city, is frightening for its unnaturalness. The worlds of house and breadwinning are so far removed. I manage to take a later train which puts me in with the fat ladies in their mink stoles going to the city to shop for more

mink stoles."⁴ He spent two full days when he finished his research com-
muting from Greenwich to Montclair, New Jersey, to duplicate the material he needed on one of the new Xerox machines.

Then he went on to Washington for several more weeks of research. All
was not work there, however. He spent some good hours with his daughter Toni, her husband, and his granddaughter Linda, and visited with old
friends Bill Zimmerman and John Cragun. Cragun was a partner in a
Washington law firm that played a major role in the settlement of some of
the tribal claims brought before the Indian Claims Commission. He and
McNickle had been friends for years, and there was catching up to do.
Then Vi Pfrommer, who was spending some time in Rochester with her
family, joined him for a few days of real vacation. Both were amazed at
how urban life had changed in the east. They were especially impressed
with the new interstate highways that encircled Washington, Boston,
Wilmington, and other large cities. McNickle, however, was there primarily to work on the La Farge biography and for the most part he devoted his time to that. The extended trip east, after he had lived in the west
for thirteen years, had reminded him once again how much he disliked
modern urban living.

McNickle's acquaintance with La Farge dated back some thirty years,
so he was probably in a better position to write the biography than Josephy would have been, at least in terms of long acquaintance with the
subject. La Farge had held a temporary appointment from Collier in the
mid-1930s to help the Hopi villages formalize a tribal government under
the Indian Reorganization Act, and McNickle, of course, was familiar
with all the details of that matter. Then in 1936, La Farge had reviewed
The Surrounded, and shortly thereafter McNickle had done the same for
The Enemy Gods. After that their paths had crossed frequently.

La Farge was elected president of the newly-reorganized Association
on American Indian Affairs in 1937, just after it had combined with the
American Indian Defense Association, a reform group that Collier had
led in the 1920s. The merger had created a united front of non-Indians
who supported Collier's policies during the 1930s and 1940s, and after

World War II, AAIA and NCAI had often joined forces in the battle against termination. Their mutual concerns through the years inevitably drew McNickle and La Farge together.

McNickle agreed to write La Farge's biography in part because he hoped to use it as a vehicle for writing a general history of Indian affairs from the 1920s through what he called "the Eisenhower misery." Admittedly, he was more attracted to the history of the period than he was to La Farge himself. "I never could get excited about the guy," he confided to a friend at the time. "My long acquaintance with him never ripened into any kind of camaraderie." La Farge was a man with a "thorny exterior" who was most accessible to others when he had been drinking heavily.[5]

McNickle was especially concerned about what he viewed as La Farge's continuing paternalism toward Indians, despite his many years of leadership in Indian affairs. He believed that La Farge's writing about Indians revealed an inner conflict regarding his own cultural values. Although *Laughing Boy* was "a sustained indictment" of his own white society, La Farge seemed unable to divorce himself from that society and relate to Indians within their own culture. It seemed to McNickle that, even though La Farge identified strongly with an essential quality of "Indianness" that he found in the Navajos, "reason cautioned that he had no business trying to escape from what he was born to be. His dilemma was real, a constant companion. He could not be Indian; he did not want to be submerged in the power class of his generation."[6]

McNickle was not the only one who felt that La Farge's stories of *Laughing Boy* and *The Enemy Gods* were written by "an outsider looking in from a defined social position upon an alien world and seeing many desirable characteristics."[7] La Farge himself, according to McNickle, was aware of this problem and struggled with himself to modify it. He recognized that his ease with his Indian acquaintances, as genuine as it was, provided an escape from his cultural ambivalence. Despite his devoted efforts on behalf of Indians, his ambivalence revealed itself in the fact that he was adamantly opposed to the idea of appointing even one Indian to AAIA's board of directors. His inner conflict contributed to an attitude of superiority and condescension that McNickle found offensive.

Even though McNickle never shared a genuine friendship with La Farge, he discovered elements of La Farge's life and work that were unexpectedly parallel to his own. La Farge was born (in 1901) to a privileged social status and McNickle obviously was not, but other similarities were striking. As boys they had both attended boarding school, and in college they revealed similar interests in drama and poetry. La Farge had contributed to the *Harvard Advocate,* as McNickle had to the *Frontier.* During his years as a graduate student, La Farge had even worked for a brief time for William Gates, McNickle's correspondent in the early 1930s. For some reason, McNickle did not mention this fact in the biography, although it is difficult to believe that he had not discovered it during his research. Both he and La Farge had known the frustration of an unhappy early marriage, and both had mourned the death of a newborn child.

Even more significantly, McNickle identified with La Farge professionally. In choosing to call himself a writer rather than an anthropologist, although anthropology was his professional field, La Farge "found himself outside the brotherhood of practising anthropologists."[8] McNickle, too, as a writer had never felt fully accepted by professionals in anthropology, although in his case it was because he lacked the academic credentials that provided legitimacy. Although both men were fellows of the American Anthropological Association, they both felt excluded at times from the professional mainstream.

McNickle identified most closely with La Farge in his unfulfilled dreams of realizing a successful literary career. Their respective first novels, created out of their youthful experiences, had presaged a shift in the direction of their lives. Despite their literary aspirations, however, their involvement in Indian affairs had preempted the time they needed to develop their creative potential. McNickle had just turned sixty when he began research on the La Farge biography and he could not help but reflect on his own writing. While interviewing La Farge's family and friends, he asked one question over and over again, as though he were asking it of himself: "What factors kept La Farge from developing into a really top-flight fiction writer?" Almost invariably, the response was that La Farge could not afford the luxury of taking the time needed to produce "art." He wrote potboilers because he could sell them and he needed the money. McNickle was grateful that he had not had to resort to potboilers, but he, too, had failed to produce a great novel. He wondered if under other circumstances he might have done so.[9]

Writing a biography, McNickle soon discovered, was more difficult than writing either a novel or a narrative history. It demanded different literary skills than had his earlier work, and he began to suspect that meeting the 1966 deadline was impossible. His greatest distraction proved to be a letter he received in December 1965, after his return from the east. Dallas W. Smythe, who was chairman of the Social Sciences Division at the University of Saskatchewan's new Regina campus, wrote to ask McNickle if he would be interested in teaching and chairing the university's infant Department of Anthropology. The appointment carried the rank of associate professor, with immediate tenure and promotion to full professor at the end of the first year. With mandatory retirement at age seventy-one, he could be productive there for five years.[10]

The invitation was a complete surprise, not because it came from Canada, where he had enjoyed professional contacts for a number of years, but because the possibility of teaching in a university anywhere had never occurred to him. Had he expressed interest in an academic career, both Sol Tax in Chicago and his friend Omer Stewart, at the University of Colorado, would have been pleased to back him. But because he lacked a college degree he had never considered teaching as one of his options. Now, for the first time, it became an attractive possibility. He wrote to tell Tax of his response to Smythe's invitation. "When I answered that I lacked the academic union card, I was told that this need not be a fatal flaw. I'm not sure I want to teach, but I have sent them my vitae and have given you as a reference. I hope you do not tire of bearing witness."[11]

Tax was pleased to "bear witness." In the past he had endorsed a number of McNickle's proposals and he was happy to do so again. He had always admired McNickle's writing ability and his administrative talents, and he had a high regard for McNickle personally. Omer Stewart, whom D'Arcy also listed as a reference, was equally enthusiastic. Stewart, a professor of anthropology at the University of Colorado in Boulder, had also known McNickle for years. He had served on the advisory board of American Indian Development, Incorporated, and had been especially supportive of the summer workshops. As a colleague, friend, and neighbor, he knew McNickle well.

Smythe contacted both Stewart and Tax. The interdisciplinary nature of the new Social Sciences Division, he explained, would require someone with a talent for working with people from a variety of backgrounds, and he wondered if they considered McNickle suited for such a role. Stewart assured Smythe that McNickle was superbly qualified.

> I have seen him function with unschooled American Indians, with Indian students, with lawyers, priests and businessmen as well as with professors of several different academic disciplines. As a top administrator in the Bureau of Indian Affairs, he had to adjust to the Indian clients as well as to bureaucrats and politicians in Washington. He made friends with both groups and gained the lasting respect of Congressmen as well as administrators.[12]

Stewart praised McNickle's talents in other areas as well, and then he revealed to Smythe what had been, until then, a closely held secret. McNickle himself certainly knew nothing of it. The University of Colorado was considering him for an honorary doctorate, to be awarded at spring commencement.

As the primary sponsor of McNickle's nomination, Stewart had requested endorsements from people who had known him since his years with the BIA, and the response was almost overwhelming. John Collier wrote, "My endorsement of D'Arcy McNickle for an honorary degree is unconditional and even ardent"; Harold Fey reported, "I have never known a group or a person to come under the influence of D'Arcy McNickle who was not lifted, made nobler and more democratic by his presence"; anthropologist Edward Spicer, at the University of Arizona, observed, "No other modern student of Indian affairs exhibits in his publications quite the comprehensiveness or depth which D'Arcy McNickle does"; and Richard K. Bennett, of the American Friends Service Committee and a board member of the Indian Rights Association, expressed a "non-professional's admiration for D'Arcy McNickle's ability to wisely tie the past to the present and the present to the future."[13]

Others also contributed their testimony. McNickle's attorney friend John Cragun observed, "His understanding and grasp of the broad problems involved [in Indian affairs] . . . has significantly advanced the cause of his people," and Alexander Leighton wrote, "His essence is educator in the broadest, deepest, and truest sense of the word." Sol Tax endorsed the nomination in a similar vein. "I am enthusiastic at the prospect of your awarding a degree to D'Arcy McNickle," he told Stewart. Then he admitted, ruefully, "I only wish we had thought of it!"[14]

When the board of regents at the university notified McNickle that they were awarding him an honorary Sc.D. degree, his surprise and delight can only be imagined. He had always regretted the fact that he had not graduated from college. Although he had been elected a fellow of both the American Anthropological Association and the Society of Applied Anthropology, he never forgot that he was "mister," not "doctor." Despite his modesty, he knew that he had become as competent a cultural anthropologist as many of his colleagues. It was a small thing in itself, perhaps, but the award meant a great deal to him, especially in light of the contract Dallas Smythe had just offered him.

Just why McNickle finally agreed to go to Canada is not wholly clear. Richard Pope, whom McNickle recruited for the faculty shortly after he arrived, speculated that it was because of Regina's proximity to McNickle's origins.[15] Although McNickle visited the Saskatchewan Provincial Archives on the Regina campus, however, and found a brief reference there to Isidore Parenteau, he did not pursue further research into his family ancestry. He neither contacted relatives in Regina, which he could have done quite easily, nor journeyed north to Batoche to examine the records of the 1885 rebellion. Pope may have been correct, but surely McNickle would have made a greater effort to investigate his roots if that possibility had been uppermost in his mind when he accepted the faculty post.

Two other factors may have been more significant in McNickle's decision. One was his financial situation. For years he had earned only a small salary as director of American Indian Development and he was keenly aware of his dependence on Roma's wage-earning capacity. If he taught for a while he might assure himself not only of a decent income but also of a small pension to augment his civil service retirement. A second and more subjective factor might well have been the professional recognition that was implicit in his becoming a tenured professor of anthropology. Whether he knew of the forthcoming degree from the University of Colorado when he signed the contract with Dallas Smythe or not, the two events were mutually reinforcing, and they provided a tremendous boost to his self-esteem.

McNickle's decision to go to Canada also provided a temporary respite from a nagging concern about his marriage. Although Roma had accepted a new job back in Washington, apparently she did not consider her move there to be a permanent separation. D'Arcy had been aware for some time that their marriage had deteriorated to one of mere convenience, but he, too, shied away from the idea of a divorce. Given the circumstances, the easiest way out, at least for the moment, was to do nothing. Roma left for the east and D'Arcy prepared to rent their house to tenants. He spent the spring and summer organizing his material for the La Farge biography and planning the introductory course in anthropology that he would teach in the fall. He wanted to take the La Farge material with him to Canada and work on it there, although it was now quite obvious that he would not meet the publisher's deadline of the end of the year.

As McNickle drove to Regina late that summer, he thought of his mother, whose grave he had visited just before leaving Boulder. He regretted that she was not there to go with him. "She would have loved coming back to Canada," he wrote in his diary, although her advanced age would surely have complicated such a visit.[16] Nevertheless, she had been on his mind much of the time as he prepared to go to Canada.

As the beginning of the term drew closer, McNickle was increasingly apprehensive about actually teaching a full-term course in anthropology. He had taught an occasional seminar at St. Regis College in Denver but had never taught a full course and the prospect was unsettling. He had confided his fears to Tax that spring: "Sometime during the summer, I hope I can sit down with you and discuss what the hell one does with an anthropology course."[17] He worried about it for months, until, when the first day of class arrived, "the tensions were shattering." "I find that nothing has stood still in anthropological literature," he observed with some distress, "and I have had to start all over again."[18] The raw edges soon wore off, but the rigors of teaching two hundred students, plus his departmental responsibilities, proved to be utterly exhausting.

The problems McNickle faced as department chairman at Regina were even greater than he had anticipated. Not only was the university itself coping with its first year, but an unexpected influx of students from the United States was stretching the new facilities to the limit. McNickle's departure for Canada had coincided with the rising tide of student unrest on college campuses in the United States, caused by the escalating war in Vietnam. As young political activists emigrated north, the Regina campus became a haven from an increasingly oppressive political atmosphere at home. Dallas Smythe welcomed the young refugees. According to Richard Pope, Smythe had "a very political vision of the new university, . . . one which stressed socially relevant research and action," and most of the politically liberal Americans were also concerned with social issues.[19] Smythe apparently believed that McNickle, as an "action" anthropologist, also shared his interests and his vision.

McNickle was not in that sense a political activist, and he had no intention of introducing a Marxist-oriented Native American studies curriculum in the anthropology department. Instead, he hoped to build a solid academic department that would encompass as much as possible of the discipline's wide spectrum. The growth of library holdings in various sub-fields while he was chairman reflected his determination to build a strong, broadly based department. Although Dallas Smythe's interdisciplinary "instructional committees" appealed to his personal interests, the new department under his direction adopted a more traditional approach to curriculum development.[20]

McNickle survived that first year, but it took its toll. He was ill in April, perhaps with a recurrent kidney stone, and Vi's perscription was for "complete rest, less smoking, and fewer cocktails." Summer seemed a long time coming. Toward the end of the term, he confessed to Tax, "After completing the academic year up here I am going to need several months in which to figure out what happened. I feel like the man who has been run over by a truck, and I didn't even get the license number."[21]

Unfortunately, the summer of 1967 proved not to be very restful. On returning to Boulder he was immediately immersed in preparations for the forthcoming student workshop, which that year proved to be a particularly frustrating one. The use of "red power" as a way of confronting Indian problems had been fermenting since the 1961 Chicago conference, and it had surfaced during the NCAI convention in 1966. Students attending the 1967 workshop were restless and more uncertain than ever about their future. McNickle struggled to find a new direction for the participants, and when the six weeks were over he was exhausted. But he got no rest. Despite his fatigue, he prepared to leave almost immediately for a conference in Austria.

Before departing, McNickle finally made the long-delayed decision about his marriage. Admitting to himself that his relationship with Roma existed only as a formality, he wrote to her and asked for a divorce. He had agonized over the matter for months, but once he had mailed the letter, he felt amazingly liberated. "It has been on my mind as a step that had to be taken for at least ten years," he confided to his diary. "Even this letter was drafted about six weeks ago, and then sat as written, while I continued to search out my own thoughts and feelings—the effect on her, etc. Finally, when it was typed out and taken to the post office, the sense of relief was truly astonishing. I had not realized what pressure I had been under."[22]

His letter came as a surprise to Roma, whose initial reaction was one of dismay and disbelief.[23] She called him tearfully and tried to dissuade him, but his decision had been made. When he stopped to see her on his return from Austria several weeks later and they had a last lunch together, he was relieved to note that their meeting was amicable, "at least so far."[24] Always the peacemaker, he had dreaded the possibility of ongoing rancor and bitterness. By that time, however, Roma had begun to recover from the shock and she seemed to have accepted what she obviously could not change.

The trip to Austria provided a much-needed tonic for McNickle, despite his fatigue and the fact that the La Farge biography still was not finished. It had been thirty-six years since he had been to Europe, and the prospect of spending a week in an old castle at the Wenner-Gren Center for Anthropological Research in Burg Wartenstein, Austria, was exhilarating. Nevertheless, it was a working vacation. Nancy Lurie and Eleanor Leacock, professor of anthropology at Polytechnic Institute of Brooklyn, had asked him to contribute a chapter for a book they were putting together on North American Indians. He and the other contributors, both American and European, were gathering in Austria to share information and ideas.[25]

The conference lived up to his expectations and McNickle, in his newly liberated emotional state, enjoyed it immensely. Nancy Lurie later recalled as one of the more memorable events an evening when McNickle, Edward Dozier, a mixed-blood anthropologist at the University of Arizona, and William Fenton persuaded the band at a nearby night club to let them use their drum. They loosened the snares of the drum to lower its pitch, sang "49" songs (social songs of post–World War II origins sung at informal gatherings of Native Americans), and showed the audience some "authentic" Indian dances. The people in the night club soon joined in, "absolutely fascinated," as Lurie later recalled, with Indians.[26] Obviously, not all their time together was spent working.

But most of it was, and the book that came out of the conference, *North American Indians in Historical Perspective,* was published by Random House in 1971 and reissued in paperback in 1988. It was a compilation of essays by regional Indian specialists, organized on a more or less chronological framework of EuroAmerican continental expansion. McNickle's chapter on pre-Columbian Indian people, "Americans Called Indians," was followed by chapters on Indian tribes of the East Coast, the Plains, the Southwest, the Pacific Coast, and the Far North. Lurie herself contributed the final chapter, "The Contemporary Indian Scene," which provided a commentary on many of McNickle's lifelong concerns. His impact on the collaborative effort was evident in much of what she wrote in that last chapter. When describing the OEO programs of the 1960s, for instance, she noted that any success in that program's Indian work "must be attributed largely to the presence of an already developed grass roots program and to effective local leadership."[27] This statement and her discussion of NCAI, the Chicago conference, and NIYC strongly suggest McNickle's input.

The Austrian conference provided the rest and recreation McNickle needed, and he returned to Regina in late August with renewed enthusiasm. The only anthropology course offered in the university catalogue during his first year had been an introductory survey, which he himself taught to over two hundred students. The second year he shared the teaching load with Richard Pope and added upper-division courses, "Culture Change" and "Culture and Personality," which reflected his ongoing concern with the social dynamics of personality development. Collier's influence was evident, too, in such survey courses as "Prehistory of the Americas" and "Culture Centers of the Americas."

Richard Pope was McNickle's first faculty recruit, and McNickle regarded him highly. Pope, a graduate of the University of Chicago, had been a member of the summer workshop staff in Boulder in 1964 and again in 1966. During the 1967–68 academic year, the two men between them taught six different courses to 350 students. The success of those offerings, especially when compared with the confusion of the first year, produced such a feeling of euphoria that McNickle reported the year's closing "in a burst of minor glory."[28]

Part of McNickle's enthusiasm at this time sprang from his optimistic hopes for the future of the Department of Anthropology. Together he and Pope planned a departmental field station, a demonstration and teaching laboratory, and a further expansion of the departmental library. As eager as he was to capitalize on the year's momentum and bring these plans closer to reality, however, there was one problem he simply could not avoid. The La Farge biography was almost two years overdue and he had found no time to work on it while he was so fully involved at the university.[29] Reluctantly, he decided to take an unpaid leave of absence for the 1968–69 academic year and finish it.

The university was not happy with this arrangement, but McNickle felt he had no choice. He flew to New Mexico that spring to attend a memorial service for John Collier, who had died several weeks earlier, and while he was there he contacted some old BIA friends in Albuquerque and arranged to spend the next year in one of their guest houses. When classes were finally over he returned to Albuquerque and settled down to write. He was not even distracted by Vi's presence. She had taken a position as advisor to American Indian students at the University of Arizona in 1966, when he had first gone to Canada, and her house was occupied by tenants.

At last he could work without distractions and the biography quickly took shape. By mid-January he had finished sixty pages, and in May the end was in sight. Despite all his work, however, he never was able to establish more than a grudging admiration for La Farge's dedication to the Indians' cause. He was well into the writing when he confided to John Cragun's wife, Pam, in Washington,

> I find that I am beginning to admire the guy a great deal, which was not the case when I began to dig into his background. I still don't like his attitude toward the Indians, in spite of what he accomplished in their behalf and the undoubted sacrifices which his Indian work required of him. He seems never to have acquired humil-

ity, which is always a great lack in a human being. But he was fearless, faithful, and a hell of a hard worker. One can settle for that.[30]

He had to settle for that, he had no choice, but the writing was more tedious because of it.

The most worrisome problem McNickle faced that year, however, was
money. Now that he was no longer married, concern over finances plagued
him once again. He had applied for a three-thousand-dollar grant from the
Louis M. Rabinowitz Foundation in New York City to carry him through,
but the foundation's review process was agonizingly slow and he watched
the gradual erosion of his meager savings apprehensively. Word that his proposal had been accepted did not arrive until May, as he was typing the final
draft of the manuscript.[31] With great relief he finished typing it, paid his bills,
and put the manuscript in the mail on July 24, 1969, more than two and a
half years past the contracted deadline. Because the manuscript was so late,
Indiana Press was forced to reschedule its publication and *Indian Man: A
Life of Oliver La Farge* was not released until 1971.

As McNickle commented wryly to a friend, the book "hit the market
with a dull thud."[32] Although it was nominated for a National Book
Award that year, press reviews were less than enthusiastic and it did not
sell well. The book was applauded as "a partial but solid" history of an important period in Indian-white relations, but it seemed "curiously incomplete" as a biography.[33] According to one reviewer, McNickle had failed
to get behind La Farge's public image to examine the private man. He had
described the activities of the AAIA and La Farge's role as titular head of
the organization, but La Farge's actual contributions to the organization
during the 1950s were never clearly described.

This omission was the source of the sharpest criticism leveled against
the biography. For some unknown reason, McNickle had failed to consult
Alexander Lesser, AAIA's executive director during the crucial period
from 1947 to 1955, while he was doing his research. McNickle sent him a
copy of the book, however, and Lesser's distraught response came by return mail. He accused McNickle, whom he had known well during the

years of the termination battles, of distorting the facts. Lesser claimed that it was he, not La Farge, who was responsible for the growing effectiveness of AAIA in the 1950s. La Farge, who had lived in Santa Fe, was little more than a figurehead, asserted Lesser. "But my friend D'Arcy," he wrote,

> credits La Farge with 8 years of my life and work. . . . What has happened to my friend D'Arcy . . . that he is so blind? . . . Am I to believe that for the 8 years that I worked 72 hour weeks every week of the year, disregarding my career in anthropology, to work for the welfare and rights of the people I had so long studied, that for all that 8 years you never even saw me, never read my articles and editorials, never knew as was obvious that all official materials were signed by La Farge as President, but who do you suppose wrote a great many of them?[34]

It was he, Lesser, not La Farge, who had brought Felix Cohen into AAIA as legal council and had enlisted Clyde Kluckhohn as a member of the board of directors, along with many others. Surely, Lesser pointed out, McNickle could not have been unaware of who was the real driving force behind the organization's activities and, of even greater importance, who was not.

By the time Lesser had read the book, of course, it was too late to change anything. D'Arcy lamely replied that he had written a biography of La Farge, not a history of the Association. He explained that, as a former administrator working within a bureaucratic structure, he, too, had written much for which he had received no credit. Lesser, however, was not mollified. He wrote two more bitter letters, to which McNickle made no reply. He regretted having offended, yet he offered no apology. Why he had not consulted Lesser during his research remains a mystery; Lesser obviously had a legitimate complaint.[35]

McNickle was tremendously relieved when he finally finished the biography that he had worked on for four years. It was a cause for celebration and he was pleased that Pfrommer had returned to Albuquerque and could celebrate with him. Although Vi had intended to stay in Tucson for only a year, she remained there until that summer of 1969. Unfortunately, their celebration was marred by the fact that she was beginning to show the first disturbing symptoms of what would later be diagnosed as Alzheimer's disease.[36]

McNickle had visited Vi in Tucson several times during the year he was in Albuquerque, and each time he saw her he noticed that she appeared a little more forgetful and disoriented. He apparently decided during this period that he wanted to marry her and assume responsibility for her care. Little is clear about that decision. Whether her illness had been diagnosed or whether either of them was aware of the long-term prognosis is not known. What is known is that Vi had doubts about the wisdom of the marriage right up to the morning of the ceremony.[37] D'Arcy pressed his case, however, and a week after he finished the La Farge biography, he and Vi married each other in a quiet Quaker ceremony at her home, attended by John and Winona Rainer from Taos Pueblo, a few friends from Laguna Pueblo, and Bainbridge and Doralene Bunting, their Albuquerque neighbors.

McNickle had looked forward to returning with Vi to Regina, but her illness, along with interdepartmental troubles that had simmered during his absence, soon dampened his enthusiasm. Teachers and students had become politically polarized while he was gone, and he found himself totally occupied trying to keep the turmoil from reaching into the classroom. As Richard Pope has recalled,

> D'Arcy found himself caught between conflicting loyalties and conflicting friends, between committed Marxists who gave lip service to Indian conditions but who were much more concerned about U.S. foreign policy, and less political anthropology students and faculty who were excited about Indians as a "cause." He was also caught between his commitments to the Social Science Division and the emerging "departmentalization" of the faculty, in which he participated because he wanted to build an anthropology program.[38]

The conflict developed into the kind of situation that McNickle disliked intensely. In the face of increasingly adversarial academic politics, he found it almost impossible to administer the department by consensus. His vision of a field station and an anthropology laboratory faded as he tried to cope with the growing unrest. One wonders how much his leave of absence had contributed to the turmoil. Perhaps if he had been present during that crucial third year, his leadership would have maintained its momentum. In his absence the disintegrative elements had moved freely and some aspects of his program became permanently sidetracked. Nevertheless, by the time he retired in 1971 the department as a whole appeared to have regained the sense of direction McNickle had brought to it in the beginning.

During those last two years in Regina, McNickle was busier even than he had been previously, if that was possible. In 1969, Indian affairs in Canada approached a crisis which was brought about, in part, by the publication of a white paper that endorsed a philosophy of termination similar to that which had produced such disastrous results more than a decade earlier in the United States.[39] Since McNickle was familiar with that policy and its impact on Indians in the U.S., he was overwhelmed with demands as a speaker and consultant. Although he was not the only one to speak out in opposition to the government dictum, his views undoubtedly carried considerable weight, and the policies outlined in the document were never implemented.

While various groups in Canada were denouncing the white paper, a renewed interest in Indian affairs was beginning to appear in the United States as part of the civil rights movement there, and publishers were beseiged for information about the country's Indian population. One by one McNickle began to update his Indian histories. While still in Canada, he started to revise *They Came Here First* and at Fey's request he updated *Indians and Other Americans*. The demands on his time quickly escalated and once again he pushed himself to exhaustion. He completed the revision of *Indians and Other Americans* in July 1970 and was attending a conference in Ottawa when he suffered a relatively mild heart attack. It may have been mild, but it was also a warning of what continuing stress and a lifetime addiction to tobacco were doing to him. He remained in the hospital for a week, with Vi at his bedside, before flying back to Albuquerque for the remainder of the summer. By September he was back in Regina declaring that he had returned to a state of good health, but the episode had taken its toll on both of them.

As busy as he was, D'Arcy was forced to accommodate his schedule to Vi's deteriorating health and, for the first time, to his own. The last year in Regina was very difficult for both of them, as Vi was increasingly disoriented even in familiar surroundings. Richard Pope, who remembered her from the summer workshops, recalled sadly, "When Vi finally came, after their marriage, she wasn't the same Vi I had known in Boulder, . . . she was slow, forgetful."[40] She must have been almost totally confined at home while D'Arcy was in the classroom or attending the numerous conferences and meetings that increasingly occupied his time when he was not teaching.

Although D'Arcy and Vi returned to Regina for that last year, McNickle looked forward to his retirement. Other opportunities had arisen that would allow him to work at home, a prospect that became increasingly attractive as the year wore on. The Smithsonian Institution had asked him to serve on the editorial board of a major new project, an extensive twenty-volume revision of the *Handbook of North American Indians* that had first been published in 1907. He was to be editor-in-chief of the concluding volume, which would focus on contemporary Native Americans. He also accepted an appointment as associate editor of *Human Organization,* the official publication of the Society of Applied Anthropology. Both of these projects he could work on at home.

These two assignments, along with several others that were pending, offered McNickle immensely satisfying prospects for continued involvement in Indian affairs after he officially retired. He had had enough of university infighting. As he wrote to an old BIA friend, "Academic life turned out to be a greater bureaucratic trap than the BIA, and I was glad to be out of it."[41] He had had enough, too, of the harsh Canadian winters. He confessed that he was no longer a northerner; Albuquerque, with its relatively mild winters, was much more appealing than Canada. He wanted time to write, to think, to take care of Vi, to sit with her under the huge cottonwood tree in their front yard and enjoy the quiet natural beauty of Albuquerque's North Valley. He might even find time to go fishing. Although he was flattered by the many educational and professional invitations that came to him almost daily, he often declined. His new editorial responsibilities would be enough to keep him in touch with those things that were most important to him.

But somehow retirement eluded him. When he and Vi returned to New Mexico in 1971, more than ten years after "retiring" from Crownpoint, McNickle felt that he had returned to an entirely different world. The orientation of his personal life had changed dramatically because of the unexpected responsibilities arising from Vi's illness. At the same time he found that his public stature as an elder statesman on Indian affairs had grown immeasurably. He was one of a diminishing number of people whose memory and experience extended as far back as the Collier years. He had helped implement the Indian Reorganization Act, had been present at the inception of the Inter-American Indian Institute, and had witnessed the signing of the Indian Claims Commission Act. He had contributed to the growing effectiveness of the National Congress of American Indians as a national Indian voice, and had observed the impact of the American Indian Chicago Conference and the growing activism of the National Indian Youth Council. He had welcomed the opportunity to reflect on those events and to assess the impact of the 1960s Civil Rights movement in the decade that followed. His views, expressed in numerous articles, inspired a new generation of readers, Indian and non-Indian alike, with a realization of the enduring Indian presence in American society.

The American public could hardly have been unaware of that presence when he began revising *The Indian Tribes of the United States* in 1971. The first edition had concluded with a lengthy excerpt from the "Declaration of Indian Purpose," the definitive document of the American Indian Chicago Conference. Almost ten years had passed since then, and the Chicago conference was increasingly being viewed as a watershed event in modern Indian history. It had resulted in an unprecedented gathering of Indians whose cultural orientation ranged from traditional and tribal to nearly total assimilationist. Historically there had more often been suspicion and distrust among various tribes. As McNickle recalled in his revision of the book, "At several critical moments the conference stood ready to dissolve, but on each such occasion an acceptable base for continuing discussion was found."[42] The "Declaration of Indian Purpose" had expressed a consensus of the various groups and particular interests represented at the conference. Through it, the movement toward cooperation among all Indian peoples that began with NCAI in 1944 had led to expanded opportunities for effective political action.

An added significance of the 1961 conference, which McNickle discussed in his revision of the book, was the fact that from it had emerged issues and personalities that were increasingly influential in national Indian affairs. As only one example, the National Indian Youth Council had become an effective rallying force for young Indian activists. In 1969 it had helped focus public attention on Indian issues by its participation in the Pacific Northwest "fish-ins" and its seizure of Alcatraz Island in San Francisco Bay, events which were led by the even more militant members of American Indian Movement (AIM).[43] Indians were discovering the uses of political power in modern society, and they were insisting on a substantive role in making the decisions that affected their own families, tribes, and modes of accommodation within the larger society.

The revised book, with its new title, *Native American Tribalism: Indian Survivals and Renewals,* was already typeset when a group of angry young Indians forcefully occupied BIA headquarters in Washington, D.C., in November 1972. In an added preface, McNickle explained how and why such an unprecedented action had occurred. Taking his theme from what the protesters had called "The Trail of Broken Treaties," he reviewed in general the history of treaties made and broken that had created an immense legacy of fear and hostility among Indians across the country. Unrealized expectations had fostered a deep anger that the younger generation of Indians, unlike their elders, did not hesitate to express. Although the uprising at Wounded Knee, South Dakota, three months after the Washington incident, reflected internal tribal dissention as well as hostility toward federal Indian policy, the real targets of these incidents, McNickle believed, "were the men in far places, of good faith and bad, who still thought of themselves as the only proper source of Indian well-being."[44] Fortunately, the second incident at Wounded Knee, unlike the first in 1890, had produced no mass slaughter. Both the Indians and the army, which had again appeared in response to the emergency, knew that this time public opinion would not tolerate the use of force.

Although these incidents were symptomatic of deep and lasting anger, McNickle assured his readers that there was reason to believe that more constructive actions might be taken in the near future. President Nixon had come closer than most previous presidents to expressing a genuine understanding of what young Indians were trying to say in their protests. In an address on July 8, 1970, Nixon had told the American public,

> The goal of any new national policy toward the Indian people [must be] to strengthen the Indian's sense of autonomy without threatening his sense of community. We must assure the Indian that he can assume control of his own life without being separated involuntarily from the tribal group. And we must make it clear that the Indians can become independent of federal control without being cut off from federal concern and federal support.[45]

For the first time since the Bureau of Indian Affairs was established in 1824, it seemed that Indian communities might, as a matter of policy, be given time and space to learn the skills necessary to accommodate themselves to the modern world without violating their traditional values.

With the publication of *Native American Tribalism*, all of McNickle's Indian histories had been revised and were once again in print. Other activities, however, continued to make demands on his time. On several occasions he was asked to consult on projected television series. The potential for education through television was obvious, and he was interested in seeing what could be developed in this area.

One such television project proposed a six-episode series titled "Peopling of the New World." Education Enterprises International involved a prestigious group of people that included Henry Steele Commager and Loren Eiseley. McNickle was disappointed, however, when he read the preliminary outline for the series. He pointed out that, as proposed, the subject would be presented within an evolutionary framework of "progress" that was obviously ethnocentric and, in his view, totally unacceptable. He insisted that Indian people were not "primitive," on their way to becoming "civilized." Their lives reflected an adaptation to the specialized environments in the New World, and they had developed a different but hardly less civilized set of priorities. Cultures could not be classified on a simple time line toward "progress," as was implied by the suggested outline, and McNickle backed away from the project.[46]

A second television group called Black Elk Productions, which was planning an even more ambitious twelve-program series, also sought his advice. McNickle even considered trying his hand at writing a script for it. Marlon Brando was to be codirector of the series, and N. Scott Momaday, whose novel *House Made of Dawn* had just won a Pulitzer Prize, was among the consultants. Although this series was more to McNickle's liking and he was eager to see something come of it, he did not live to see any of it in production.

Regardless of the value of these and similar proposals, McNickle's response to them all was less than wholeheartedly enthusiastic because of Vi's illness. On their return to Albuquerque in 1971, they built a new home on property adjacent to the house that Vi had bought ten years earlier. Designing and building his own house must have meant a great deal to D'Arcy, for he went ahead with it despite Vi's objection to the whole idea. Although their new home was lovely, she was never happy in it. As her illness more and more reflected the tragedy of Alzheimer's disease, she was increasingly fearful of new places. Finally, tragically, D'Arcy was unable to care for her by himself and was forced to put her into a nursing home. As he reported to Vi's sister, "Her physical health is good, but she no longer functions in the present. A great sorrow to me."[47]

Fortunately, McNickle's new editorial responsibilities did permit him to work at home during this difficult period. After establishing the content for the concluding volume of the Smithsonian's *Handbook of North American Indians,* he began contacting potential authors for the various sections, a task that he could do easily by telephone and mail. And finally, once again, he found time to work on the "Feather Boy" novel.

Over the years McNickle had repeatedly returned to the manuscript, adding to it, deleting, changing its plot and its cast of characters. He was still haunted by the loss of the holy artifact and by what it symbolized of the cultural clash between the Native Americans and the EuroAmericans who denigrated all other religions as they propagated their own. He knew that the "Feather Boy" incident would make a wonderful story if he could just discover the right context for it.

The evolution of McNickle's third novel from an early romance to a final complex tragedy reflected his deepening understanding of the underlying causes of Indian-white conflict.[48] Each time he returned to the material he wrestled with some new approach. As originally conceived, the novel's conflict was between a young B I A agent, the federal bureaucracy, and some ranchers who ran their cattle on land leased from the Little Elk Indians. The agent hoped to restore the land to Indian use. First, however, he had to deal with the Indians' refusal to consider becoming ranchers themselves unless and until they could recover their sacred medicine bundle. The agent was caught in the middle of this initial plot, which was confused by irrelevant subplots and a spurious romance between him and an attractive anthropologist. When the sacred bundle was finally dropped among them from a low-flying airplane, the agent, not the Indians, opened it as Thunder Bird, representing the power of Feather Boy, rumbled in the distance "like a great sea pounding against the Mountains."[49]

The evolution of the story from this inauspicious beginning was as complicated as was that of *The Surrounded.* Over time the focus of conflict changed from grazing leases to a dam on the Little Elk Reservation. The Indian agent, Toby Rafferty, no longer fought the federal bureaucracy and the white ranchers but his own and other white people's cultural predispositions. Henry Jim, the leading Indian protagonist, acquired a brother, Bull, and the conflict between them became a major element in the story. Sometime during this evolution McNickle also introduced the young Indian boy Antoine, who learned the ways of his people through the careful tutoring of his grandfather, Bull. The only element that remained unchanged was the loss of the sacred artifact, Feather Boy, and the determination of the Little Elk people to recover it.

The change of focus from land leases to a dam that "killed the water" of the Little Elk Indians was an idea that emerged from events in the late 1940s, after an earlier version of the novel had been rejected by Dodd, Mead. As a BIA field director, McNickle was personally involved in congressional hearings on several dam projects on Indian land after World War II. One of those dams, on the Flathead Reservation itself, had been on the drawing board since before the war. McNickle had gone to Montana in 1946 to help the Flathead Tribal Council and the BIA negotiate with the Bonneville Power Company over lease rights on the reservation. In fact, he later admitted that he had set the novel in the Flathead country.[50] Other dam projects that he knew well involved Kinzua Dam in New York State, the subject of lengthy court battles between the Iroquois and government authorities, and Garrison Dam on the Missouri River in North Dakota, which eventually flooded more than a third of the Fort Berthold Reservation, part of which had been Hidatsa territory.[51] The dam on the Little Elk Reservation, a fictional composite of these various sites, became in the novel a universal representation of the white people's exploitation of Indian resources in the name of progress.

By the time McNickle returned to the novel in the 1970s, the story had rewritten itself repeatedly in his mind. At that time, however, he discarded all previous efforts and spent six months creating what was essentially a new story with a universal theme. As he told Douglas Latimer, who later edited the manuscript for Harper and Row, "I would like the reader to see the Little Elk episode not as an isolated tragedy, about which one need not get too concerned, but as a critical statement about the quality of human behavior when people of different cultures meet."[52] Once again he focused on the question that had concerned him since he worked on *The Surrounded* in the 1930s: How do people communicate (or fail to do so) across cultural barriers when language itself, the basic tool of communication, derives from radically different modes of perception? This time he framed the question in an elegiac novel that was finally published, posthumously, as *Wind from an Enemy Sky*.

The new novel's chief protagonists, as in the earlier versions, took their identities from the Indian and the non-Indian cultures. Bull, the traditional chief of the Little Elk people and younger brother of Henry Jim, hopes to recover the tribe's sacred medicine bundle, and he appeals for help from Toby Rafferty, agent on the Little Elk Reservation. Rafferty listens sympathetically to Bull's request, then passes it on to Adam Pell. Pell, representing the best intentions of the non-Indian world, is also sympathetic to Bull's appeal. But Bull, Rafferty, and Pell live according to different "maps of the mind," and their lives intersect only at a point of explosive collision.

Some thirty years before McNickle's story begins, Bull and his brother Henry Jim had become estranged over the leadership of the Little Elk people. Bull, the traditionalist, was named instead of his older brother to succeed his father as chief, so Henry Jim stole the tribe's sacred Feather Boy bundle and turned it over to a local missionary. The presence of Feather Boy had traditionally assured the tribe's well-being and Henry Jim hoped to reduce his brother's power by getting rid of it. The missionary, of course, was more than happy to relieve the tribe of this reminder of its "pagan" past, and he donated Feather Boy to the Americana Institute in New York City. Meanwhile, Henry Jim left his people and settled in the valley, where he lived in a house like a white man and became a model farmer for the Little Elk Agency. Bull, however, kept the Little Elk people as far away as possible from the white man's world. Each year they retreated farther into the mountains, recalling a time and a place "where the plover cried and the song of the meadowlark held the world together."[53] Henry Jim and Bull did not speak to each other in the thirty years that followed.

The reader learns of this tribal history in a series of flashbacks. As the story begins, Bull and his grandson Antoine are hiking an old Indian trail to a place where they can see the new dam the white man has built, thus beginning what McNickle calls their "journey into the world." The lake impounded behind the dam has flooded a meadow that was sacred to the Little Elk people. It had been a place, Bull explains to Antoine, "where anger was to be left out of men's thoughts."[54] Bull makes a futile gesture of defiance toward the dam by shooting his rifle into its concrete face, but there is no indication that the bullet ever reaches its target—there is no flash from the gun barrel, no evidence of impact. Even the sound of its firing is lost in the roar of the water and the whirr of the dam's machinery. Antoine watches, his eyes bright with fear when he sees his grandfather's anger and impotence in the face of the white man's massive construction. The next day Bull's hot-headed nephew, Pock Face, repeats his uncle's defiant act, but this time the shot is far from harmless: a young man working at the dam is killed.

While Bull broods over the white man's dam, Henry Jim comes to regret his earlier actions and the gulf that has separated him from his brother. He is aware that his fellow tribesmen are struggling to hold on to their traditions and their tribal identity, and he believes that only the return of Feather Boy will let them maintain their viability as a tribe. Learning in a dream that he will not live much longer, Henry Jim makes his way to Bull's camp and appeals for a reconciliation. He entreats Bull to appeal to the white man, Rafferty, who might be able to recover the sacred bundle. Rafferty talks differently from the other whites, Henry Jim assures his brother. He might be willing to help.

McNickle interweaves these three threads, the brothers' conflict, the white man's dam, and the recovery of the medicine bundle, in the structure of the novel. In one of several parallels in the story, the young man killed by Bull's nephew is the nephew of Adam Pell, who coincidentally is both a member of the engineering firm that built the dam and a director of the museum that acquired the Feather Boy bundle. Toby Rafferty, who has begun to develop rapport with the Little Elk people, stands between Bull and Pell as an intermediary. Despite the killing, when Rafferty realizes Pell's connection with the Americana Institute, he conveys Bull's request and asks for Pell's help in recovering Feather Boy.

Rafferty's middle-aged Indian interpreter and general aide, Son Child, whose Indian name has been mistranslated by the whites as The Boy, is Rafferty's Indian counterpart. He, too, plays the role of cultural mediator.[55] In a passage reminiscent of McNickle's description of Archilde's grandmother as she prepared for the dance in *The Surrounded*, Rafferty watches The Boy as he tends a fire in the tepee where Henry Jim lies dying. "Rafferty watched The Boy's deft movements as he worked on the fire— the delicate touch of the large hands, the ease of his crouch—and he could see the fitness of the man in his situation."[56] Like those of Archilde's mother, Son Child's movements are completely suited to his task. He is totally competent in his own world, and who is to say that his world is less desirable than the white man's? As Rafferty watches The Boy tend the fire, he begins to see new value in the Indian's way of life, where nothing is done extraneously, but all things are done well and with care. But even though he is respected by both Rafferty and the Indians, The Boy has no real power to alter the course of events.

Bull's grandson Antoine, who is learning tribal ways from his grandfather, represents the continuity of tribal identity. In some ways, he resembles Archilde in *The Surrounded*. He, too, has been away for several years, attending an off-reservation boarding school in Oregon. On his return he, like Archilde, gradually finds his place as a member of the group by participating in a ceremonial dance. Antoine, however, does not carry the white man's blood in his veins as Archilde did. He has no desire to learn the white man's ways, only the ways of his people. Readers familiar with *The Surrounded* may expect Antoine to play a larger part in the story than he does, given the opening scene. John Purdy asserts that Antoine's education in the ways of his people is the primary theme of the story.[57] But

the character of Antoine was inserted into the novel late in its development, and by introducing him McNickle may only have been returning to
a literary device that had served him well in *The Surrounded* and *Runner in
the Sun*. Although Antoine is not entirely passive, he is essentially an observer. McNickle uses him to convey information about the traditional
life of the Little Elk people and to help define the context of the story, but
the character does little to carry the action forward. Although the reader is
given a strong sense of his presence, Antoine, like The Boy, does nothing
to determine the flow of events.

The Little Elk women also have a very limited role in *Wind from an Enemy Sky*, although McNickle portrays them with gentleness and humor.
Veronica, Bull's first wife, is a woman of great strength and wisdom, and
his second wife, Catharine, who is Veronica's niece, is also a sympathetic
character. The scene where Marie Louise, one of the women in Bull's village, is wearing several dresses as she tries to mount a horse that is already
burdened with all her other possessions is very funny.[58] But even though
the women contribute to the tribal context, they are not the movers that
Catharine and Elise La Rose are in *The Surrounded*. They maintain the
camp, and they squabble and bicker and have their petty jealousies, but
they are not essential to the development of the plot.

The novel's main theme, that of conflict deriving from the difficulty of
communication between peoples of different cultures, despite the best of
intentions, is played out against a countertheme of reconciliation between
Bull and Henry Jim. These two strong and resolute men, whom McNickle
describes with considerable artistry, finally meet across the barrier of
thirty years of silence. Their reconciliation is possible because, despite
Henry Jim's apparent sellout to the white man's ways, the brothers are
rooted in the same culture and ultimately they share the same tribal values.
Their reconciliation is reminiscent of Salt's acceptance of Dark Dealer and
his people—Henry Jim and Bull look beyond themselves to the welfare of
their people and find their essential meaning in the unity of the tribe.
Their ability to communicate from within a common set of values restores
the tribe to wholeness. Two Sleeps, the wonderful old shaman in the

story, senses this basic truth as he searches for the meaning of what has happened to the people. "A man by himself was nothing, a shout in the wind. But men together, each acting for each other and as one—even a strong wind from an enemy sky had to respect their power."[59] When the reconciliation between Bull and Henry Jim is realized, the followers of both men ride out together to tell their people of the tribe's newly restored unity. As one people they approach the agent and ask for the return of Feather Boy.

The theme of reconciliation between Henry Jim and Bull is complemented by another sibling rivalry, this one involving Adam Pell and his sister, the mother of the young man killed by Pock Face's bullet. Here also is conflict, hurt, and misunderstanding. The strained relationship between these two, however, is never resolved. There is no larger sense of shared values to provide a bridge between them, and family ties are not strong enough to heal the breach. Unfortunately, McNickle is not enough interested in their relationship to deal with it in any depth. He might have constructed a more satisfying contrast between the two pairs of siblings, but he becomes diverted by describing Pell's engineering venture in South America. Pell's sister and her husband remain enigmatic.

It is clear from the correspondence with his editor, Douglas Latimer, at Harper and Row, that McNickle considered Pell the novel's central character, although he does not appear until more than halfway through the book.[60] Pell is a composite of all the "friends of the Indians" that McNickle had known over the years. John Purdy asserts that he is drawn from George Heye, founder of the Museum of the American Indian in New York City, which is possible, but elements of Pell's life and character in the novel suggest Oliver La Farge and anthropologist Allan Holmberg as well.[61] Pell is well-born and well-educated, a professional man of sensitivity and good will. He is also a creature of his own culture who has never really questioned the underlying values that have shaped his life. As a young civil engineer, he spent some months in South America, building a hydroelectric dam to bring to the "Cuno" Indians the benefits of electricity. But as he tells his sister about his experience in Peru, it becomes ob-

vious that he never met the Indians as individuals, and he has no appreciation of the fact that their world view may not be the same as his own. Although he is appalled at their exploitation by the ruling powers, he is
oblivious to their traditional values and their life and culture.

McNickle wrestled with his delineation of Pell, and he was not as successful with that portrayal as he was with some of the other principal characters. He argued at length with Latimer about whether to delete the long
narrative description of Pell's engineering project (chapter 18), which in-
terrupts the dramatic flow of the story. As Latimer pointed out, "Only in
Adam [Pell's] case is character revealed through long flashbacks of events
which really have at best just tangential connection with the main story."[62]

McNickle, however, insisted that this sequence was necessary. "My
strategy here was to make Adam attractive, if somewhat eccentric, as a human being; a man of accomplishment and compassion," he told Latimer.
"I must say that I have gone back to that chapter several times with the intention of reducing the detail and speeding the action. But each time I
have had to conclude that it stands on its own feet and the detail is essential to an understanding of the basic theme of cross-cultural confrontation."[63] The sequence was also essential because it prepared the reader for
the introduction of the gold statuette that Pell offers the Indians as a sub-
stitute for Feather Boy when he discovers that return of the artifact is not
possible. Latimer suggested that McNickle invent some other literary device that would provide the same information without such an obvious in-
trusion into the main story, but McNickle was adamant, and the passage
remained.

McNickle's insistence on retaining this intrusive element reflected his
interest in the continuing discussion among professional anthropologists
about the correct procedures for their field work. Pell's Peruvian adventure is a composite of Allan Holmberg's community development project
among the Vicos Indians, which had coincided with McNickle's project at
Crownpoint, and an earlier *communidad* experience at Muquiyauyo, Peru,
in which peasant miners invested in a hydroelectric plant that revolu-
tionized their way of life.[64] As "participant observers," Holmberg and the

director of the Muquiyauyo project had initiated dramatic changes in the Indians' culture by using methods that were contrary to McNickle's non-directive approach.

Procedural questions about field work were still being discussed at professional gatherings in the 1970s as McNickle was rewriting the novel. Holmberg himself, in describing the Vicos project, had acknowledged its departure from the noninterventionist norm. He admitted that his work had required the control and manipulation of elements of environment, society, and culture until such time as the subjects of his study were ready to assume responsibility for continuing the changes that had been introduced. Describing the process concisely, he stated, "We used our power to share power to a point where we no longer held power."[65] McNickle's telling use of the two Peruvian projects in the novel reveals his own belief that participant intervention, with its element of "control and manipulation," brings no new understanding of the process and dynamics of culture change. The South American incident in *Wind from an Enemy Sky* discloses how little Pell had really learned about Indians.

It is Toby Rafferty, superintendent of the Little Elk Agency, who comes closest to real communication with the Indians, at the cost of seeming to be out of step with his own culture. Rafferty is the product of what McNickle describes as the "new settlement-house humanism," suggestive of John Collier's background. He is at first clearly bewildered by the Indians' desire to recover the medicine bundle. He is also uncertain of his own responsibility in facilitating that recovery, although he has reluctantly agreed to do so. "I'm trying to keep a sense of direction," he confides to the agency doctor as he tries to find a rationale for his action. "I wasn't sent here to rescue bits and pieces of the past." But he wonders whether he is taking the people forward or backward in attempting to restore the medicine bundle. Rafferty's training as agency superintendent has provided him with no guidance for a situation of this kind. He has never been told that the people on the reservation are different from the people in his home town in Ohio. "Just carry on as you would in Marietta, give guidance and leadership, and the people will respond"—that was the official position.[66] Bull's request that Rafferty find and return the medicine bundle is clearly outside the scope of those instructions. Nevertheless, he agrees to help recover the bundle, and when he discovers that it has been sent to Adam Pell's museum, he tells Pell of Bull's desire to retrieve it for the Little Elk people. Pell institutes a search for the bundle, but when it is finally found in the basement of the museum, it is seen to be irreparably damaged.[67] It is not possible to return Feather Boy—the holy artifact has been destroyed.

While Rafferty gropes for an understanding of Bull's request on behalf of the Little Elk Indians and begins to develop a sense of the gulf that exists between their world view and his own, Pell also searches for some relationship between the loss of Feather Boy and his nephew's death. Despite his best intentions, however, he is unable to grasp the medicine bundle's meaning for the Indians. He fails to make the connection between the dam and the ultimate destruction of Feather Boy as they affect the Little Elk people. His subsequent actions inevitably reflect his own cultural values. He attempts to atone for the destruction of Feather Boy by offering in its place the golden figurine from Peru, an object which possesses great monetary value and academic interest to any museum in America but is meaningless to the Indians. Bull and his followers are stunned when they realize that Feather Boy no longer exists. Pell's announcement of the demise of Feather Boy precipitates the novel's final catastrophe in which he, Rafferty, and Bull all die. For the Little Elk people at that moment, "no meadowlarks sang, and the world fell apart."[68]

McNickle's use of the meadowlark as a symbol first of the tribe's prosperity and then of its disintegration is quite purposeful. The meadowlark has been so closely tied to the folklore of the nothern plains tribes that it is sometimes called "the bird that spoke Lakota," or even "the Sioux Bird." Always it is a benefactor, bringing new hope or healing, warning of danger, reporting the latest news, ensuring the people's survival. Although Thunder Bird, which is represented by Feather Boy, is a mythical creation and not identical to the meadowlark, McNickle obviously suggests one as a symbol of the other. When the meadowlark is first mentioned, its song "wove the world together." In the final scene, "no meadowlarks sang, and the world fell apart."[69]

Although the destruction of Feather Boy happens in Pell's museum, Pell is not the villain in McNickle's novel—the story has no real villain. Pell represents neither the government nor any other particular segment of society, but, in the broadest sense, every American citizen. This is precisely McNickle's point. Over the years, the government's Indian policies have reflected a consensus morality that derives from the laws and religion of society itself, and the government's actions have reflected and been supported by that society. McNickle's essential argument is that "most critics of government policy in Indian affairs seem unaware of their own involvement in support of the very morality which informs that policy."[70] La Farge, Collier, even he himself, are included in this indictment. At the same time all the characters in the novel, Indian and non-Indian alike, share responsibility for the ultimate outcome. All are limited by their own thoughts, language, and cultural values.

Here is the source of the novel's universal tragedy. All the characters, despite their good intentions and considerable understanding, are never completely value-free in their cultural relations, nor can they be. Perhaps McNickle had been too hard on La Farge, and was unwilling to accept the fact that people must of necessity act from within their own value system. Men and women, by definition of their humanity, make value judgements about their world. More than most people, McNickle was able to put aside his own predilections and "walk in the Indians' moccasins," but he, too, had a strong sense of his own values. That was why he was so depressed at the conclusion of the Crownpoint experiment. The tragic element in the novel, and in McNickle's life if the novel reflects it, is the seeming inevitability of the final collision.

As an imaginative expression of McNickle's deepest understanding of Indian-white relations, the tone of his last novel is profoundly pessimistic. The assurance of Indian continuity, which is so clearly his theme in *Runner in the Sun* and *Native American Tribalism: Indian Survivals and Renewals,* gives way in *Wind from an Enemy Sky* to a sense of overwhelming futility. He had perceived in his own life a unique opportunity to live in both the Indian and the non-Indian world, and he had tried everything he knew to bring the two closer together. In his last novel he seems to say that it cannot be done. He had tried to speak for both worlds in his professional life, in his writing, and by living through the consequences of his Indian identity, but in *Wind from an Enemy Sky* he seems to say that there simply is no way for Indians and whites truly to understand one another.

Despite its pessimism, the novel contains evocative passages of great beauty. When Douglas Latimer first read the manuscript, he was moved to write McNickle and tell him of his immediate reaction. "It's a beautifully written and extremely moving story, told with great power. Bull's character is so strong, his death so heroic and so inevitable, that it has all the elements of a Greek tragedy. It made me sad, but sad in a way which still uplifted my spirit."[71] *Wind from an Enemy Sky* was McNickle's lament and his elegy for a world that was about to be lost forever.

But this was fiction, written during the last painful months of Vi's life, and McNickle was understandably depressed. He may have revealed his own deepest feelings in the novel, but he could not, would not, did not want to change the direction of his life. There was still work to be done. In fact, even as he wrote the final draft of the novel, he was deeply involved with the project that would become the primary interest of the rest of his life. That was where he found new hope for the future of his people.

9

The Legacy

Although *Wind from an Enemy Sky* had gestated for forty years and was part of McNickle's legacy to the future, its final revision occupied only about six months while he stayed home with Vi. During the years after they returned from Canada he also worked on the Smithsonian's *Handbook of North American Indians,* and he wrote a long, devastating reprise on Indian affairs from the 1920s through the Indian Self-Determination Act of 1973 for the American Indian Policy Review Commission.[1] As one of a diminishing number of survivors of the Collier era, McNickle often was called on to assess the former commissioner's significance and to reflect on the impact of the Indian Reorganization Act and subsequent Indian policy. Collier's role as commissioner of Indian affairs was still being critically reviewed by historians, and McNickle provided an insider's view.

Time had provided a moderating perspective, and although he remained as loyal as ever to Collier, McNickle recognized and admitted the flaws and weaknesses of the commissioner's reform program. He worked out his final evaluation of Collier, in part, for an address he delivered at a

1974 symposium in Canada. He then incorporated his more fully developed ideas into his report for the American Indian Policy Review Commission, as well as into chapters he was preparing for two different publications, both of which, as it happened, were published posthumously.[2]

McNickle prefaced his remarks to his Canadian audience by introducing himself as one of Collier's assistants, thus identifying his own participation in the Indian New Deal. "I was a member of staff during the Collier
administration," he confessed, "so if I question the performance of those
days, I am, in fact, questioning my own insights of the time, . . ."[3] Then he
explained to his audience the theoretical basis for the Indian New Deal.
He told how, during Collier's first visit to the Southwest, he had perceived an enduring sense of community among the Pueblo Indians. Although he knew little about other Indian tribes, Collier then convinced
himself that most Indian tribes had survived because they were rooted in
age-old communities that had retained enough of their traditional power
structure to become self-governing again if given the freedom to do so.
According to McNickle, the Collier administration's deepest concern was
to restore that tribal autonomy.[4]

Looking back at those years, McNickle discerned three major attempts
to discover and implement methods for achieving that goal. The first was
the Indian Reorganization Act itself. Despite various limitations and conditions imposed by Congress, the act had set the stage for further reform.
Second, Collier's desire to use the social sciences to develop Indian policy
was a crucial innovation, although the Applied Anthropology Unit was
vigorously opposed by certain "cave dwellers" in Congress, to use
McNickle's colorful phrase. Collier's third and most ambitious effort,
which was never fully realized, was the Personality Study, whose beginning, unfortunately, coincided with the onset of World War II. With Collier's departure in 1945, Congress was determined "to avert a recurrence
of administrative innovation" such as Collier had attempted, and the Indian New Deal became history.[5]

Despite congressional attempts to clip Collier's wings, however, his
administration had had long-term implications for Indian people, and he

had succeeded in bringing about some significant changes in federal policy. The alienation of Indian land was halted for twenty years, and some tribal holdings were actually enlarged. More than two-thirds of the tribes had moved toward constitutional government within the defined body of federal law. Modest advances were also made in tribal health care, and new reservation day schools kept families intact while providing the children with at least a rudimentary education. Financial credit had been extended for the development of tribal resources, although, because of budgetary restrictions, not at the rate Collier had hoped. Although the momentum of Collier's program had been halted by termination, not all had been lost. Some reforms had remained, and since then some others had even been reinstated.[6]

Ultimately, McNickle told his Canadian audience, "the true antagonist of Collier's reform efforts was his own social insight, an inheritance which he shared with others of his class, his generation, his cultural conditioning." Collier had inherited the Progressive reformer's faith in rational man. He believed that Indians, as rational men and women (and he never doubted that they were in full possession of that quality), would perfect themselves given the incentive and the opportunity. His enlightened and well-intentioned attempts to involve social scientists in the development of Indian policy reflected his underlying belief in the perfectability of Indian life, ultimately circumscribed by his own definition of the perfect. McNickle explained that, "as a man of his class and generation, he [Collier] saw no reason why he should not speak for the Indian people, no reason why they should not be satisfied to have him speak. His efforts to fulfill this mission is the the story of his administration."[7]

McNickle was not entirely consistent in his assessment of Collier's administration, however. From the perspective of the 1970s, Collier had not been behind his time but ahead of it. In retrospect, the Indian New Deal appeared as a "miscalculation in a calendar count—an aberration in time."[8] Although McNickle described Collier's ideology as a derivative of the Progressive era, he also extolled the commissioner's vision of a pluralistic society that hardly fit the "melting pot" concept of most Progressive reformers. Much of Collier's program, flawed as it was by the cultural baggage of his paternalism, would become the basis for political action by Indians themselves in the 1970s. By that time, *they* were the ones who were insisting on their rights of self-government, of resource control and maintenance, of cultural autonomy. The Indians, McNickle claimed, had finally caught up with John Collier.[9]

In thus offering his explanation of Collier's reform philosophy, McNickle was confessing the rationale for his own actions, especially his community development project at Crownpoint. There he had wanted to be a catalyst who would help the Navajos identify their needs and utilize the opportunities available on the reservation for meeting those needs. Like Collier's, his mission as a man of reason was to create the opportunity for change toward what he considered a better life. When that did not happen as he had anticipated, when various cultural elements intervened, he saw only his own failure.

As he identified himself with Collier's program, McNickle recognized his own culpability. He had been critical of La Farge for interpreting Indian cultural patterns from a "foreign" perspective; now he saw Collier, and by inference himself, as subject to the same limitations of culture. Adam Pell and Toby Rafferty in *Wind from an Enemy Sky* confronted the truth and, despite their good intentions, they were powerless to deflect the ultimate collision of the two cultures. McNickle had been unable to finish the Feather Boy novel until he understood and accepted this reality.

Despite the final tragic scene in *Wind from an Enemy Sky,* which perhaps can never be fully explained, McNickle believed that Native Americans do have a future. "Where, then, have we come?" was a final rhetorical question he asked of his Canadian audience in 1974. Answering it himself, he told them that Indian survival must ultimately be the responsibility of the Indians themselves. Their old traditional response to danger, retreating to fight another day, would no longer serve. If they resorted to that strategy in the modern world, they would be completely overwhelmed. But Indian people were instead developing new strategies for defense. Instead of retreating they were learning to adapt to the new realities of political life by identifying and becoming articulate about issues that affected not just their own tribes but all Indian people. They were demanding the right to control their own resources, to educate their own children, to determine their own destiny.[10] He was pleased that he had had some part in making all this happen.

Although McNickle had, in theory, retired, he continued to write, to consult, and to participate in professional conferences. Despite all these activities, however, his primary concern after retiring from academic life was an exciting new research center being developed at the Newberry Library in Chicago. The Newberry is an excellent research library that is noted for a variety of scholarly interests, including cartography, illuminated manuscripts, early printing, and the genealogy of regional, national, and tribal families. In addition to its holdings in those fields, it has two notable collections of western Americana, the Edward Ayer and the Everett D. Graff collections, which between them contain more than one hundred thousand volumes relevant to Indians and Indian-white relations. Under the leadership of Director Lawrence W. Towner, the library was increasingly concerned with the question of how to make those collections better known and more accessible to Indian scholars. By 1971, a tentative plan had been developed for the creation of an interdisciplinary research center devoted to the study of American Indian history. In January of that year, Matt P. Lowman, a staff member at the Newberry, wrote to McNickle and other eminent Indian scholars for their assessment of such a plan.

Although McNickle knew of the prestigious Newberry Library, he had been unaware of the Ayer and Graff collections. The possibility that the Newberry might sponsor a research center based on those collections and concerned exclusively with Native American history was unexpected and tremendously exciting. Such a center would attract an increasing number of young people like those who had attended the summer workshops, who were eager to take advantage of any opportunity to learn more about the history of their people. In the back of his mind also was the old dream of creating the kind of Indian archive he had hoped would evolve, and never did, under the Indian Claims Commission.[11]

McNickle's enthusiastic response to Lowman's letter then led Towner to invite him to participate directly in the project. The library intended to apply for an initial six-hundred-thousand-dollar matching grant from the National Endowment for the Humanities (NEH). If the grant was received, the new center would need as a spokesperson someone who could encourage the white establishment to provide matching funds and at the same time establish the center's credibility with both the scholarly and the Indian communities. Towner believed that McNickle, as both an Indian and a scholar, was more than qualified to serve in this dual capacity, and he invited him to serve as principal investigator for the NEH proposal. If the funds were forthcoming, McNickle would then be given the position of the new center's first program director. McNickle accepted, on condition that he be able to do most of the preliminary work from his home in Albuquerque and that he be considered only as a part-time, temporary director. He believed that the center, if and when it became operational, would need a full-time resident director, but if the Newberry people would continue their search for someone to fill that position on a more permanent basis, he would be pleased to contribute his name and his talents.[12]

McNickle wrote the proposal and he was in Washington with Towner when they received word that it had been accepted. They celebrated appropriately with dinner at the Jockey Club, where McNickle, appointed to the task, selected the best wine available with no consideration of cost. The matching grant of $597,000 was announced to the public at a press conference in Chicago on October 20, 1972. Private donors who matched the initial funding included the W. Clement and Jessie V. Stone Foundation, the Woods Charitable Fund, and the Ford Foundation. With funding assured, McNickle's appointment as director for the new Center for the History of the American Indian (CHAI) became official. He would receive an annual stipend of $4,000.[13]

McNickle's initial excitment about the center's potential soon translated itself into hard work. As he and the people at the Newberry struggled to realize the kind of program that would best utilize the library's resources and most effectively serve the country's Indian communities, they identified several areas of primary concern. Basic to all others was their desire to develop a new conceptual basis for Indian history. They hoped to employ a multidisciplinary approach, using history, literature, and anthropology to discover and describe the Indians' view of their own past. As McNickle had pointed out when he first responded to Lowman, the greatest disadvantage American Indians had had in dealing with the incoming Europeans was their lack of a written history, some record of their achievements, their insights, and their values. "No people," he had told Lowman, "should have to depend on another and possibly hostile party to give its account to the world."[14] The center's concern, therefore, was not to produce a variation on the theme of Indian-white relations, but to attempt a historical reorientation based on the fact that Indian people do indeed have a history of their own, quite apart from their interaction with non-Indians. By using the techniques of anthropology and history, they hoped to reconstruct the story of Indian people from the Indians' point of view.

Such a reorientation of Indian history would necessarily involve Indians themselves in all aspects of its program. Just as the new history could not be written without the assistance of Indian people, it would be useful to them only if they had access to it. To encourage Native American participation, therefore, the center planned to establish a scholarship program for Indians at the pre- and postdoctoral levels in various social sciences. An obvious need for teachers trained in the new Indian history would be met through the development of a series of summer workshops designed to acquaint educators with the latest research and methodology. In addition, the center was to be linked academically to a consortium of Big Ten universities and the University of Chicago, so that graduate students from these institutions, many of whom would become America's teachers, would have access to the Ayer and Graff collections and the other resources to be developed at the center.[15]

McNickle endorsed the center's high academic standards, at least in principle. It soon became painfully evident, however, that there were very few Indians who could qualify if a pre- or postdoctoral level of scholarship were required. He therefore began to urge the acceptance of Indians who had only bachelor's or master's degrees until a larger pool of advanced scholars became available. The center then extended its fellowship program to include tribal historians and other Indian scholars, thus bringing Indians to the center for research regardless of their educational level.[16] These fellowships also provided financial support, and a growing list of well-known activists, scholars, teachers, and authors in the field of Indian history who are themselves Indian testifies to the success of the program. Blue Clark (Creek), R. David Edmunds (Cherokee), Donald Fixico (Sauk and Fox, Shawnee, Creek, and Seminole), George Horse Capture (Gros Ventre), Bea Medicine (Lakota), and Veronica Tiller (Jicarilla Apache) are only a few of a growing number of Native Americans who have benefited from, and contributed to, the center's programs as D'Arcy McNickle fellows.

Non-Indians, too, have availed themselves of the opportunities for study and research offered by the center, and many of them today are recognized authorities in the field of Indian history. Frederick E. Hoxie, the center's director since 1983, was one of its early fellows. Gary C. Anderson, James Axtell, Raymond J. DeMallie, Michael D. Green, Peter Iverson, Calvin Martin, David Miller, Jay Miller, Clyde A. Milner II, Donald Parman, Willard Rollings, Richard White, and many others have learned to look at Indian history in new and creative ways and have published seminal works that reflect the new Indian history.

In addition to providing opportunities for individual study and research, the center's fellowship programs have created opportunities for fledgling scholars to interact informally with better-established Indian historians and anthropologists from all over the country. Serving at various times on the advisory council have been, among others, Robert F. Berkhofer, Roger Buffalohead (Ponca), Henry F. Dobyns, Robert V. Dumont, Jr., William T. Hagan, Robert F. Heizer, Nancy O. Lurie, N. Scott Momaday (Kiowa), Alfonso Ortiz, Paul Prucha, S.J., Father Peter J.

Powell, Sol Tax, Robert K. Thomas (Cherokee), Robert M. Utley, Dave Warren, and Wilcomb E. Washburn. Not only have these men and women served on the advisory council, they and a host of others have participated in seminars and workshops open to current fellows and the community at large. Such professional contacts have offered the fellows both inspiration and guidance. This expanding network of scholars has been crucial in supporting the work of graduate students and in creating a new awareness of Native Americans' vital participation in the nation's past, its present, and its future. Above all, it has provided opportunities for Indians themselves to discover and reclaim their own history. As Fred Hoxie, the center's director, has observed, "It is an extraordinary legacy of both D'Arcy's and Bill's [Towner] that this fellowship program exists. The opportunities it has provided for Indian people and the contacts it has made possible between Indians and non-Indians has been remarkable."[17]

McNickle had correctly foreseen that over time an increasing number of McNickle fellows would arrive at the center with at least some academic background. At first, however, a number of tribal historians lacked the research skills that would allow them to take full advantage of the facilities that were available to them. For others, just coming to Chicago from the reservation was a traumatic experience. Helping these people find their way in the urban world of Chicago and the academic milieu of the Newberry Library provided another challenge for the center. The library, in turn, had to adapt its urbane identity to those people, Indian and non-Indian alike, who often lived far from the nation's cosmopolitan cities. Different perceptions and expectations occasionally created frustrating situations, and the center learned how best to cope primarily on an ad hoc basis.

The controversies that inevitably surfaced from time to time over policy matters reminded McNickle of his years at the University of Saskatchewan and perhaps also of Crownpoint. In each case a new institution was struggling toward self-definition, and opposing views were often strongly held and vigorously defended. Differences of opinion were inevitable as those who held them explored various options. Former colleagues involved in those discussions, when asked about McNickle's role in them, have without exception characterized his leadership as one of mediation. Francis Jennings, who succeeded McNickle as the center's director in 1976, described him during those moments as "unflappable." "He seemed to think that his job was to promote unity rather than be a partisan," Jennings observed. Fussing with his pipe, he would slow the pace of the discussion until tempers cooled and ideas began to coalesce. Father Paul Prucha, who served several terms on the center's advisory council while McNickle was there, observed the same delaying tactic. He remembers McNickle acting "as a sort of moderating force between the whites and the Indians on the board and between the historians and the anthropologists." Rolland Wright, who had taught at the Boulder workshops in the 1960s, described McNickle's leadership there the same way. "He was never intrusive with faculty or staff, but rather was always helpful and interested in everything that was going on. . . . Despite his interest and concern, however, he was absolutely non-directive with the faculty and staff, always expecting them to find their own way." Richard Pope, from the Regina campus, commented similarly on McNickle's efforts to achieve consensus in the Department of Anthropology there. "To those of us who knew Indians," Pope recalled, "he ran the Department in a very Indian way."[18]

As a leadership technique, struggling for consensus was more Indian than white; for McNickle, it had become almost axiomatic. Lawrence Towner has maintained that McNickle seemed more "Indian" every time he came to Chicago, and his passion for consensus was a large part of that definition.[19] Some people perceived this search for a common ground among adversaries as a weakness. Vine Deloria, Jr., for instance, observed, "My impression of [McNickle] was that he would never take any controversial positions on anything."[20] For those who were accustomed to working within an adversarial framework of majority rule, McNickle's modus operandi could indeed be very frustrating, but it was also very Indian. In a profile of characteristic Indian behavior, Nancy Lurie describes this reach for consensus and notes, "While often baffling to whites, the process is patterned, and Indian people of widely varying tribal backgrounds are able to conduct business together according to mutually understood 'rules.'"²¹

Throughout the 1970s, McNickle remained devoted to and involved with the new center at the Newberry Library. As program director he attended quarterly board meetings in Chicago, and he kept in close touch by telephone from Albuquerque. Daily administrative duties, however, were initially handled by Newberry president Lawrence Towner (his title had been changed from director); Richard Brown, director of research and education; and Robert Bieder, McNickle's assistant. They were the ones who in those first years labored to bring the center to a more focused definition. As a liaison between the center and its potential constituency, however, McNickle showed a sense of what was possible and profitable that ensured stability and maintained the center's sense of direction.

By 1976, however, CHAI was once again searching for a full-time program director. Robert Bieder had left to pursue other academic interests, as had his replacement, Martin Zanger, and Lawrence Towner and Richard Brown were concerned with finding someone of McNickle's stature to take over this crucial post. The problem at that time was that the position was conceived and funded as a short-term one, and acceptance would amount to time-out in a professional academic career. A retired scholar of McNickle's stature seemed to offer the best alternative. Various people were considered, but after reading Francis Jennings's *The Invasion of America*, which was still in galley proofs, McNickle wrote to Richard Brown, "I think we've got our man!" Much to everyone's relief, Jennings accepted the appointment, and he served as director until 1981.²²

Towner, however, was unwilling to let McNickle separate himself completely from the Newberry Library. At his suggestion, the center's advisory council elected McNickle to serve as its chairman, a position with fewer responsibilities that yet kept him in touch.²³ McNickle was pleased to serve in that capacity. By this time, he and Towner had become close friends, and Towner was not reluctant to express his appreciation for McNickle's contributions. In a letter dated August 1, 1973, he had told

McNickle, "Without your help, we would never have gotten funded by the White community, and without your help, we would never have been accepted by either the scholarly or the Indian community. You have been the CRUCIAL factor in our success, and I thank you on behalf of the Library, the financial sponsors, the scholarly community, and, if I may be so bold, the Indian community." Anticipating McNickle's next visit to Chicago, he had concluded by telling McNickle, "Rachel and the children look forward to having their most favorite Indian of all near by once again."[24]

Vi's illness had prevented D'Arcy from taking a more active role at the Newberry, and although she was no longer aware of his presence, he was reluctant to leave town for more than a few days at a time. When her death finally came in the summer of 1977, it was a blessing for them both. Towner eased McNickle's pain by helping him establish a scholarship at the center in Vi's memory, to which her family in New York has contributed generously.[25] McNickle then began to pick up the pieces of his life— he even returned to St. Ignatius on the Flathead Reservation, for the first time since his sister Ruth's funeral in 1946. His daughter Toni visited him in September, and later that month he greeted a group of fellows from Chicago who had arrived in Albuquerque for a field trip. Francis Jennings accompanied them and McNickle met them at the airport. Their itinerary included a visit to Taos Pueblo for its annual San Geronimo feast day celebration, and Jennings later recalled McNickle's pleasure as he watched the antics of the koshares, or clowns. "He was accompanied by an old buddy from the BIA, and the two of them glowed like grandfathers looking on as beloved grandchildren do tricks."[26] The "old buddy" was probably John Rainer, his friend from Taos Pueblo whom he had known for more than twenty-five years.

McNickle had not yet learned of it, but just days before the fellows' visit the Newberry Library's board of directors had nominated him to its most esteemed position, that of distinguished research fellow. This singular honor included a generous stipend, gratuitous housing whenever he could come to Chicago, and freedom while there to work on his own projects. Richard Brown wrote to inform him of the honor and assured him, "You are very much a part of the 'Newberry family' and it would give us great pleasure indeed to have you here."[27] McNickle wanted very much to accept—he needed only to find someone to care for his house in Albuquerque if he were to leave for extended periods of time. He promised to inform them of his decision at the October advisory council meeting.

McNickle looked forward to that meeting as eagerly as the board members anticipated his being there. The meeting coincided with that of the American Society for Ethnohistory, also in Chicago that year, and he planned to arrive early so that he could attend sessions of that conference, as well. When he failed to arrive as expected, Towner and the other council members became increasingly concerned. They finally decided to contact the Albuquerque police and ask them to investigate. McNickle had lived alone since Vi's death, and conceivably something had happened to him. The police called back a short time later to report that they had found D'Arcy lying on the floor of his home, the victim of a massive heart attack. Newspapers at the front door suggested that he had died several days earlier.[28]

The council members were stunned. A short recess was called so that they might absorb the first shock of what they had just learned. A number of those present, including Nancy Lurie, Alfonso Ortiz, Sol Tax, Robert Thomas, and Dave Warren, had known D'Arcy for years, and the news came almost as a physical blow. The other members, too, realized the nature of their loss. According to the minutes of the meeting, they reconvened briefly "for the single purpose of recommending the creation of a memorial to McNickle in recognition of the veneration usually accorded him and the invaluable services he has given to this Center."[29] The distress of his friends made continuation of the meeting impossible and it was adjourned. By that time, several council members were weeping openly.

It cannot be said that McNickle's death was totally unexpected, in view of his medical history. But to those who had seen him recently, to the center's fellows on their recent field trip and to his daughter Toni, who had just returned to Washington after her visit with him a few weeks earlier, his death came as a tragic surprise. A brief service was attended only by members of the family, Alfonso Ortiz, and Francis Jennings, who represented the Newberry Library.[30] A short time later, however, McNickle's daughters invited a larger group of friends and associates to a memorial gathering at McNickle's home that might almost have been called a celebration. Good food and good wine evoked loving memories and, as someone who knew him well observed, "D'Arcy would have liked that." Jonah Yazzie, a Navajo friend from Crownpoint days who had helped build the new house, observed that the showers falling gently that day were evidence that D'Arcy McNickle had not really left his people. His presence would continue among them as the blessing of rain.[31]

Had he been given the choice, McNickle would probably have preferred going the way he did, but he would have said, "Not yet, please." He had commitments, and there were still things he wanted to do. He was looking forward especially to a return to Regina. Richard Pope had invited him to come and see the results of one of the projects they had planned together a few years earlier. When Pope heard of McNickle's death, he wrote, in a memorial letter to his colleagues,

> D'Arcy worked to create an Indian presence at this University through the Department of Anthropology, but political factors both within and without the University prevented these aspirations from coming to fruition as a visible result of his efforts. Is it historical irony or a Divine Hand that has brought the Saskatchewan Indian Federated College, so much the model of what D'Arcy had been striving for, into existence on this campus? I was looking forward very much to his planned visit here [in] January, an invitation which he accepted a few days before his passing.[32]

McNickle, also, was looking forward to the visit; he would have liked to see that new college.

There were other pleasures, as well, that he had begun to enjoy, not the least of which was freedom from worry about his personal finances. In addition to a modest government pension, he was receiving a small pension

from the University of Saskatchewan. Even more satisfying, all his books
on Indian history were in print again and earning respectable royalties.
He had also been pleased to note a small but growing demand for republication of *The Surrounded*. Robert Bigart, who worked on the Flathead
Reservation in Montana, had suggested that he write a new introduction
to bring the novel into a contemporary context and offer it for Montana's
bicentennial. McNickle admitted that he might be interested in doing
that, although he was also contemplating a new novel on the subject
rather than an introduction to the earlier one. He took requests for *The
Surrounded* seriously enough, however, to obtain the publishing rights
from Dodd, Mead in January 1974, and Bigart did his best to interest the
Montana Bicentennial Commission in its republication.

Meanwhile, unknown to Bigart, others were also interested in seeing
The Surrounded back in print. The success of N. Scott Momaday's *House
Made of Dawn* (1968) and its winning the Pulitzer Prize the following year
marked the beginning of renewed interest in contemporary Native American literature. Helen Bannon, who had been a fellow at the center, and
Geary Hobson, professor of Native American literature, both at the University of New Mexico, contacted Hugh Treadwell, director of that university's press, about the possibility of reissuing *The Surrounded*. In the
summer of 1977, Treadwell wrote to McNickle to see if he was interested.
McNickle was surprised at this overture from an unexpected source and
also very pleased; apparently he had been unaware of the local effort on his
behalf. He accepted UNM's offer and suggested that Lawrence Towner be
asked to write an introduction. "I have published so few things," he confided to Towner, when he wrote to tell him of UNM's interest. "I am glad
that this one is to be kept in print a while longer."[33]

Towner had hardly begun to write that introduction when word came
of McNickle's death. Thus his introduction became an afterword, aeulogy
for a man whom he had once described as "my great and good friend."[34]
He and McNickle had shared the excitement of watching the center come
into being, and their relationship had deepened over the years. Towner
understood and appreciated the complexities of McNickle's personality

and his extraordinary gifts. In his afterword, he described McNickle as "a man with the breadth of intellect to live in two worlds, with the compassion to love them both, and with the talent to write so effectively about where they tragically intermesh that he could share his experience with others."[35] Unfortunately, McNickle did not live to see *The Surrounded* in print again. He died before either that novel or *Wind from an Enemy Sky* reached the market.

By 1978, when those two novels were released, a new and more sophisticated generation of critics was awaiting them. *Wind from an Enemy Sky* was reviewed in several library and publishing journals, where it received mixed reviews. F. Whitney Jones, writing for *Library Journal*, called it an "engrossing" story, even though it "relie[d] heavily on romantic conventions." In *World Literature Today*, Charles Larson characterized it as both tragic and nonviolent. In the same review, he described *The Surrounded* as "the most significant novel by an American Indian written before World War II." *The Surrounded,* however, attracted critics because of its original publication date of 1936. Although it had been out of print for forty years and was almost unknown, literary scholars now sought to make room for it in what some have called a renaissance in Native American literature.[36]

Here, unexpectedly, was an antecedent for N. Scott Momaday's *House Made of Dawn*, James Welch's *Winter in the Blood* (1974), and Leslie Marmon Silko's *Ceremony* (1977). Momaday's novel, like *The Surrounded,* is the story of a young man, Abel, who has been overseas (in this case serving in Vietnam), is spiritually wounded, and returns home to the reservation in search of healing and of his Indian identity. Silko's Tayo has also experienced the war and bears psychic wounds that refuse to heal. Abel and Tayo move toward wholeness through reconnecting with the traditional religion of their people. Welch's anonymous hero suffers from a different kind of anomie, but he, too, finds new meaning for his life through discovering his tribal roots. McNickle's lived-through experience of moving between two worlds had given Archilde in *The Surrounded* a unique and powerful voice decades before Abel and Tayo struggled with their own alienation. As a new kind of Indian hero, Archilde, returning to the reservation, had turned away from the white people's world and discovered new values in the old ways of his people. Abel and Tayo, even Welch's hero, would do the same.

Since it was reissued in 1978, *The Surrounded* has been subjected to much textual analysis.[37] Many contemporary critics, like the earlier ones, have described it as depressing, fatalistic, despairing. Louis Owens views the novel as part of a naturalist literary tradition in which "the protagonist simply cannot understand much less order and control the world he inhabits."[38] The theme of the novel, in Owens's view, is fatal misunderstanding and failed communication. McNickle himself, in choosing to flee from similar circumstances, undoubtedly viewed Archilde's predicament that way.

John Purdy, on the other hand, views *The Surrounded* as a story of Archilde's (and also, he contends, McNickle's) vision quest. In fact, he views all three of McNickle's novels in this context. Whereas Owens sees Archilde as neither understanding nor controlling his world, Purdy sees him acquiring new understanding through his growing acceptance of the Salish life-ways, thus ensuring his survival.[39]

In attempting to move away from Owens's bleak, fatalistic approach, other critics have suggested a broader interpretation. James Rupert, for instance, considers *The Surrounded* a multidimensional story in which Archilde's experience transcends the tragedy of his circumstances. He maintains that "human value is created by the protagonist's struggle, not his victory." On a more sophisticated level, William Bevis takes a position similar to Rupert's, but he frames it in a different context. The most important works in Native American literature today, by McNickle, Momaday, Silko, and Welch, are about what Bevis calls "homing in." The hero returns to his home and his people for identity and meaning. In marked contrast to modern American views,

> most Native American novels are not "eccentric," centrifugal, diverging, expanding, but "incentric," centripetal, converging, contracting. The hero comes home. "Contracting" has negative

overtones to us, "expanding" a positive ring. These are the cultural choices we are considering. In Native American novels, coming home, staying put, contracting, even what we call "regressing" to a place where one has been before, is not only the primary story, it is a primary mode of knowledge and a primary good.[40]

The "homing in" plots used by McNickle and the others all present the tribal past "as a gravity field stronger than individual will." When "homing in" is read in the tribal context, "tribalism is respected, even though it is inseparable from a kind of failure."[41]

It was the circumstances of his birth, of course, that gave D'Arcy McNickle the opportunity to live in the two worlds he wrote about so tellingly. Each of the three McNickle children, given the same option, had made a different choice. D'Arcy's older sister Ruth remained in Montana, married a mixed-blood Flathead, and raised her family as tribal members on the reservation. The younger of his two sisters, Florence, became a nurse, moved to Canada, married a non-Indian, and raised her children as part of white society. D'Arcy, however, followed a third path. He married non-Indian women, raised his children as members of white society, yet lived his own Indianness to the end, living in both worlds, as Lawrence Towner noted, with equal grace.[42]

Despite claiming his tribal affiliation, however, McNickle never conformed to a stereotypical Indian identity. He did not adopt an Indian costume or lifestyle and he attended Indian dances and powwows only as a spectator, although he did, on occasion, participate in ritual sweatbaths. Although the limited vision of some critics allowed the acculturated Indian like himself only two choices, either to conform to the demands of the Indian tribal community or to give up any claim to being Indian, McNickle refused to do either. He felt no need to invent new behavior strategies to prove that he was Indian and he refused to pretend that he was someone (or some thing) other than himself. Nevertheless, since his childhood he had instinctively developed patterns of Indian behavior that permitted him to move comfortably and acceptably within the Indian world.

The most serious threat, in his view, to his Indian identity had occurred in the fall of 1968, after he had decided to spend the academic year in Albuquerque working on the La Farge biography. The Tribal Council of the Confederated Salish and Kootenai Tribes, in updating its tribal rolls, had recorded his Canadian address, but he had neglected to tell them that he would be there for a limited period of time. They presumed that he had become a permanent resident of that country and therefore was no longer a tribal member. The postal service was slow in forwarding his mail from Regina to Albuquerque, and by the time the letter from the tribe asking for verification reached him, the deadline for corrections had passed. He had been stricken from the rolls. This was, indeed, a serious matter, and he lost no time in correcting the misinformation. His residence in Canada, he assured the council, was only temporary. He was still officially a resident of the United States and should continue to be carried on the rolls as an enrolled member of the tribe.[43]

Even though he maintained his own name on the tribal rolls, however, McNickle never inquired about the possibility of enrolling his children. Between 1935 and 1960 the tribe redefined its membership several times and Toni and Kathleen might have been enrolled, but McNickle never suggested the possibility, either to them or to the tribal council.[44] This is not surprising; even if his own blood quantum had been verifiably larger than twenty-five percent, his children had never been exposed to Indian culture in any of its multitudinous forms, and their personalities would have had no shaping into an Indian configuration. Neither he nor they would have claimed that they were Indians. His gifts to them as his children were otherwise.

In still another area, too, McNickle lacked what many people consider an Indian characteristic. For all his devotion to Indian people and his concern for maintaining his tribal enrollment, McNickle did not consider the Flathead Reservation his home after his departure in 1925. Though it is true that there were times when he regretted having sold his allotment, his regrets came thirty years after the fact, and he never considered returning there to live. As Alfonso Ortiz noted in the memorial he prepared for the friends who gathered after D'Arcy's death, "When McNickle sold his land and went off to Europe, he gave himself over to history, and from this time on he did not again have any sense that his Indianness was ultimately rooted in a place to return to in any way."[45] The heroes of his three novels, Archilde, Salt, and Antoine, all return to the place of their birth— McNickle himself did not, except in his imagination. His Indian forebears, after all, were Canadian Cree, not Flathead.

But the Canadian north country did not appeal, either. He was drawn instead to the land of the Southwest. Perhaps Albuquerque attracted him because its setting bears some resemblance to the Mission Valley of Montana. The abrupt rise of the Sandia Mountains to the east, which he could see from his home in the North Valley, may have touched some deep-seated memories of the Mission Range and of the place where he had lived as a boy. In his later diaries he often commented on the wonderful variety of birds and wildlife in his Albuquerque neighborhood. He had come to love the southwestern landscape. He knew the Navajo names of all the features of the eastern reservation country, as well as the stories of how those names came to be, and he felt a kinship to that place that he had not known anywhere else.[46]

And now D'Arcy McNickle's name bespeaks his legacy to all American people, Indian and non-Indian alike, in his novels and his other writing and in his tireless efforts on behalf of young Indian people everywhere. Three institutions, especially, bear his imprint. One is the center at the Newberry Library. Its efforts to train scholars in a new approach to Indian history, to collect and make accessible previously unknown tribal materials, to train teachers, and to help tribal historians create a meaningful history for their own people, reflect his lifelong concerns. A new generation of Indian scholars, trained at the center, is making an important contribution to the Indians' understanding of their own past. In 1983 his daughter Toni contributed her father's papers to the Newberry Library, and the center was renamed the D'Arcy McNickle Center for the History of the American Indian in his honor.

Another institution that traces its intellectual lineage to D'Arcy McNickle is Native American Educational Services, a university without walls in Chicago that is perhaps better known as NAES.[47] NAES has developed an accredited academic degree program that provides Indian students with training in two primary areas. The first is concerned with the overall generalized Indian experience. In this part of the curriculum, students tackle such subjects as federal law and policy, academic and professional studies in the social sciences and literature, and the socioeconomic analysis of tribes as generic, common units. The other thrust of the program is site specific. It involves the in-depth study of individual tribal environments, including the religion, the wisdom embodied in the tribes' oral traditions, and federal-tribal relations as experienced by particular tribes. Such studies of the Assiniboine and Sioux tribes are well advanced, and others are being planned.[48] Thus NAES students are exploring ways to follow both "maps of the mind." They are developing a meaningful web of knowledge that will allow Indian people to take for themselves the best of both worlds as they anticipate a stronger and brighter future for Native American people everywhere.

Such a program has obvious similarities to the curriculum of the Leadership Training Workshops, and not surprisingly it has been developed by people who were workshop participants. Faith Smith, NAES's current president, was a workshop participant in the 1960s. One of NAES's originators, Robert V. Dumont, Jr., attended the 1960 workshop, and has recalled the significance of that event in his later life. It "was probably the most important academic experience of my life, because it provided a framework for learning which was related to my environment. Certainly we have modelled NAES on this notion—the functional role of tribal knowledge and learning for the student and the community."[49]

NAES has not only derived its inspiration from McNickle, it has used his Indian histories in its curriculum. A number of its students also have worked on their tribal histories at the McNickle Center. In addition, Sol

Tax and Robert Thomas, both involved in the workshops for years, have been active members of N A E S's board of directors. N A E S has become a vital extension of McNickle's interest and concern that Indian people develop their own educational format and tell their own story to the world.

A third institution, one that reflects McNickle's influence in a less direct way, is the D'Arcy McNickle Library at Salish Kootenai College on the Flathead Reservation in Pablo, Montana. Although McNickle had maintained little contact with the Flathead Tribe during his lifetime, he had memorialized its mixed-blood heritage in the figure of Archilde Leon, and young people from the reservation who attended the workshops knew that his concern was for all Indian young people, even those from the little reservation towns in Montana. The new library at the college was dedicated in McNickle's name in October 1987, ten years almost to the day after his death. The powwow and feast that accompanied the ceremony were an affirmation of McNickle's life and his devotion to the future of all Indian people. He had called himself a "breed," but he never allowed that "marginality" to be more than a temporary obstruction. It seems fitting that the library serving the new community college on the Flathead Reservation should bear his name.

So what exactly was D'Arcy McNickle's contribution to American Indians in the modern world? He may not have been a truly innovative thinker—except for his novels, his ideas were not original. When working for the Bureau of Indian Affairs he whole-heartedly supported John Collier's reforms. The National Congress of American Indians did not originate with him, nor did the Indian Claims Commission. It was Collier who suggested that he be offered the contract for his first historical monograph, his collaboration with Harold Fey fell into his lap by accident, and Alvin Josephy recommended him for the La Farge biography. Others, notably Sol Tax, drew him into the Leadership Training Workshops and the American Indian Chicago Conference, and still others initiated his role at the University of Saskatchewan and the Newberry Library.

But without McNickle's willingness to assume leadership and responsibility for these various projects, they would not have happened as they did; they would perhaps not have happened at all. Although he was not an innovator, he was, nevertheless, a visionary who possessed a keen instinct for what was not only desirable but possible. He made things happen because he could inspire people to action and because he was an extremely able and tireless organizer, administrator, and fund raiser. In this sense, he was a real risk-taker. He was indefatigable when there was work to be done, and there is nothing in his papers to suggest that he ever took a real vacation—if he did, it was not of sufficient interest for him to have recorded it.

In retrospect, it is not difficult to see why the Crownpoint Project was so important to him and also why he so seldom spoke of it. Of all his various projects, this one had been most completely his own and he had invested himself completely in it. It brought all his gifts into sharp focus in a way that provided him great pleasure and equally great pain. Crownpoint represented the climax of all that he had learned, and he felt that it had failed. No wonder he seldom spoke of it.

In his novels and poetry McNickle revealed his true artistry. He was both a realist and a romantic, and he struggled to temper his romantic sensitivity with the often tragic reality of the Indians' situation that he knew so well. The balance that he finally achieved between the two in his fiction was the result of considerable determination and a great deal of effort.

If there is any one word that those who knew him best have used to describe D'Arcy McNickle, that word is "gentle." He was a wise and gentle man, sensitive always to the feelings and needs of those around him, attuned to the way they used the language, and concerned for the human and natural environment in which he lived. Yet he was also, in his later years, a lonely man who rarely shared his private thoughts and feelings even with those closest to him. Although his knowledge and wisdom were impressive, he was largely self-taught, and he seldom found himself in situations that nurtured his intellectual hunger.[50] He found his milieu among anthropologists during the Collier years, at the 1967 conference in Austria, and at the First Convocation of American Indian Scholars at Princeton in 1971, but such times were relatively rare. His intellectual tastes and accomplishments were both broad and deep, but he never flaunted his knowledge. He was always available to those who sought him out for advice and companionship.

For many young Indian people, D'Arcy McNickle became a superb role model as he showed that it was possible to maintain an Indian identity in twentieth-century America. He believed that he was truly born "of the opposition," born to adhere to a different world view than that of the dominant society. Identifying his world view with the ethical and moral standards of Indian culture, he wanted to see it survive by wisely and selectively adapting to modern technology.

D'Arcy McNickle was a mixed-blood, a Métis, who called himself a "breed" at a time when, to most non-Indian Americans, that was a pejorative word. But carrying a dual ancestry offered some compensations. It gave him an unusual self-consciousness of his unique sociocultural position, and it allowed him to enjoy the best of two worlds. His uncommon endowment of insight, intellect, and personality opened doors to a future that he could not have imagined for himself in his youth. Although he was certainly endowed with exceptional gifts, D'Arcy McNickle created his own place. Living in two worlds, he gave everything he had to bring together the peoples who were united in his own person. His legacy will serve them both for many years to come.

Notes

PREFACE

1. See Dorothy R. Parker, "D'Arcy McNickle," 55–75.

PROLOGUE

1. George Woodcock, *Gabriel Dumont,* 33–36. For a firsthand account of the organization of the buffalo hunt, see Alexander Ross, *The Red River Settlement: Its Rise, Progress, and Present State* (London: Smith, Elder & Co., 1856). The definitive work on the Métis people is Marcel Giraud, *Le Métis Canadien,* translated by George Woodcock as *The Métis in the Canadian West.*

2. Woodcock, *Gabriel Dumont,* 84.

3. Joseph Kinsey Howard, *Strange Empire,* 294. See especially chap. 15, "The Prince of the Prairies," for information about Gabriel Dumont.

4. Howard, *Strange Empire.* This book contains a detailed account of the life of Louis Riel and reveals his messianic sense of destiny as leader of the Métis people.

5. Genealogical information on the Parenteau and Plante families has been provided by D'Arcy McNickle's niece, O. Jahala Currie, of Calgary, Alberta. Mrs. Currie has investigated the records of baptisms, marriages, and deaths in the

Roman Catholic churches of Duck Lake, Batoche, and St. Laurent, Saskatchewan, and the 1891 census records for the province, p. 7, no. 30.

6. D'Arcy McNickle to Mrs. Judy Jordan, Mar. 17, 1972, General Correspondence, McNickle Papers, Special Collections, Newberry Library, Chicago, Illinois (hereafter cited as MP, NL). Nancy Lurie has recalled McNickle speculating that his grandmother was born in a tipi, possibly under similar circumstances. There is no other family recollection of this, but it is possible. Letter from Nancy Lurie to author, May 1988.

7. Woodcock, *Gabriel Dumont*, 81–82.

8. Louis Riel, *The Diaries of Louis Riel*.

9. Desmond Morton, *The Last War Drum*. Morton provides a military history based on primary sources.

10. A list of those involved in the battles includes a number of Parenteaus, but not Isidore. List sent to O. J. Currie from the Chancery Office, St. Boniface, Manitoba, Oct. 6, 1986; copy in author's files.

11. Statutory Declaration, Homestead File no. 806684, Dec. 14, 1904, Saskatchewan Archives Board, Saskatoon, Sask.; from O. J. Currie, copy in author's files.

CHAPTER ONE

1. D'Arcy McNickle, *The Surrounded*, 43–44.

2. John Fahey, *The Flathead Indians*, 272–77.

3. *St. Ignatius Mission*.

4. McNickle, *The Surrounded*, 35–36.

5. *Inventory of the County Archives of Montana*, prepared by the WPA and the Montana Historical Records Survey, 1940, Newberry Library. See also Fahey, *Flathead Indians*, appendix, 314, n. 14.

6. Verne Dusenberry, "Waiting for a Day That Never Comes," 27–30.

7. Verne Dusenberry, "The Rocky Boy Indians," 3.

8. Copy of baptismal records are in author's file. Canadian Census, 1891, District 200, Prince Albert County, Saskatchewan. See also J. E. Chamberlain, *The Harrowing of Eden*, 34–36.

9. Telephone interview with Robert Thomas, Tucson, Arizona, Sept. 4, 1986.

10. Records of St. Ignatius Mission School, Bureau of Catholic Indian Missions, series 1/2, box 15, folder 5, Department of Special Collections and University Archives, Marquette University, Milwaukee, Wisconsin (hereafter cited as Records of St. Ignatius Mission School).

11. Letter from Agent Smead to Indian Commissioner, Apr. 27, 1904, Reports of Changes in School Employees, Flathead Boarding School, Central File, Flat-

head Agency, 26647-1904, 29423-1904, Records of the Bureau of Indian Affairs, National Archives, Record Group 75 (hereafter cited as NA, RG75).

12. This assumption is based on the fact that Philomene was the only one of the Parenteaus to request enrollment in 1904. Despite their enrollment, Philomene did not want the children to be considered Indian. In fact, this may have become a volatile element within the marriage. Quote is from a letter from O. J. Currie to author, dated Feb. 20, 1986.

13. Records of St. Ignatius Mission School.

14. Philomene McNickle to Indian Commissioner, 32386-39-803 to 33036-27-820, Central Classified File, Flathead Tribe, 1907–1939, NA, RG75. See also Morgan memo, Oct. 27, 1914, MP, NL. Philomene claimed that the children were only one-eighth Indian, and that she wanted to raise them as white.

15. Special Agent Downs to Commissioner of Indian Affairs, Feb. 14, 1905, quoting from letter from Commissioner to Special Agent McNichols, Sept. 25, 1902, Selected Records of the BIA relating to the Enrollment of Indians on the Flathead Reservation, 1903–8, microfilm production M1350, National Archives, Washington, D.C. These records are also on microfilm at the Flathead Tribal Land Office, Pablo, Montana (hereafter cited as Flathead Tribal Records). McNickle family allotment numbers are 43–46; D'Arcy is no. 46.

16. Downs to Commissioner, May 25, 1905, ibid.; ibid.; Council Proceedings, Apr. 18, 1905, Flathead Tribal Records.

17. Council Proceedings, April 18, 1905, Flathead Tribal Records. In a letter dated August 23, 1962 to her granddaughter Helen, Philomene says, "Grampa had me and children adopt at the Flathead" (letter provided by O. Jahala Currie, Calgary, Alberta).

18. McNickle to Robert Bigart, Oct. 15, 1974, General Correspondence, MP, NL.

19. Separation decree, Oct. 30, 1912, Flathead Tribal Records.

20. The records of the Salem Indian School at Chemawa and related correspondence (including that between Philomene and Morgan), as well as copies of material relating to the McNickle divorce, are in the National Archives and Records Service, Seattle, Washington (hereafter cited as Federal Records Center, Seattle). Copies are also included in the Flathead Tribal Records.

21. Fred Morgan to Indian Commissioner, July 22, 1913, ibid.; Fred Morgan to Indian Commissioner, Apr. 22, 1913, ibid.; Fred Morgan to Indian Commissioner, July 22, 1913, ibid.

22. Divorce decree, Apr. 16, 1913, ibid.

23. Father Taelman to Commissioner of Indian Affairs Francis Leupp, Dec. 27, 1908, Central Classified File, Flathead Agency, 1907–1939, NA, RG75.

24. Father Taelman to Commissioner Leupp, Dec. 11, 1908, ibid.

25. McNickle to Robert Bigart, Oct. 15, 1974, General Correspondence, MP, NL.

26. Ibid. Some buffalo escaped the roundup, and the remnant became the original herd of the National Bison Range, Moiese, Montana.

27. McNickle to Karen Fenton, Oct. 15, 1974, General Correspondence, M P, N L.
28. Francis Paul Prucha, *The Churches and the Indian Schools, 1888–1912*, especially chap. 4.
29. Fahey, *Flathead Indians*, 272–77; *Statistics of Indian Tribes, Agencies, and Schools, Compiled to July 1, 1903*, 21.
30. Robert S. Hamilton and Mary Lemery to Senator Charles S. Curtis, Apr. 30, 1920, 137-21-053 to 72408-19-054, Central Correspondence File, Flathead Agency, N A, R G75.
31. Mother Superior to Supt. Morgan, Oct. 22, 1914, Flathead Tribal Records. See also O. J. Currie to author, Nov. 19, 1986. Currie describes a recent visit to Montana, where she had talked to a man who had seen the runaway boy.
32. Fred Morgan to Wadsworth, Oct. 7, 1914, Salem Indian School Records, Federal Records Center, Seattle. Sworn testimony from the school physician, the cook, the head matron, and an assistant matron refute the charges that D'Arcy apparently made.
33. Philomene to Department of Indian Affairs, Oct. 27, 1914, Flathead Tribal Records.
34. D'Arcy McNickle, "The Hungry Generations." A holographic copy of this early unpublished manuscript is in the McNickle Papers. See also McNickle, *The Surrounded*, 90–97.
35. O. J. Currie to author, Feb. 2, 1987.
36. D'Arcy McNickle, *Wind from an Enemy Sky*, 106–10.
37. George D. Spindler and Louise S. Spindler, "American Indian Personality Types and Their Sociocultural Roots," 148.
38. Mrs. Gus Dahlberg to Superintendent Wadsworth, Mar. 15, 1914, Salem Indian School Records, Federal Records Center, Seattle. See also Dahlberg to My Dear Boy, June 8, 1916, ibid.
39. O. J. Currie to author, Feb. 20, 1985.
40. Woodcock, *Gabriel Dumont*, 250.
41. Flathead Tribal Records.
42. *Frontier*, Winter, 1924–25, in Special Collections, Mike Mansfield Library, University of Montana (hereafter cited as Mansfield Library, University of Montana). McNickle's contributions to the *Frontier* include "The Silver Locket," vol. 4, no. 1, 18–21; "Clod the Magician," vol. 4, no. 3, 8–10; "Cycle," vol. 5, no. 1, 1; "The Mountains," vol. 5, no. 1, 10–11; "Sailing a-Sailing," vol. 6, no. 1, 22–25; and "Man Hesitates But Life Urges," vol. 6, no. 2, 16.
43. *The Sentinal*, University of Montana Yearbook, 1924, 100, Special Collections, Mansfield Library, University of Montana.
44. Files of the Alumni Association at the University of Montana contain some later material from Joran, who maintained her university contacts for many years.
45. A. B. Guthrie, Jr., *The Blue Hen's Chick*, 51.

46. McNickle to Carey McWilliams, n.d., General Correspondence, M P, N L.
47. McNickle to Superintendent Charles Coe, Apr. 2, 1924, Flathead Tribal Records.
48. McNickle's application for patent in fee, Mar. 17, 1925, ibid.
49. McNickle to John Collier, May 25, 1934, General Correspondence, M P, N L.
50. *Missoula Missoulian,* June 21, 1925.
51. H. G. Merriam, "To Whom It May Concern," Sept. 29, 1925, General Correspondence, M P, N L. Merriam's acquaintance with John Joseph Mathews, an Osage from Oklahoma who was also a Rhodes scholar, suggested to him that McNickle, too, should go to Oxford. Mathews's novel *Sundown* was published in 1934.

CHAPTER TWO
1. D'Arcy McNickle, "Sailing, a-Sailing," 22, 24.
2. Ibid., 25.
3. Alfonso Ortiz, "D'Arcy McNickle (1904–1977), 13; McNickle to Wilcomb Washburn, Aug. 22, 1973, General Correspondence, M P, N L.
4. McNickle Diary, Oct. 3, 1932, M P, N L. McNickle kept a diary, or journal (hereafter cited as Diary, with the date), for most of his adult life. The sequence, however, is incomplete, and some of the entries are not dated, others only partially so. McNickle's assessment of the New York years was written over a period of two months, with entries on August 11, August 23, and October 3, 1932.
5. Walter Lippmann, *Interpretations, 1931–1932,* 335–36.
6. Diary, Aug. 11, 1932.
7. Ibid.
8. Ibid.
9. Diary, Aug. 23, 1932.
10. Ibid.
11. Diary, Aug. 11, 1932.
12. McNickle to H. G. Merriam, June 11, 1932, H. G. Merriam Papers, Mansfield Library, University of Montana. By 1932, the magazine had expanded its name to *Frontier and Midland: A Literary Magazine.* By that time it was accepting contributions from outside writers as well as from students and alumni. The Mansfield Library has a complete run of this publication.
13. Diary, May 30, 1932.
14. Ibid., Apr. 27, 1933, and Jan. 1, 1956.

15. Ibid., 1932; Richard Hofstadter, *The Progressive Historians,* 349–51. Hofstadter describes the excitement generated at the time by Parrington's *Main Currents in American Thought.*

16. McNickle to Collier, May 4, 1934, General Correspondence, MP, NL. This is a draft of McNickle's initial application for employment with the Bureau of Indian Affairs.

17. D'Arcy made no mention of his father's death in his diary, and it is possible that he did not know of it at the time. William died in St. Ignatius, Montana on November 28, 1929. A copy of William McNickle's obituary is in author's files.

18. Diary, July 1931.

19. Ibid.

20. Diary, Aug. 23, 1932.

21. McNickle to IRS, 1934, General Correspondence, MP, NL; diary, May 25, 1933. The suicide incident is described in D'Arcy McNickle, "The Indian New Deal as Mirror of the Future," in *Political Organization of Native North Americans,* ed. Ernest L. Schusky, 107.

22. Ronald Steele, *Walter Lippmann and the American Century.* See especially chap. 24, "A Reluctant Convert."

23. Writings and Periodicals, MP, NL.

24. See D'Arcy McNickle, *The Hawk Is Hungry: An Annotated Anthology of D'Arcy McNickle's Short Fiction* for McNickle's short stories. A handwritten draft of "The Hungry Generations" is included in McNickle's papers at the Newberry Library.

25. McNickle, "The Hungry Generations," 108, MP, NL; ibid.

26. Ibid., 117.

27. Superintendent Coe to McNickle, Apr. 13, 1932, General Correspondence, MP, NL. In response to D'Arcy's inquiry and his telling Coe that he had not heard from his mother in two years, the superintendent supplied him with her Milwaukee address. D'Arcy then apparently wrote to her. He commented in his diary on August 19, 1933, that his mother was making a "tolerable living," for which he was grateful. He was in no position to help her himself.

28. Harcourt, Brace & Co. to McNickle, Apr. 6, 1929, Correspondence esp. re *The Surrounded,* MP, NL.

29. K. S. Crichton to McNickle, Dec. 28, 1931, ibid.

30. Lois Dwight Cole to McNickle, Dec. 28, 1933, ibid.

31. McNickle to Collier, May 25, 1934, General Correspondence, MP, NL.

32. John Lloyd Purdy, *Word Ways,* 14–17.

33. McNickle, *The Surrounded,* 207.

34. Ibid., 297.

35. "Manuscript Report," Oct. 23, 1934, publisher not identified, Correspondence esp. re *The Surrounded,* MP, NL.

36. Ibid.

37. Block to McNickle, Oct. 29, 1934. Letters from McNickle to Lewis Gannett, Feb. 5, and to Harrison Smith, Feb. 7, reveal McNickle's frustration and disappointment at this latest rejection. Correspondence esp. re *The Surrounded,* MP, NL.
38. McNickle, *The Surrounded,* 222.
39. Ibid., 211.
40. Purdy, *Word Ways,* 53, 59.
41. McNickle, *The Surrounded,* 108.
42. Mourning Dove, *Cogewea, the Half-Breed*; Mourning Dove, *Mourning Dove;* Jay Miller, "Mourning Dove"; Charles R. Larson, *American Indian Fiction,* 173–80.
43. Purdy, *Word Ways,* 16.
44. Alfred Kazin, *An American Procession,* 360–62.
45. See Correspondence esp. re *The Surrounded,* MP, NL, and McNickle's diaries during this period.
46. McNickle to Skinner, July 18, 1935, General Correspondence, MP, NL. See also letters from Skinner to McNickle dated Feb. 3, 1936 and Oct. 10, 1935, ibid.
47. Skinner to McNickle, Oct. 10, 1935, MP, NL.
48. Monty Noam Penkower, *The Federal Writers Project,* 1–8.
49. McNickle Personnel File, Office of Personnel Management, Federal Records Center, St. Louis (hereafter cited as McNickle Personnel File); George Cronyn to McNickle, Sept. 4, 1935, General Correspondence, MP, NL; Cronyn to McNickle, Sept. 6, 1935, Records of the Works Progress Administration, box 140 M–Q, 1935–37(je), no. 258, NA, RG69.
50. McNickle to Skinner, Oct. 6, 1935, General Correspondence, MP, NL.
51. Oliver La Farge, "Half-breed Hero," *Saturday Review of Literature,* March 14, 1936, 10; Mary Heaton Vorse, "End of the Trail," *New Republic,* April 15, 1936, 295.
52. Florence Milner, *Boston Transcript,* March 4, 1936, 3.
53. Fred T. Marsh, "A Novel of Old and New Americans," *New York Times,* February 16, 1936, 7.
54. Skinner to McNickle, Feb. 3, 1936, Correspondence esp. re *The Surrounded,* MP, NL. Her review of *The Surrounded* in *Booklist* 32 (April 1936): 233 echoed her letter to McNickle.
55. Dusenberry to McNickle, Mar. 30, 1936, General Correspondence, MP, NL.
56. Ibid, June 3, 1936.

CHAPTER THREE
1. Robert Brunhouse, *Pursuit of the Ancient Maya,* 128–67.

2. McNickle to Gates, Mar. 25, 1934, General Correspondence, MP, NL. According to Richard Slobodin in *The Métis of the Mackenzie District,* 15, "The Red River Métis commonly refer to themselves as 'breed' and 'half-breed' without apparent strain or pain." In Mourning Dove's *Cogewea,* the heroine's use of the word in the context of life on the Flathead Reservation suggests that it was commonly used there during McNickle's childhood.

3. McNickle to Gates, Mar. 25, 1934, General Correspondence, MP, NL.

4. Ibid.

5. Gates to McNickle, May 14, 1934, General Correspondence, MP, NL.

6. Ibid.

7. McNickle to Collier, draft, May 4, 1934, General Correspondence, MP, NL.

8. Gates to McNickle, May 14, 1934, ibid.

9. Gates to Collier, May 11, 1933 and Collier to Ickes, Jan. 18, 1934, entry 178, box 5, Office Files of Commissioner John Collier, NA, RG75 (hereafter cited as Collier Office Files, NA, RG75); Lawrence Kelly, "Anthropology and Anthropologists in the Indian New Deal," 9. Kelly suggests that Ruth Underhill was the first anthropologist to be appointed by Collier, but Gates's appointment would seem to predate that of Underhill by at least six months.

10. McNickle to Collier, May 25, 1934, General Correspondence, MP, NL.

11. McNickle to E. R. Burton, July 20, 1934, ibid.

12. Ibid. It is of note that McNickle makes no explicit comments in this letter on the nature of his own boarding school experience. See also Margaret Szasz, *Education and the American Indian,* 65.

13. McNickle to Gates, July 26, 1934, General Correspondence, MP, NL.

14. Gates to McNickle, Sept. 7, 1934, ibid.

15. Benjamin Lee Whorf, *Language, Thought and Reality,* edited and with an introduction by John B. Carroll. Carroll elaborates on what has become known as the Sapir-Whorf thesis. He states that among those who were most impressed with the relationship of language to cultural perceptions were Clyde Kluckhohn, Dorothea Leighton, and Laura Thompson, all of whom became associated in some way with the BIA.

16. McNickle to Gates, July 26, 1934, General Correspondence, MP, NL.

17. Gates to McNickle, Sept. 7, 1934, ibid.

18. "Indians in a Democratic Society," Feb. 26, 1959, unpublished address delivered by McNickle to the Conference on Indian Affairs in Canada, sponsored by the Welfare Council of Greater Winnipeg; copy in author's files.

19. Entry 178, box 5, Collier Office Files, NA, RG75.

20. McNickle to Collier, draft, May 4, 1934, General Correspondence, MP, NL. It is not clear that this draft is the letter McNickle actually sent to Collier.

21. Application for Employment, Oct. 21, 1935, McNickle Personnel File.

22. Ibid.; documents dated Oct. 22, 1935; Nov. 21, 1935; Feb. 17, 1936; and Mar. 16, 1936. McNickle was hired under Section 12 of the Indian Reorganization

Act, establishing the so-called Indian civil service. He was not covered by federal civil service until 1944, when he was appointed field representative.

23. McNickle to Rae, Sept. 27, 1936, General Correspondence, M P, N L. For the first accounting on *The Surrounded,* see Correspondence esp. re *The Surrounded,* M P, N L.

24. Ruth Rae to Joran McNickle, [Oct. 1936?], M P, N L. Joran translated three works by the Norwegian author Gosta of Geijerstam, all of which were published by E. P. Dutton and Company. They included *Northern Summer* (1937), *Storevik* (1938), and *Northern Winter* (1939).

25. Using her maiden name of Birkeland, Joran published an account of her trip as *Birchland: A Journey Home to Norway* (New York: E. P. Dutton & Co., 1939).

26. Antoinette McNickle Vogel, personal interview, July 23, 1986, Silver Spring, Md.; Katherine Simons, personal interview, June 5, 1987, Albuquerque, N. Mex.

27. McNickle Personnel File; George M. Weber, "Indians Employed in the Indian Service," *Indians at Work,* August 1938, 5.

28. Descriptions of McNickle's various responsibilities are included in his application for the position of chief of the tribal relations branch of the B I A, McNickle Personnel File; Graham Taylor, *The New Deal and American Indian Tribalism,* 37–38.

29. D'Arcy McNickle, "Hill 57," 19–21; see also D'Arcy McNickle, "We Go On from Here," 16.

30. Dusenberry, "Waiting for a Day," 39.

31. LaRouche replaced Mary Heaton Vorse, who had come under increasingly heavy fire for supposedly being a Communist. Her third husband, whom she had divorced, had been a member of the C P - U S A, and she was considered tainted. House Committee on Indian Affairs, *Wheeler-Howard Act, Exempt Certain Indians, Hearings on S.2103,* 76th Cong., 3rd sess., 1940, 160, 309–10 (hereafter known as House Comm. Hearings on S.2103). Quote is from Floyd LaRouche to John Collier, Aug. 25, 1938, reel 15, Collier Papers, microfilm, Special Collections, Zimmerman Library, University of New Mexico, Albuquerque (hereafter cited as Collier Papers, U N M).

32. Kelly, "Anthropology," 10–11. See also Taylor, *New Deal,* 37.

33. Taylor, *New Deal,* 12–13; Scudder Mekeel, "An Appraisal of the Indian Reorganization Act," 209–17; John Collier, "Collier Replies to Mekeel," *American Anthropologist* 46 (1944): 422–26.

34. Memo, McNickle to Collier, June 30, 1937, entry 178, box 15, Collier Office Files, N A, R G75. McNickle's suggestion was supported by H. Scudder Mekeel, the first director of the A A U. See D'Arcy McNickle, "Anthropology and the Indian Reorganization Act," 55.

35. Memo, McNickle to Collier, June 30, 1937, entry 178, box 15, Collier Office Files, N A, R G75.

36. Nancy Oestreich Lurie, "The Will-O'-the-Wisp of Indian Unity," 23; John Collier, Jr., foreword, in Lawrence C. Kelly, *Assault on Assimilation,* xv.

37. Kelly, *Assault on Assimilation,* 119–20; John Collier, *The Indians of the Americas,* 307.

38. Kenneth R. Philp, *John Collier's Crusade for Indian Reform,* 239–40; Laurence M. Hauptman, *The Iroquois and the New Deal,* 29.

39. Harold E. Fey and D'Arcy McNickle, *Indians and Other Americans,* 132–33.

40. D'Arcy McNickle, "A U.S. Indian Speaks," 10. In this article, which he described to Helen Peterson as "one of the best background statements I have written," McNickle said that assimilation is inevitable and that the problem lies in determining how it can be directed or accelerated (McNickle to Peterson, Mar. 18, 1954, box 19, Individual Correspondence, Smithsonian Archives). By the 1960s his position had changed and he came to believe that selective adaptation would lead to Indian survival. But he rarely echoed Collier's mystical approach to the subject.

41. Kelly, *Assault on Assimilation,* chaps. 6–10; Robert Berkhofer, Jr., *The White Man's Indian,* 185.

42. Hauptman, *The Iroquois and the New Deal,* 41–50; House Comm. Hearings on S.2103, 162.

43. "Report for Commissioner Collier from Mr. McNickle," c. Nov. 5, 1943, 2, Silvershirts of America, entry 178, box 15, R–S, Collier Office Files, NA, RG75.

44. House Comm. Hearings on S.2103, 157.

45. Ibid., 157.

46. Ibid.

47. House Comm. Hearings on S2103, 158–59, for the full text of McNickle's review. See D'Arcy McNickle, "The Straddle Between Cultures," 29–30, for the review.

48. House Comm. Hearings on S.2103, 157–58.

49. Ibid., 162.

50. Ibid., 160.

51. Ibid., 310–12.

52. Ibid., 315.

53. McNickle to Indiana University Press, "Author's Publicity Material," Sept. 19, 1970; copy in author's file.

54. Edwin Lieuwen, *United States Policy in Latin America,* 72–73.

55. House Comm. Hearings on S.2103, 93.

56. Houptman, *The Iroquois and the New Deal,* 41–50.

57. John Collier, "A Permanent Institute on American Indian Life," 1–7; Collier, *The Indians of the Americas,* 291–306.

58. Press Release, Dept. of Interior, Nov. 30, 1941, Studies-Research-General, Planning File, General, McCaskill Office Files, NA, RG75.

59. Senate Committee on Appropriations, *Interior Department Appropriations Bill for 1950, Part I, Hearings on HR 3838,* 81st Cong., 1st sess., 1949, 461.

60. Ibid.

61. McNickle to John W. Ford, July 27, 1974, General Correspondence, MP, NL.

CHAPTER FOUR

1. John Collier, *From Every Zenith,* 217–25. The Indian Personality, Education, and Research Project will hereafter be cited as the personality study.

2. Guide to the Papers of Robert J. Havighurst, *Handbook Series,* vol. 2, no. 30, National Anthropological Archives, Smithsonian Institution, Washington, D.C. (hereafter cited as Smithsonian Archives). The papers of Dorothea Leighton and Laura Thompson, in the same repository, also contain material related to this project.

3. Kelly, "Anthropology," 19–22.

4. Memorandum for the office, Dec. 30, 1941, Office Organization, Planning File, General, McCaskill Office Files, NA, RG75.

5. "Removal of Indian Office to Chicago Complete," *Indians at Work,* July–September, 1942, 7.

6. An undated carbon copy of "Memorandum ofUnderstanding between the Secretary of War, the Secretary of the Interior, and the Coordinator of the War Relocation Authority" is in box T–W, Collier Office Files, NA, RG75. Reel 25 of the Collier Papers, UNM, details the role of the BIA in developing the War Relocation Center at Poston, Colorado. See correspondence between March 1 and April 15.

7. McCaskill to Collier, Mar. 2, 1942, Internment of Japs on Indian Lands, part 1, box 17, entry 178, Collier Office Files, NA, RG75.

8. This agreement is in entry 178, WRA, box T–W, Collier Office Files, NA, RG75. This agreement revised the original Memorandum of March 18.

9. Collier to Ickes, July 9, 1943, Myer to Ickes, Sept. 16, 1943, Office Records of Assistant Commissioner William Zimmerman, 1935–48, NA, RG75; Alexander Leighton, *The Governing of Men,* 104, n. 12; Audrie Girdner and Anne Loftis, *The Great Betrayal,* 226–27.

10. McNickle's draft became the basis of an article by Carey McWilliams concerning the management of the relocation centers. See "Japanese Evacuation: Policy and Perspectives," 65–72.

11. Alexander Leighton, "The Psychiatric Approach in Problems of Community Management," Miscellaneous Records Relating to WRA, box 480, entry 178, NA, RG75.

12. Edward Spicer et al., *Impounded People.*

13. Collier to Beulah Head, Apr. 23, 1942, reel 25, Collier Papers, UNM; Collier to Laura Thompson, Apr. 24, 1942, ibid. Collier to John Provinse, June 19, 1942, ibid.

14. Collier to Guggenheim Foundation, Nov. 11, 1937, reel 15, Collier Papers, UNM. McNickle's second application was made on October 11, 1945. He did not receive a Guggenheim Fellowship until 1963.

15. Collier to Morris Rubin, editor of *Lafollette's Progress,* Dec. 10, 1943, reel 26, ibid. Collier referred to McNickle as "my associate here," and told Rubin, "He can write a better article than I ever could. He is a rather distinguished author."

16. As quoted by Donald Smith in "Now We Talk—You Listen," (Royal Ontario Museum, Toronto), August 1990; draft copy in author's file.

17. Kelly, "Anthropology," 19–20.

18. Laura Thompson, "Action Research among American Indians," 34–40.

19. W. Lloyd Warner to Collier, June 1942, Personality study, box 11, entry 178, Collier Office Files, NA, RG75.

20. D'Arcy McNickle, "Toward Understanding," 4.

21. Ibid., 6. Laura Thompson, in "Some Perspectives in Applied Anthropology," describes in detail the rationale for the project.

22. D'Arcy McNickle and Willard Beatty, "Science and the Future."

23. Personality Study, folder 4, box P, Collier Office Files, NA, RG75.

24. Collier to Paul Fejos, Nov. 3, 1944 and Collier to Laura Thompson, Oct. 21, 1943, box 12, Collier Office Files, NA, RG75.

25. Provinse to Thompson, May 15, 1947, ibid.; Kelly, "Anthropology," 23.

26. Laura Thompson wrote at least two articles about the personality project. See Thompson, "Some Perspectives," 12–16, and Thompson, "Action Research," 34–40.

    The following are publications that came out of the personality project: Laura Thompson and Alice Joseph, *The Hopi Way;* Clyde Kluckhohn and Dorothea Leighton, *The Navaho;* Gordon Macgregor, *Warriors without Weapons* (Chicago: University of Chicago Press, 1946), on the Sioux; Dorothea Leighton and Clyde Kluckhohn, *Children of the People;* Alice Joseph, Rosamond Spicer, and Jane Chesky, *The Desert People;* Laura Thompson, *Culture in Crisis;* and Dorothea Leighton and John Adair, *People of the Middle Place,* on the Zunis.

27. Edna A. Gerkin to Collier, Jan. 30, 1943, A. H. Leighton and D. C. Leighton folder, box 7, Collier Office Files, NA, RG75.

28. John Collier, in the foreword to Alexander H. Leighton and Dorothea Leighton, *The Navajo Door,* xiii–xv.

29. McNickle to Alexander Leighton, Apr. 24, 1943, box 7, Collier Office Files, NA, RG75.

30. Collier to Roger Scaife at Harvard Press, June 23, 1944, reel 26, Collier Papers, UNM. The cover was indeed handsome, with a centered embossed katchina figure in turquoise and red.

31. Milton S. Eisenhower, *The President Is Calling*, 123, 125, 111.

32. Dillon Myer, *Uprooted Americans*. For Myer's informal account of his years of government service, see "An Autobiography of Dillon Myer," oral history transcript, Bancroft Library, University of California, Berkeley, 1970, Oberlin College Library (hereafter cited as Myer, "Autobiography").

33. U.S. Department of Interior, War Relocation Authority, *Community Government in War Relocation Centers;* Leighton, *Governing of Men*. These books detail the main issues that were problematic during the formation of policy for the WRA. Collier noted McNickle's draft when he wrote to John Provinse, who had been appointed to head WRA's community services program: "The enclosed commentary on the Tentative Statement of Policy, by D'Arcy McNickle, deserves attention. McNickle is one of our most thoughtful people" (June 19, 1942, Collier Papers, UNM). McNickle contributed to several volumes produced by the government on the relocation experience, but they are without ascribed authorship.

34. Collier to Ickes, Sept. 13, 1942, reel 25, Collier Papers, UNM.

35. Collier to Langdon Warner, July 1, 1942, ibid.; diary, Sept. 9, 1942, MP, NL; Collier to Laura Thompson, Nov. 2, 1942, reel 25, Collier Papers, UNM.

36. A hearing on the Poston trouble was held in Los Angeles in May 1943. House Special Committee on Un-American Activities, *Investigation of Un-American Propaganda Activities in the United States, Report and Minority Views,* 78th Cong., 1st sess., 1943, vols. 15 and 16.

37. Michi Weglyn, *Years of Infamy*. Despite its title, Weglyn has, in the author's view, produced the most balanced account of the Japanese-American internment problems during World War II.

38. Collier to Laura Thompson, Dec. 14, 1942, reel 25, Collier Papers, UNM.

39. McNickle's memorandum for Mr. Zimmerman, n.d. [July ?, 1943], Office Records of Assistant Commissioner William Zimmerman, 1935–48, NA, RG 75.

40. Head to McNickle, Aug. 6, 1943, ibid.

41. Head to Collier, Aug. 11, 1943, ibid.

42. Ickes to Myer, Aug. 24, 1943, ibid.

43. Myer to Ickes, Sept. 16, 1943, ibid.; McNickle to Zimmerman, Oct. 8, 1943, ibid.

44. For the negotiations on the transfer of land and personnel after the BIA's withdrawal, see letters between Ickes and Myers dated August 24, September 16, and October 7, 1943, ibid. The final land tranfers are described in the Annual Report of the Commissioner of Indian Affairs, fiscal year ending June 30, 1945, 238.

45. Hazel Hertzberg, *The Search for an American Indian Identity,* 289–91.
46. Elizabeth Clark Rosenthal, "'Indian Interest Organizations' and the American Indian Community, 1882–1982," draft, February 1982, 52–53, copy in author's files; Taylor, *New Deal,* 146–47.
47. McNickle to Helen Maynor, Aug. 13, 1959, Individual Correspondence, box 19, series 4, Records of the National Congress of American Indians, Smithsonian Archives (hereafter cited as NCAI Records, Smithsonian Archives).
48. Fey and McNickle, *Indians and Other Americans,* 238–39.
49. McNickle to Helen Maynor, Aug. 13, 1959, Individual Correspondence, box 19, series 4, NCAI Records, Smithsonian Archives.
50. Ibid.
51. Lois E. Harlin, "The National Congress of American Indians," 20–22. See also box 1, Policies and Procedures, NCAI Records, Smithsonian Archives, for subsequent revisions of the NCAI constitution and by-laws.
52. McNickle to Helen Maynor, Aug. 13, 1959, NCAI Records, Smithsonian Archives. See also Peter Iverson, "Building toward Self-Determination," 165–68; Fey and McNickle, *Indians and Other Americans,* 239.

CHAPTER FIVE

1. O. J. Currie to author, Sept. 10, 1986.
2. Interview with Erma Walz (née Hicks), Apr. 8, 1985, Albuquerque, New Mexico.
3. "Snowfall" was from McNickle's new novel. Other pieces published in *Common Ground* at about the same time included "Afternoon on a Rock" and "Golden Myth."
4. McNickle spoke of the Hidatsa sacred bundle in an address before the Fifth Annual Spring Conference of the Missouri Archeological Society in 1940. His talk was printed in the *Missouri Archeologist,* the organization's newsletter, later that year; copy in author's file.
5. U.S. Dept. of Agriculture Press Release, Dec. 31, 1937, Office Records of Ass't. Commissioner William Zimmerman, Correspondence 1935–48, box M–P, NA, RG75. Quote is from "An Indian Thinks 'Sacred Bundle' Brought Too Much Rain," *Indians at Work,* September 1938, 11.
6. R. T. Bond to McNickle, May 12, 1944, Correspondence esp. re *The Surrounded,* MP, NL.
7. D'Arcy McNickle, *Indian Man,* 119; Oliver La Farge, *As Long As the Grass Shall Grow* (New York: Longmans, Green & Co., 1940); Collier, *The Indians of the Americas.*

8. Carey McWilliams, *The Education of Carey McWilliams,* 134; Collier to Adamic, Jan. 31, 1944, reel 26, frame 723, Collier Papers, UNM.

9. See Bernd C. Peyer, *The Singing Spirit,* for McNickle's short stories.

10. Fey and McNickle, *Indians and Other Americans,* 126–29; D'Arcy McNickle, *Native American Tribalism,* 152–54.

11. "Statement of Superior Accomplishment," July 28, 1946, McNickle Personnel File.

12. Ibid.; Oscar Chapman to McNickle, Aug. 15, 1946, McNickle Personnel File.

13. D'Arcy McNickle, *They Came Here First,* 9. McNickle condensed his sketch "Afternoon on a Rock" for the preface. See n. 3.

14. See preface of McNickle, *They Came Here First.*

15. Lewis Gannett, *New York Herald Tribune,* July 27, 1949; Anne Whitmore, *Library Journal* 74 (1949): 1098; Stanley Vestal, *Saturday Review of Literature,* October 15, 1949, 21; Paul Bestor, *Survey* 85 (December 1949) 695; Anne Whitmore, *Library Journal* 74 (1949): 1098; anonymous review, *Maryland News,* July 22, 1949, MP, NL; anonymous review, *Americas,* January 1951, 382–84.

16. Gabriel Menager to McNickle, Sept. 6, 1949, and Ruth Dishrow to McNickle, Sept. 5, 1949, General Correspondence, MP, NL.

17. Pierce to McNickle, Mar. 14, 1955, ibid.

18. Clyde Kluckhohn, review of *They Came Here First,* by D'Arcy McNickle, *New York Herald Tribune Book Review,* November 13, 1949, 30.

19. William N. Fenton, review of *They Came Here First,* by D'Arcy McNickle, *American Anthropologist,* 546–47.

20. American Anthropological Association to McNickle, Sept. 20, 1949, General Correspondence, MP, NL.

21. See D'Arcy McNickle, "Basis for a National Indian Policy," 3–12, and Imre Sutton, ed., *Irredeemable America,* 381.

22. Harvey D. Rosenthal, "Indian Claims and the American Conscience," 35–70; Felix S. Cohen, "The Erosion of Indian Rights, 1950–1953," 371; Felix S. Cohen, *The Legal Conscience,* esp. 264–72.

23. Nancy Oestreich Lurie, in the epilogue to Sutton, ed., *Irredeemable America,* 381.

24. Rupert Costo, ed., *Anthropology and the American Indian,* 56.

25. Nancy O. Lurie, in the epilogue to Sutton, *Irredeemable America,* 375; see also Nancy Oestreich Lurie, "The Indian Claims Commission," 100. See also McNickle's account of the passage of the Indian Claims Commission Act in Fey and McNickle, *Indians and Other Americans,* 104–6.

26. Ibid. Some archives of original tribal documents have been established and their material made available on a limited basis, but they are a far cry from what McNickle had envisioned originally as resulting from the Indian Claims Commission.

Notes to Pages 123–129

27. McNickle Personnel File; *Official Organizational Handbook,* U.S. Department of the Interior, 1949–1950, Office File of Assistant Commissioner John H. Provinse, 1946–50, NA, RG75. The chief of tribal relations was "responsible for the correlation of plans of Indian communities and of the Bureau; for providing technical advice in perfecting Indian community organization; and for obtaining prompt and sympathetic review of tribal ordinances and resolutions requiring Departmental or Bureau approval" (ibid.).

28. Clayton Koppes, "From New Deal to Termination," 556–57.

29. Ibid., 548–50.

30. McNickle, *Indian Man,* 109

31. McNickle, *They Came Here First,* 298. See also Wilcomb Washburn, "A Fifty-Year Perspective on the Indian Reorganization Act," 281.

32. D'Arcy McNickle, "A Battle Yet to Wage" (a contribution to the Institute on American Indian Assimilation conducted by the Association on American Indian Affairs, Washington, D.C., May 8, 9, and 10, 1952; copy in author's files).

33. McNickle, "Basis for a National Indian Policy," 3–12.

34. Clayton Koppes, "Oscar L. Chapman." See also Koppes, "From New Deal to Termination."

35. NCAI notes on Myer's confirmation hearing before the Senate Committee on Interior and Insular Affairs, April 10, 1950, box 72, series 16, NCAI Records, Smithsonian Archives. A transcript of the hearing was not published, but it is available on microfiche as "United States Senate Report of Proceedings, Committee on Interior and Insular Affairs, April 17, 1950."

36. Cohen, "The Erosion of Indian Rights." The Collier Papers, UNM, especially reel 43, contain numerous documents and letters prtinent to Myer's administration.

37. D'Arcy McNickle, "It's Almost Never Too Late," 227.

38. John Collier, "Memorandum on why Dillon Myer should not be reappointed as commissioner of Indian Affairs," Oct. 18, 1952, reel 43, Collier Papers, UNM; Felix S. Cohen, "The Erosion of Indian Rights," 383. Collier to McNickle, Aug. 21, 1951, reel 39, Collier Papers, UNM.

39. John Collier, *From Every Zenith,* 369.

40. Myer's denunciation of what he called a "piecemeal" approach to Indian self-government, that is, a gradual shift of responsibility, was spelled out in "Address by Dillon S. Myer, Commissioner of Indian Affairs, at the Eighth Annual Convention of the National Congress of Indian Affairs, St. Paul, Minnesota, July 25, 1951," reel 43, Collier Papers, UNM. See Nancy Oestreich Lurie, "Menominee Termination: From Reservation to Colony," 257–70, for an unhappy case history of the termination of one particular tribe.

41. Dillon S. Myer, *Uprooted Americans,* 342–43. In 1946 the Japanese-American Citizens League presented Myer with a citation in gratitude for his labor on their behalf.

42. McNickle described Myer's attitude in chapter 16, "The Dispossessed," of *Indians and Other Americans.*

43. Kenneth R. Philp, "Stride toward Freedom," 175–90.

44. Myer, "Autobiography," 170.

45. In one such instance, McNickle wrote in his diary for April 12–13, 1962 of his being at a loss for words. "But it was more a matter of being unable to make a plea. . . . I can never think fast enough or find the right words at such a time." For insight into his view of Myer, see Fey and McNickle, *Indians and Other Americans,* 122, 135–36, 150, and 156; McNickle, *Indian Man,* 159, 162–64, 177, and 189; and McNickle, "It's Almost Never Too Late."

46. Tom Holm, "Fighting a White Man's War," 69–81. See also D'Arcy McNickle, "The Indian Tests the Mainstream," 279. An unidentified clipping from the Alumni Files at the University of Montana, dated November 1, 1948, cites McNickle as saying that the only future for thousands of Indians is to leave their reservations. This was hardly an unqualified endorsement of termination, however. "Such legislation, conceived in good intentions, may completely wreck this country's policy of respecting Indian ownership and paying for what we take," he said.

47. William J. van den Heuvel, Esq., "Arrow, Inc., and the National Congress of American Indians: An Appraisal of their Relationship," 1958, Arrow, Inc., and NCAI, box 74, NCAI Records, Smithsonian Archives (hereafter cited as van den Heuvel, "Arrow, Inc.," NCAI Records, Smithsonian Archives).

48. Ruth Bronson to N. B. Johnson, Aug. 8, 1951, Individual Correspondence, box 20, ibid.

49. Ruth Bronson to Commissioner Dillon Myer, May 11, 1951, box 3, Desk File, Office of Commissioner of Indian Affairs, Commissioner Dillon S. Myer, NA, RG75.

50. Department of Interior Information Press Release, Sept. 5, 1951, series 1, box 295, folder 11, Jesuit Archives, Bureau of Catholic Indian Missions, Marquette University, Milwaukee, Wisconsin (hereafter cited as Jesuit Archives, Marquette University); Willard Beatty to Father Tennelly, S.J., Sept. 4, 1951, ibid.; Szasz, *Education and the American Indian,* 122.

51. This is from an untitled manuscript that appears to be McNickle's address to the 1952 NCAI convention, 5, box 3, Correspondences, Towner/McNickle Papers, Newberry Library, Chicago, Illinois (hereafter cited as Towner/McNickle Papers, NL).

CHAPTER SIX

1. "American Indian Development Community and Home Improvement Demonstration Workshops, July 13–18, 1953," series 1, box 300, folder 44, Jesuit Archives, Marquette University.

2. D'Arcy McNickle, "The Crownpoint Project in Health Education: A Summary Report," n.d. [1955?]; copy given to author by John Adair (hereafter cited as McNickle, "The Crownpoint Project").

3. James F. Canan, "Grazing District 7: A Factual Survey of Conditions among the Navajo Indians Living Off the Reservation in New Mexico," Window Rock, Arizona, 1950, as cited in D'Arcy McNickle and Viola Pfrommer, source notes, chapter two, "Dine Txah: A Community Experience," MP, NL (hereafter cited as "Dine Txah," MP, NL). This 250-page manuscript is the report of McNickle's Crownpoint Project. It is currently being prepared for publication by Dr. Jennie Joe, a Navajo who has interviewed many of the people still living on the reservation who worked with the Navajo Development Committee.

4. Peter Iverson, *The Navajo Nation*, 47–50.

5. D'Arcy McNickle, "The Indian in American Society," 68–77.

6. Alexander and Dorothea Leighton, *The Navajo Door*, esp. chaps. 5–7; D'Arcy McNickle and Viola Pfrommer, "It Takes Two to Communicate." See also John Adair, Kurt W. Deuschle, and Clifford R. Barnett, *The People's Health*, 31. Adair, who was working with the Cornell-Navajo Field Health Research program, was unaware at the time of McNickle's role in the publication of the Leightons' book, but he much appreciated the contribution AID was making to the understanding of the process of health education (personal interview with John Adair, Gallup, New Mexico, Oct. 19, 1989).

7. Personal interview with Robert Young, Shiprock, New Mexico, Oct. 16, 1990.

8. McNickle to Ruth [Bronson?], July 13, 1952, box 19, series 4, Individual Correspondence, NCAI Records, Smithsonian Archives.

9. Donald Parman, *The Navajos and the New Deal*, esp. chaps. 3, 6. Parman gives a detailed account of all aspects of Collier's program for the Navajos, with a balanced assessment of their impact. See also Collier, *From Every Zenith*, 247–58 and Taylor, *New Deal*, 126–30.

10. Charles R. Griffith, "Crownpoint and Shiprock: Two Eastern Navajo Agency Communities and Their Environs, Past, Present, and Future," San Juan Basin Regional Uranium Study, Working Paper no. 52, U.S. Department of the Interior, Sept. 1980, 10–11.

11. Herbert C. Stacher, "Rebuttal of a book by Richard Wetherill: Anasazi, by Frank McNitt, 1964," 8, Special Collections, Zimmerman Library, UNM. See also Herbert C. Stacher, "History of Crownpoint, New Mexico, 1910 to 1935," 1986, Fellin Public Library, Gallup, New Mexico. This manuscript contains some excellent photographs of the early school and hospital.

12. Kenneth Philp, *Indian Self-Rule*, 86; Parman, *Navajo and the New Deal*, chap. 6; Collier, *The Indians of the Americas*, 279.

13. Memo, Collier to Ickes, July 29, 1937, J. C. Morgan Activities, box 8, Collier Office File, NA, RG75.

14. Adair, Deuschle, and Barnett, *The People's Health,* 26.
15. McNickle to Ruth [Bronson?], July 13, 1952, box 19, series 4, Individual Correspondence, NCAI Records, Smithsonian Archives.
16. Personal interview with Antoinette Vogel, Silver Spring, Maryland, July 16, 1986.
17. Andy Cogswell to D'Arcy McNickle, Aug. 8, 1949, University of Montana Alumni Files, Missoula, Montana; Joran Birkeland to Andy Cogswell, Nov. 7, 1949, ibid. The announcement of Toni's marriage is also in this file.
18. Personal interview with Antoinette Vogel, Silver Spring, Maryland, July 16, 1986.
19. McNickle to Ruth [?], July 13, 1952, box 19, NCAI Records, Smithsonian Archives.
20. Don Owens to Lawrence W. Towner, Dec. 1, 1980, Towner/McNickle Papers, NL. Owens was Viola Pfrommer's brother-in-law. He sent a brief biographical sketch of Viola to Towner at the Newberry Library after her death. See also a reference to a letter from Evelyn Robin to McNickle in his diary entry for January 12, 1953.
21. Diary, Feb. 5, 1953.
22. Ibid.
23. Diary, May 12, June 20–23, 1953.
24. Dr. Arthur Warner to author, March 1987. Dr. Warner was chief medical officer at the Crownpoint Hospital from 1955 to 1957.
25. Personal interviews with Charles Griffith, Albuquerque, New Mexico, on Aug. 23, 1985 and subsequent dates.
26. McNickle to Walter Taylor, Mar. 4, 1962, General Correspondence, MP, NL.
27. Iverson, *Navajo Nation,* 154–60; McNickle to Pfrommer, Feb. 23, 1955, Correspondence with Viola (1953–1968) MP, NL; Mary Carroll Nelson, *Annie Wauneka,* 47–58; diary, Aug. 3, 1956; personal interview with Arlene Hobson, Albuquerque, New Mexico, June 28, 1987.
28. McNickle, "The Crownpoint Project," 7–8; McNickle to Pfrommer, Feb. 23, 1955, Correspondence with Viola (1953–1968), MP, NL; McNickle and Pfrommer, "It Takes Two to Communicate"; personal interview with Annie Dodge Wauneka, Gallup, New Mexico, Oct. 19, 1989. According to John Adair, Pfrommer and McNickle "played an important part not only in developing an understanding of modern medicine in that community, but also in being instrumental in the calling of annual conferences which did so much to further more effective communications between the Navajo patients and the staffs in the off-reservation contract sanatoria" Adair, Deuschle, and Barnett, *The People's Health,* 244, nn. 3 and 4.
29. Dr. Frederick Margolis, M.D., to author, Oct. 15, 1987.
30. In "Dine Txah," MP, NL, which was written as a case study in anthropology, McNickle followed standard professional practice and changed the names of

the people involved. John Perry became John Begay. McNickle included biographical information on Perry in chapter 8 of "Dine Txah." There is some suggestion in McNickle's papers that he was considering writing Perry's biography.

31. "Dine Txah," 44, MP, NL.

32. A parallel study in community development was in process at the same time (1952–62) among the Vicos Indians in Peru, but there the outsiders offered concrete solutions to problems the people faced. The anthropologists, from Cornell University, were actively involved in "directed change." At Crownpoint, McNickle refused to assume that he had a better way of doing things. It was for the people themselves to determine what was better for them. For Nancy O. Lurie's definition and description of action anthropology, see Costo, *Anthropology and the American Indian*. McNickle was a participant at this symposium. See also Hortense Powdermaker, *Stranger and Friend: The Way of an Anthropologist* (New York: W. W. Norton & Co., 1966), 285–311; Sol Tax, "The Fox Project," 17–19; Wilcomb Washburn, "Ethical Perspectives in North American Ethnology," 50–64; and Laura Thompson, "Is Applied Anthropology Helping to Develop a Science of Man?" 277–87.

33. Collier, *The Indians of the Americas,* 278–79.

34. McNickle to Dr. A. R. Stunkard, Sept. 26, 1955, General Correspondence, MP, NL.

35. "Dine Txah," 47–49, 140–47, 58, MP, NL. Trading posts in the early days of the reservation often had guest hogans adjacent to the premises, where overnight visitors could stay. Such an arrangement seemed satisfactory to all concerned. See Frank McNitt, *The Indian Traders*, 78. A food distribution program that had been abandoned earlier was resumed in 1955 because of Pfrommer's intercessions (personal interview with Lillian Coy, Santa Fe, New Mexico, Mar. 18, 1986). Coy was a case worker with the New Mexico Department of Public Welfare and assisted in the distribution of food at Crownpoint through the Surplus Commodity Program, Department of Agriculture.

36. McNickle to Helen Peterson, Mar. 18, 1954, box 19, series 4, Individual Correspondence, NCAI Records, Smithsonian Archives.

37. McNickle to Helen Peterson, Oct. 28, 1957, ibid.; diary, Aug. 13, 1960.

38. McNickle to Pfrommer, Aug. 26, 1953, Correspondence with Viola (1953–1968), MP, NL; McNickle, American Indian Development's "Program for the Eastern Navajo Indians at Crownpoint New Mexico," 1955, 3, McNickle/Towner Papers, NL. See also Adair, Deuschle, and Barnett, *The People's Health,* 244, n. 4.

39. Note, box 19, series 4, NCAI Records, Smithsonian Archives.

40. McNickle to Pfrommer, Nov. 18, 1955, Correspondence with Viola (1953–1968), MP, NL.

41. See Adair, Deuschle, and Barnett, *The People's Health,* for a description of the Cornell-Navajo Field Health Research Project.

42. Dr. Arthur Warner to author, March 1987; "Dine Txah," 103, 104, M P, N L. Several of Dr. Warner's siblings were directors of the summer work camps.

43. Dr. Arthur Warner to author, March 1987.

44. Pfrommer to McNickle, Dec. 5, 1954, Correspondence with Viola (1953–1968) M P, N L.

45. Pfrommer to McNickle, Feb. 18, 1956, Correspondence with Viola (1953–1968), M P, N L. Such difficulties are also alluded to in McNickle's diary of the time and in the N C A I papers at the Smithsonian Archives.

46. Warner to author, March 1987; interviews with Charles Griffith, Albuquerque, New Mexico, 1986–88.

47. McNickle to Pfrommer, Nov. 18, 1955, Correspondence with Viola, (1953–1968), M P, N L; Pfrommer to McNickle, Feb. 18, 1956, ibid.; ibid, Sept. 7, 1954; ibid.

48. Carl Tjerandson, *Education for Citizenship,* 33, 41. The Emil Schwartzhaupt Foundation's executive director has summarized and evaluated the various programs sponsored by the foundation in this single volume.

49. Joseph Garry to Louis Bruce, Jan. 3, 1957, Sherman folder, box 21, series 4, Individual Correspondence, N C A I Records, Smithsonian Archives, and van den Heuvel, "Arrow, Inc.," ibid.

50. McNickle to Pfrommer, Feb. 7, 1957, Correspondence with Viola (1953–1968) M P, N L. The corporation's dissolution date was furnished by the Colorado Secretary of State's office to author, Apr. 1, 1987. For information on the N C A I Fund, see Helen Peterson to "Dear Friend," Apr. 24, 1958, box 5, Chronological Correspondence, 1949–64, N C A I Records, Smithsonian Archives. This solicitation letter was sent to members of the American Anthropological Association.

51. Tjeransden, *Education for Citizenship,* 26.

52. "Dine Txah," 197–98, M P, N L. In 1957, when the Navajo Tribal Council authorized the construction of twelve new community centers across the reservation, Crownpoint was to serve as a model. Needless to say, McNickle was delighted.

53. As quoted in Tjerandson, *Education for Citizenship,* 37.

54. Iverson, *Navajo Nation,* 78.

55. "Dine Txah," 188, M P, N L.

56. Ibid., 194–96.

57. Ibid., 207–10. McNickle himself was not opposed to the use of peyote for ceremonial purposes. For his position on the use of peyote, see his article "Peyote and the Indian," 220–29.

58. "Dine Txah," 234–36, M P, N L.

59. Ibid., 227–28.

60. Nancy Lurie, "The Contemporary American Indian Scene," in *North American Indians in Historical Perspective,* by Eleanor Burke Leacock and Nancy Oestreich Lurie, 439; McNickle, *Indian Man,* 164–66; idem, *Native American Tribalism,* 105–6; Philp, *Indian Self-Rule,* 17.
61. Philp, *Indian Self-Rule,* 17.
62. Vine Deloria, Jr., ed., *Of Utmost Good Faith,* 208–13; "Emergency Conference of American Indians on Legislation," Washington, D.C., February 25–28, 1954, series 9, NCAI Records, Smithsonian Archives; Burt, *Tribalism in Crisis,* 107ff.
63. Joint Committee on Interior and Insular Affairs, Subcommittee on Indian Affairs, *Termination of Federal Supervision over Certain Tribes of Indians, Part 7, Hearings Pursuant to Joint Resolution 108, on S.2750 and HR 7319,* 83rd Cong., 2nd sess. See also McNickle, *Native American Tribalism,* 103–12, the updated and revised version of *The Indian Tribes of the United States,* Burt, *Tribalism in Crisis,* 22–23, 36–38.
64. Roma McNickle to Helen Peterson, Nov. 14, 1954, box 19, series 4, Individual Correspondence, NCAI Records, Smithsonian Archives. Newspaper clippings in the Alumni Association Files, University of Montana, Missoula, give accounts of McNickle's trips to that state. There is no indication of the source of the clippings.
65. McNickle's report to the NCAI annual convention, Phoenix, Arizona, 1953, audio tape 114, NCAI Records, Smithsonian Archives. In this recording McNickle's respiratory problems are evident.
66. "Dine Txah," 212, MP, NL.
67. Diary, Feb. 2, 1961. McNickle's daughter described the ring as his favorite. It disappeared shortly after his death.
68. "Dine Txah," 237–40, 243.
69. As quoted in Tjerandson, *Education for Citizenship,* 30.
70. "Dine Txah," 244, MP, NL.
71. Ibid., 178.
72. Ibid., 242.
73. "1966 Workshop Report," box 5, Towner/McNickle Papers, NL. This report contains the most complete statement of McNickle's understanding of the problems of Indian leadership.

CHAPTER SEVEN
1. Alfonso Ortiz, in the afterword to D'Arcy McNickle, *Runner in the Sun,* 236.
2. McNickle, *They Came Here First,* 48; McNickle, *Runner in the Sun,* ix–x.
3. Joseph Campbell, *The Hero with a Thousand Faces,* 30. According to Alfonso Ortiz, McNickle's library contained many volumes of folklore, including those

of Joseph Campbell. After he died, most of his books were donated to the Navajo Community College in Tsaile, Arizona.

4. Ibid., 30.

5. Purdy, *Word Ways,* 97.

6. Ortiz, afterword to *Runner in the Sun,* 243–45.

7. Lawrence Lindley, *Indian Truth* 31 (Winter 1954): 8; Learned T. Bulman, *Saturday Review of Literature,* November 13, 1954, 90; Maxon, *Library Journal,* December 15, 1944, 2501; A. LaVonne Brown Ruoff, *American Indian Literatures,* 72–73.

8. McNickle, "The Indian in American Society," 73–74. See also Parker, "D'Arcy McNickle."

9. Harold Fey to author, Feb. 16, 1989. See also Harold Fey, *Indian Rights and American Justice.*

10. McNickle to Collier, June 20, 1958, reel 57, Collier Papers, UNM.

11. *Indians and Other Americans* folder, box 20, series 4, Individual Correspondence, NCAI Records, Smithsonian Archives; D'Arcy McNickle, "United States Indian Affairs, 1953," 263–73.

12. Fey and McNickle, *Indians and Other Americans,* 197–200.

13. Ibid., 200.

14. Harold Fey to author, Feb. 8, 1989. Fey loaned the author his files on this collaboration.

15. Richard L. Neuberger, "A Senator Surveys the Land of the Braves," *Saturday Review,* May 9, 1959, 14–15.

16. Angie Debo to Helen Peterson, May 23, 1959, and June [?], 1959, series 4, box 17, Individual Correspondence, NCAI Records, Smithsonian Archives. Although no correspondence exists today between Debo and McNickle, they were familiar with each other's work. McNickle had read Debo's *And Still the Waters Run* for Collier when it was first submitted for publication in 1936 (Suzanne H. Schrems and Cynthia J. Wolff, "Politics and Libel," 191–92).

17. John Rainer to Helen Peterson, May 29, 1959, series 4, box 17, Individual Correspondence, NCAI Records, Smithsonian Archives. Box 20 of this collection also contains additional letters with positive responses to the book.

18. Roma McNickle, *The Changing West.*

19. Helen Fee to author, Feb. 9, 1987. See also Roma to Helen Peterson, Apr. 23, 1954, Individual Correspondence, box 4, NCAI Records, Smithsonian Archives.

20. Philomene to her granddaughter, Helen, and family, Aug. 23, 1962; copy to author from O. J. Currie.

21. Interview with Katherine Simons, Albuquerque, New Mexico, June 6, 1987. Simons was Roma's classmate at Grinnell College, where Roma was Phi Beta Kappa. Interview with Antoinette McNickle Vogel, Silver Spring, Maryland, July 15, 1986.

22. Donald and Florette Owen to Lawrence W. Towner, Dec. 1, 1980, Towner/ McNickle Papers, NL; interview with Doralene Bunting, Albuquerque, New Mexico, Dec. 9, 1986.

23. McNickle to Pfrommer, Dec. 19, 1954, Correspondence with Viola (1953– 1968), MP, NL; also, Pfrommer to McNickle, Dec. 5, 1954, ibid.

24. See, generally, Correspondence with Viola (1953–1968), MP, NL, and McNickle's diaries for this period.

25. McNickle to Pfrommer, Dec. 18, 1962, ibid.

26. Personal interview with Antoinette Vogel, Silver Spring, Maryland, July 16, 1986 and discussion with Mary Collier, wife of John Collier, Albuquerque, New Mexico, fall 1988. D'Arcy and Roma had spent some time with the Colliers at the summer home of Dorothea and Alexander Leighton in Nova Scotia in 1948, and Mary Collier recalled much tension between them then. Toni Vogel's comments suggested the same.

27. Personal interview with Elizabeth Clark Rosenthal, Santa Fe, New Mexico, June 28, 1987. See also Elizabeth Clark Rosenthal, "'Indian Interest Organizations' and the American Indian Community, 1882–1982," 72, unpublished draft, 1982, in author's file.

28. Helen Peterson to Pascal Sherman, Sept. 27, 1957, box 21, Roe Cloud, series 4, NCAI Records, Smithsonian Archives.

29. Rosalie H. Wax, "A Brief History and Analysis of the Workshops on American Indian Affairs Conducted for American Indian College Students, 1956–1960, together with a Study of Current Attitudes and Activities of Those Students," October 1961, 3, Workshops on American Indian Affairs, box 74, series 17, NCAI Records, Smithsonian Archives (hereafter cited as Wax, "Workshops"). Wax later wrote of her work at Tule Lake during World War II in *Doing Fieldwork: Warnings and Advice* (Chicago: University of Chicago Press, 1971).

30. Wax, "Workshops," 2.

31. Ibid.

32. Ibid., 8.

33. McNickle to Dr. Frederick Wacker, Monteith College, Feb. 1, 1975, General Correspondence, MP, NL.

34. Wax, "Workshops," 14–15.

35. Ibid., 10.

36. Ibid.

37. Tjerandson, *Education for Citizenship,* 687. See also ibid., 27–44 and 594–655 for an evaluation of the Crownpoint Project, based on McNickle's periodic and final reports.

38. The NCAI Records in the Smithsonian Archives and the Towner/McNickle Papers at the Newberry Library both contain a number of porposals for leadership training programs and follow-up studies, none of which were successful in raising the necessary funding.

39. The most comprehensive account of the American Indian Chicago Conference is Nancy Oestreich Lurie's, "The Voice of the American Indian," 478–500. Specific documents are in the NCAI Records, boxes 74 and 75, Smithsonian Archives. See also Omer C. Stewart, "The Indians in Chicago," 9–14.
40. Telephone interview with Sol Tax, Chicago, Illinois, July 8, 1986.
41. Vine Deloria, Jr., *Of Utmost Good Faith,* 216–19. Deloria declared that AICC's "Declaration of Indian Purpose" was a "mere formality" and that it echoed various resolutions passed by NCAI conventions in the late 1950s. He was correct in part. McNickle had had a role in writing many of those earlier resolutions, and he incorporated some sections of them verbatim. But the "Declaration of Indian Purpose" went far beyond the earlier resolutions and reflected the views of a much larger number of American Indians.
42. *Gallup* (N. Mex.) *Navajo Times,* April 19, 1961; Form letter to "Dear ....," from Gerald Wilkinson, NIYC Director, n.d., folder 4, box 136, Sol Tax Papers, Regenstein Library, University of Chicago.
43. Nancy O. Lurie to author, July 23, 1988.
44. McNickle to William Zimmerman, July 11, 1961, Towner/McNickle Papers, NL.
45. Stan Steiner, *The New Indians.* Steiner described the founding of the National Indian Youth Council in August 1960 (his mistaken date) in Gallup, New Mexico. He echoed Wax's concern about college dropouts, with the same diagnosis (Ibid., 32), and described the caucus of Indian college students at the Chicago Conference in 1961 (ibid., 32). According to Alfonso Ortiz, NIYC expanded at that time from the Southwest Regional Indian Youth Council, of which he was a member. SRIYC was organized in 1955 under the aegis of the Southwest American Indian Association (interviews with Alfonso Ortiz, Sept. 19, 1988 and Oct. 23, 1990).
46. Information on the founding of NIYC is in folder 4, box 136, Sol Tax Papers, Regenstein Library, University of Chicago.
47. Washburn, "Ethical Perspectives," 55–56. See Lurie, "The Voice of the American Indian," 481–82, for a discussion of action anthropology as it related to the conference.
48. Lurie, "The Voice of the American Indian."
49. Diary, end of 1961.
50. McNickle to Sol Tax, Dec. 24, 1962, Sol Tax File, MP, NL; McNickle's proposal for the Guggenheim Fellowship is in "Vita" folder, MP, NL.
51. McNickle and Pfrommer returned for a last visit to Crownpoint in 1969 to authorize transfer of a small bank balance from NDC's account to the Crownpoint chapter. John Perry had died, but they met once again with Manuelito, who was so moved by their visit that he cried (diary, July 24, 1969).
52. McNickle to John Collier, Nov. 9, 1964, reel 57, Collier Papers, UNM.

53. Several letters from Vi during this time reflect her encouragement in response to D'Arcy's pessimism. See Correspondence with Viola (1953–1968), MP, NL.

54. Vine Deloria, Jr., *Custer Died for Your Sins,* 90–91. Emphasis is Deloria's. Clyde Warrior was one of Deloria's angry friends, who succumbed to the ravages of alcohol in 1968. Warrior had been a workshop participant of much promise, and McNickle was deeply saddened by his death. When Murray Wax wrote to tell him of it, McNickle responded:

> I, too, had hoped that the [John Hay Whitney] fellowship—and the vote of confidence which that represented—might turn the trick of encouraging the guy to take a serious interest in his potentialities. The John Hay Whitney committee was willing to take the gamble, even though the record and the prognosis were on the gloomy side. About the only real thing going for us was the knowledge that you and Bob Thomas were on his side and might pull him through.
>
> Anyhow, it was certainly worth the effort, whatever the ultimate outcome.

(McNickle to Murray L. Wax, Mar. 1, 1968; copy in author's file.)

55. McNickle to Kenneth Porter, Feb. 6, 1974, General Correspondence, MP, NL. The anthropology profession responded vigorously to Deloria's "Manifesto" at its 1970 annual meeting in San Diego. See Costo, *Anthropology and the American Indian.* McNickle attended this session on November 20, 1970.

56. McNickle to Collier, Jan. 12, 1963, reel 57, Collier Papers, UNM.

57. McNickle to Dr. Frederick Wacker, Feb. 1, 1975, General Correspondence, MP, NL. See also Shirley Hill Witt and Stan Steiner, eds. *The Way,* 108–13.

58. McNickle to Pfrommer, Apr. 13, 1962, Correspondence with Viola (1953–1968), MP, NL.

59. Robert V. Dumont, Jr., to author, Apr. 4, 1990.

60. McNickle, *Native American Tribalism,* 119. See also tape 303, transcribed, 16–19, Navajo Series, Doris Duke Project, Special Collections, Zimmerman Library, UNM. Other tapes in the Navajo Series also discuss community development and leadership training as these topics pertain to other parts of the reservation.

61. McNickle, *Native American Tribalism,* 119.

62. Washburn, "Ethical Perspectives," 56.

CHAPTER EIGHT

1. Van de Mark to McNickle, 1963, reel 58, Collier Papers, UNM.

2. Diary, Apr. 12, 1963. See also Anderson to Pfrommer, Aug. 1, 1966, box 5, Towner/McNickle Papers, NL.

3. Alvin Josephy, Jr., to author, Nov. 11, 1986.
4. McNickle to Pfrommer, Oct. 15, 1965, box IIA-13, Towner/McNickle Papers, NL. Oliver La Farge's papers have been donated to the University of Texas, Austin.
5. McNickle to John Warner, Dec. 11, 1971, General Correspondence, MP, NL; ibid.
6. McNickle, *Indian Man,* 69; Writings, La Farge Biography I, Notes, MS Draft, MP, NL. See also McNickle, *Indian Man,* 204 and 210.
7. Ibid., 54.
8. Ibid., 207.
9. Writings, La Farge Biography I, Notes, MS Draft, MP, NL; McNickle, *Indian Man,* 102.
10. McNickle to Pam Gragun, Feb. 15, 1969, General Correspondence, MP, NL; McNickle to Royal Hassrick, Mar. 16, 1969, ibid.; and McNickle to Sol Tax, Aug. 14, 1968, Sol Tax File, MP, NL discuss McNickle's difficulties in writing the biography. For reference to Smythe's correspondence to McNickle, see McNickle to Sol Tax, Jan. 5, 1966, ibid.
11. McNickle to Sol Tax, Jan. 5, 1966, General Correspondence, MP, NL.
12. Omer Stewart to Dallas Smythe, Jan. 14, 1966. A number of letters were loaned to author by Dr. Stewart.
13. These quotations are from the material loaned to the author by Omer Stewart which was returned to Stewart and subsequently donated to the McNickle Papers at the Newberry Library.
14. Ibid.
15. Richard Pope to author, June 23, 1986. Smythe is now at Simon Fraser University in British Columbia. The author is indebted to Pope for relevant information in this chapter regarding McNickle's career at Regina.
16. Diary, Aug. 7, 1966.
17. McNickle to Sol Tax, Mar. 8, 1966, and May 9, 1967, Sol Tax File, MP, NL.
18. McNickle to Rolland Wright, Oct. 16, 1966; copy in author's file.
19. Richard Pope to author, June 23, 1986.
20. Richard Pope to author, June 27, 1991, and June 23, 1986. For a description of the "instructional committees," see Smythe to Stewart, Jan. 7, 1966, Omer Stewart Papers, now with the McNickle Papers at the Newberry Library.
21. Pfrommer to McNickle, Apr. 9, 1967, Correspondence with Viola (1953–1968), MP, NL; McNickle to Tax, May 9, 1967, General Correspondence, MP, NL.
22. Diary, July 23, 1967.
23. Interview with Antoinette McNickle Vogel, Silver Spring, Maryland, July 23, 1986.
24. Diary, Aug. 1967.
25. Leacock and Lurie, *North American Indians,* preface.

286   *Notes to Pages 211–218*

26. Nancy O. Lurie to author in Reader's Report, Apr. 19, 1988.

27. Leacock and Lurie, *North American Indians,* 442, 453, 464–65.

28. Diary, May 1967.

29. Richard Pope provided the author with printed material describing the departmental offerings and McNickle's duties at the University. This material has been copied and is now at the Newberry Library. For discussion of his progress on the biography, see McNickle to Pam Cragun, Feb. 15, 1969. He wrote, "The book moves slowly . . . since it involves so many interruptions of putting together bits and pieces from correspondence, published material, etc." (General Correspondence, M P, N L).

30. McNickle to Pam Cragun, Feb. 15, 1969, General Correspondence, M P, N L. In this letter McNickle described Cragun as "one of the very few really close friends I have" (ibid.). Cragun was in the hospital when McNickle wrote this letter to his wife. Cragun died on March 31, 1969.

31. Louis M. Rabinowitz Foundation to McNickle, May 22, 1969, General Correspondence, M P, N L.

32. McNickle to John Warner, Dec. 11, 1971, General Correspondence, M P, N L.

33. The most perceptive review of *Indian Man* was written by John Clifton for the *Saturday Review,* October 23, 1971, 32, 98. A National Book Committee press release, Mar. 27, 1972, was included in information furnished to the author by Indiana University Press. McNickle's biography competed with Barbara Tuchman's *Stillwell and the American Experience in China, 1911–1945* (New York: Macmillan, 1971) and Joseph P. Lash's *Eleanor and Franklin* (New York: W. W. Norton, 1971).

34. Lesser to McNickle, Feb. 7, Mar. 18, and Mar. 19, 1972, General Correspondence, M P, N L.

35. See Lesser to McNickle, Feb. 2, 1972, General Correspondence, M P, N L; McNickle to Lesser, Mar. 14, 1972, ibid.; and Lesser to McNickle, Mar. 18, 1972 and Mar. 19, 1972, ibid.

36. The events of this period are described in McNickle's diaries and also in the author's interview with Arlene Hobson (who replaced Pfrommer as the American Indian Advisor at the University of Arizona, Tuscon in 1969) on June 14, 1987.

37. Vi's reluctance was described by Doralene Bunting in an interview with the author on December 9, 1986.

38. Richard Pope to author, June 23, 1986.

39. The "Statement of the Government of Canada on Indian Policy," by the Minister of Indian Affairs and Northern Development, Ottawa, 1969, is discussed in McNickle, *Native American Tribalism,* 145–50.

40. Pope to author, June 23, 1986.

41. McNickle to Michael Harrison, Dec. 18, 1971, General Correspondence, M P, N L.

42. McNickle, *Native American Tribalism,* 117.
43. Fish-ins were a form of protest over violation of fishing rights guaranteed by treaty to several Northwest tribes. See Frederick E. Hoxie, *Indians in American History,* 265–66. 290–91.
44. McNickle, *Native American Tribalism,* x–xii.
45. Ibid., 125.
46. McNickle to Brian A. Rosborough, President of Education Expeditions International, n.d., box II B, 7, Towner/McNickle Papers, MP, NL.
47. McNickle to "Lu" Spahn, Aug. 12, 1976, General Correspondence, MP, NL.
48. See Purdy, *Word Ways,* for an in-depth study of the development of all of McNickle's novels. *Wind from an Enemy Sky* is the subject of chapter four. Although the present author disagrees with Purdy's overall interpretation, he (Purdy) does offer valuable insight into the long evolution of this novel. There are several partial manuscripts of the novel in the McNickle Papers.
49. Roger Dunsmore, "Reflections on *Wind from an Enemy Sky,*" 28–57; Purdy, *Word Ways,* 112; Birgit Hans, "Surrounded: The Fiction of D'Arcy McNickle," unpublished master's thesis, University of Arizona, Tucson, 1988; McNickle, "Snowfall."
50. McNickle to Douglas Latimer, Mar. 23, 1977, General Correspondence, MP, NL; William Kittredge, review of *Wind from an Enemy Sky,* by D'Arcy McNickle, *Missoula Missoulian,* March 3, 1979.
51. Senate Subcommittee on Appropriations, *Hearing before a Subcommittee on Appropriations, on H.R. 4805,* 79th Cong., 1st sess., was one of the hearings on Garrison Dam at which McNickle appeared.
52. McNickle to Latimer, July 6, 1976, General Correspondence, MP, NL.
53. McNickle, *Wind from an Enemy Sky,* 30.
54. Ibid., 1 and 6. An early title of the story was "Where Anger Died."
55. Ibid., 91.
56. Ibid., 125.
57. Purdy, *Word Ways,* 132.
58. McNickle, *Wind from an Enemy Sky,* 97–99.
59. Ibid., 197.
60. Douglas Latimer to McNickle, Dec. 30, 1976, General Correspondence, MP, NL.
61. Purdy, *Word Ways,* 119.
62. Douglas Latimer to McNickle, Dec. 30, 1976, General Correspondence, MP, NL.
63. McNickle to Douglas Latimer, July 6, 1976, ibid.
64. Ibid. See also Collier, *The Indians of the Americas,* 309–10; McNickle to Latimer, July 6, 1976, General Correspondence, MP, NL.
65. Allan Holmberg, "The Research and Development Approach to the Study of Change," 13.

66. McNickle, *Wind from an Enemy Sky,* 37; ibid.; McNickle, *Wind from an Enemy Sky,* 35.
67. McNickle was concerned that this part of the story be as authentic as possible. He contacted Nancy Lurie at the Milwaukee Public Museum to ask her if such a disaster could happen, and Lurie assured him that it was quite possible, even with the best of intentions, in some of the older museums. Nancy O. Lurie to author in Reader's Report, Apr. 19, 1988.
68. McNickle, *Wind from an Enemy Sky,* 256.
69. Julian Rice, "How the Bird That Speaks Lakota Earned a Name," 425. McNickle also may have echoed John Keats's reiterated "And no birds sang," from "La Belle Dame sans Merci," for his meadowlark image, and taken "the world fell apart" from William Yeats's "Byzantium."
70. McNickle to Douglas Latimer, Mar. 23, 1977, General Correspondence, MP, NL.
71. Latimer to McNickle, May 25, 1976, ibid.

CHAPTER NINE

1. D'Arcy McNickle, "The Right to Choose," 31–54.
2. Ibid.; D'Arcy McNickle, "The Surfacing of Native Leadership," 7–15; McNickle, "Anthropology and the Indian Reorganization Act," 51–60; D'Arcy McNickle, "Indian New Deal," 107–19. Schusky dedicated this book to McNickle.
3. McNickle, "Surfacing of Native Leadership," 8.
4. McNickle, "Anthropology and the IRA," 52.
5. Ibid., 60.
6. McNickle, "Indian New Deal," 115–16.
7. McNickle, "Surfacing of Native Leadership," 11; ibid.
8. McNickle, "Anthropology and the IRA," 51.
9. Ibid., 60.
10. McNickle, "Surfacing of Native Leadership," 15; McNickle, "Indian New Deal," 117; McNickle, "The Right to Choose," I-52-3.
11. McNickle to Matt P. Lowman II, Feb. 1, 1971, CHAI Correspondence, MP, NL.
12. Interview with Lawrence Towner, Chicago, Illinois, July 11, 1986.
13. Information on the establishment of the Center for the History of the American Indian was provided by personal interviews with Lawrence W. Towner on July 11, 1986, and July 14, 1989; Richard Brown on July 24, 1989; and John Aubry on July 23, 1989, at the Newberry Library.

14. McNickle to Matt P. Lowman II, Feb. 1, 1971; Dave Warren, "Why Tribal Archives?" v–viii.

15. Leading the effort to supply printed material for the new Indian history, the Newberry Library itself has printed as occasional papers a number of addresses delivered by scholars at conferences at the center, as well as proceedings of those conferences. In addition, the university presses of Indiana and Oklahoma have produced a number of tribal bibliographies and other curriculum materials. The University of Oklahoma Press has also published *Atlas of Great Lakes Indian History,* edited by Helen Hornbeck Tanner, that was in preparation for eleven years at the Newberry. Distribution of this material has substantially extended the center's influence throughout the country.

16. Robert Bieder to author, Dec. 29, 1986.

17. Frederick Hoxie to author, May 25, 1990.

18. Francis Jennings to author, Nov. 14, 1986; Francis Paul Prucha, S.J., to author, Feb. 12, 1987, Rolland Wright to author, Apr. 4, 1990; Richard Pope to colleagues, Apr. 19, 1978; copy in author's file.

19. Interview with Lawrence Towner, Chicago, Illinois, July 11, 1986.

20. Vine Deloria, Jr., to author, Aug. 30, 1986.

21. Nancy Oestreich Lurie, "The Contemporary Indian Scene," in *North American Indians,* ed. Leacock and Lurie, 444.

22. Richard Brown to author, Jan. 20, 1989. Herbert T. Hoover was acting director from 1981 to 1983 and Frederick E. Hoxie has served in that position since 1983.

23. Lawrence Towner to McNickle, Sept. 18, 1976, CHAI Correspondence, MP, NL.

24. Lawrence W. Towner to McNickle, Aug. 1, 1973, ibid.

25. Richard H. Brown to D'Arcy McNickle, Sept. 23, 1977, ibid. Roma, McNickle's second wife, suffered a stroke shortly after D'Arcy died in 1977. She died in 1980.

26. Francis Jennings to author, Nov. 14, 1986.

27. Richard H. Brown to D'Arcy McNickle, Sept. 23, 1977, CHAI Correspondence, MP, NL.

28. Interview with Alfonso Ortiz, Albuquerque, New Mexico, Sept. 9, 1988. He is the one who called the police.

29. Minutes of the Advisory Board Meeting, Oct. 15, 1977, Sol Tax Papers, box 140, folder 9, Regenstein Library, University of Chicago.

30. Alfonso Ortiz, "D'Arcy McNickle," 12.

31. Telephone interview with Jean Parrish (a neighbor of McNickle's who attended the gathering), February 19, 1985. Others who were also present at the second memorial gave details to the author, namely Margaret Connell-Szasz (interview in Albuquerque, New Mexico, on February 24, 1985) and Helen Bannon (interview in Albuquerque, New Mexico, on February 19, 1985).

32. Richard Pope, "To Friends of D'Arcy McNickle," Apr. 19, 1978; copy in author's files.

33. McNickle to Lawrence Towner, Sept. 20, 1977, CHAI Correspondence, MP, NL.

34. Lawrence Towner to McNickle, Sept. 18, 1976, ibid.

35. Lawrence W. Towner, in the afterword to McNickle, *The Surrounded,* 304.

36. *Library Journal,* November 1, 1978, 2262, and *World Literature Today* 53 (Spring 1979): 247. Kenneth Lincoln, *Native American Renaissance* (Berkeley: University of California Press, 1983).

37. Priscilla Oakes, "The First Generation of Native American Novelists," 57–65; Charles Larson, *American Indian Fiction,* 68–78; Louis Owens, "The 'Map of the Mind,'" 275–83; idem, "The Red Road to Nowhere," 239–48.

38. Owens, "The Red Road to Nowhere," 247.

39. Purdy, *Word Ways,* 71.

40. James Rupert, "Textual Perspectives and the Reader in *The Surrounded,*" 99; William Bevis, "Native American Novels," 582.

41. Bevis, *"Native American Novels,"* 585, 583. See also William W. Bevis, *Ten Tough Trips.*

42. Lawrence W. Towner, in the afterword to McNickle, *The Surrounded,* 304.

43. McNickle to Confederated Salish and Kootenai Tribes, Sept. 19, 1968, General Correspondence, MP, NL.

44. Ronald L. Trosper, "Native American Boundary Maintenance," 267.

45. Alfonso Ortiz, "D'Arcy McNickle," 12.

46. Personal interview with Alfonso Ortiz, Albuquerque, New Mexico, Oct. 13, 1990.

47. NAES College Students and Faculty, *Contemporary Issues, Reader One: A Humanistic View of Diversity and Commonality in the Tribal and American Indian Community,* (Chicago: NAES Publications, 1981).

48. *NAES College Catalogue, 1989–1991* (Chicago: NAES Publications, 1988).

49. Robert Dumont to author, Apr. 4, 1990.

50. Interview with Alfonso Ortiz, Albuquerque, New Mexico, Sept. 9, 1988.

Bibliography of the
Published Works of
D'Arcy McNickle

NOVELS

Runner in the Sun: A Story of Indian Maize. New York: Holt, Rinehart and Winston, 1954. Reprint, with an afterword by Alfonso Ortiz. Albuquerque: University of New Mexico Press, 1987.

The Surrounded. New York: Dodd, Mead, 1936. Reprint, with an afterword by Lawrence W. Towner. Albuquerque: University of New Mexico Press, 1978.

Wind from an Enemy Sky. New York: Harper & Row, 1978. Reprint, edited and with a foreword by Louis Owens. Albuquerque: University of New Mexico Press, 1988.

POETRY AND SHORT STORIES

"The Silver Locket." *Frontier: A Literary Magazine,* November 1923, 18–21.

"Clod the Magician." *Frontier, A Literary Magazine,* May 1924, 8–10.

"Cycle." *Frontier: A Literary Magazine,* November 1924, 1.

"The Mountains." *Frontier: A Literary Magazine,* May 1925, 10–11.

"Man Hesitates but Life Urges." *Frontier: A Literary Magazine,* March 1926, 16.

"Meat for God." *Esquire,* September 1935, 86, 120, 122.

"Snowfall." *Common Ground* 4 (Summer 1944): 75–82.

"The Hawk Is Hungry": An Annotated Anthology of D'Arcy McNickle's Short Fiction. Edited by Birgit Hans. Tucson: University of Arizona Press, 1992.

BOOK-LENGTH NONFICTION

Indian Man: A Biography of Oliver La Farge. Bloomington: Indiana University Press, 1971.

The Indian Tribes of the United States: Ethnic and Cultural Survival. London: Oxford University Press, 1962. Revised and updated as *Native American Tribalism: Indian Survivals and Renewals.* London: Oxford University Press, 1973.

Native American Tribalism: Indian Survivals and Renewals. London: Oxford University Press, 1973.

They Came Here First: The Epic of the American Indian. The Peoples of America. Philadelphia: J. B. Lippincott Co., 1949. Rev. ed. New York: Harper & Row, 1975.

With Harold E. Fey. *Indians and Other Americans: Two Ways of Life Meet.* New York: Harper & Brothers, 1959. Rev. ed. New York: Harper & Row, 1970.

ARTICLES

"Sailing, a-Sailing." *Frontier: A Literary Magazine,* November 1925, 22–25.

"Alaska—Getting Acquainted." *Indians at Work,* November 1936, 5–7.

"Hill 57." *Indians at Work,* February 1, 1937, 19–21.

"In Maine." *Indians at Work,* October 15, 1937, 15–18.

"The Straddle Between Cultures." *Indians at Work,* December 1, 1937, 29–30.

"Four Years of Indian Reorganization." *Indians at Work,* July 1938, 4–11.

"Indian Arts, A Collective Force." *Indians at Work,* July 1940, 27.

"The American Indian Today." *Missouri Archaeologist.* Presented at the Fifth Annual Spring Conference of the Missouri Archaeological Society, ca. 1940.

"The Art of Basketry." *Indians at Work,* January 1941, 14–16.

"What Do the Old Men Say?" *Indians at Work,* December 1941, 24–26.

"Toward Understanding." *Indians at Work,* May–June 1942, 4–7.

With Willard Beatty. "Science and the Future." *Indians at Work,* May–June 1943, 43.

"We Go on from Here." *Indians at Work,* November–December 1943, 14–21. (Also published in *Common Ground* 3 [Autumn 1943]: 26–31).

"Peyote and the Indian." *Scientific Monthly* 57 (September 1943): 220–29.

"Afternoon on a Rock." *Common Ground* 5 (Spring 1945): 71–76.

"Rescuing Sisseton." *American Indian* 3 (1947): 21–27.

"Basis for a National Indian Policy." *American Indian* 5 (1949): 3–12.

"Golden Myth." *Common Ground* 9 (Summer 1949): 65–74.

"United States Indian Affairs, 1953." *America Indigena* 13 (October 1953): 263–73.

"Indian Crisis: A Challenge to Social Science." *University of Chicago Roundtable,* February 21, 1954, 14–18.

"A U.S. Indian Speaks." *Americas* 6 (1954): 8–11, 27.

"Indian Crisis, U.S.A." *Colby Junior College Bulletin,* April 1954, 11–13.

"Indians of North America." *Encyclopaedia Britannica,* 14th ed. Chicago: 1954.

"The Indian in American Society." In *Social Welfare Forum,* 68–77. New York: Columbia University Press, 1955.

"The Healing Vision." *Tomorrow* 4 (January 1956): 25–31.

"Indian and European: Indian-White Relations from Discovery to 1887." *Annals of the American Academy of Political and Social Science* 311 (May 1957): 1–17.

"Process or Compulsion: The Search for a Policy of Administration in Indian Affairs." *America Indigena* 17 (July 1957): 261–70.

"It's Almost Never Too Late." *Christian Century* 74 (1957): 227–29.

"The Indians of the United States." *America Indigena* 18 (April 1958): 99–118.

With Viola Pfrommer. "It Takes Two to Communicate." *International Journal of Health Education,* July 1959, n.p.

"Private Intervention: The Role of Private Welfare Groups in Indian Affairs Administration in the U.S. and Canada." *Human Organization* 20 (Winter 1961): 208–15.

"Indian Expectations." *Indian Truth* 38 (July 1961): 1–7.

"The Indian Tests the Mainstream." *Nation,* September 26, 1966, 275–79.

"The Dead Horse Walks Again." *Nation,* December 25, 1967, 677–68.

"John Collier's Vision." *Nation,* June 3, 1968, 718–19.

"The Sociocultural Setting of Indian Life." *American Journal of Psychiatry* 125 (August 1968): 2.

"American Indians Who Never Were." *Indian Historian* 3 (1970): 4–7.

"They Cast Long Shadows." In *Look to the Mountain Top,* edited by Charles Jones, 19–28. San Jose, Calif.: H. M. Gousha Co., 1972.

"Americans Called Indians." In *North American Indians in Historical Perspective,* edited by Eleanor Leacock and Nancy O. Lurie, 29–63. New York: Random House, 1971.

"Clash of Cultures." In *World of the American Indian,* edited by Melville Bell Grosvenor, 311–53. Washington, D.C.: National Geographic Society, 1974.

"Commentary." In *Indian-White Relations: A Persistent Paradox,* edited by Jane F. Smith and Robert Kvasnicka, 251–57. Washington, D.C.: Howard University Press, 1975.

"The Surfacing of Native Leadership." Presented at symposium, "Patterns of Amerindian Identity," Montmorency, Quebec, October 1974. Quebec: Les Presses de L'Université Laval, 1976.

"The Right to Choose: A Policy for the Future." In *Captives Within a Free Society: A Review of the American Indian Policy Review Commission,* prepared for the American Indian Policy Review Commission by D'Arcy McNickle, Mary E. Young, and W. Roger Buffalohead. N.p., 1976.

"Anthropology and the Indian Reorganization Act." In *The Uses of Anthropology,* edited by Walter Goldschmidt, 51–60. Washington, D.C.: American Anthropological Association, 1979.

"The Indian New Deal as Mirror of the Future." In *Political Organization of Native North Americans,* edited by Ernest L. Schusky, 107–19. Washington, D.C.: University Press of America, 1980.

References

ARCHIVAL SOURCES

Flathead Agency, Pablo, Montana
BIA Land Services Records
Marquette University, Milwaukee, Wisconsin, Department of Special Collections
and University Archives
Bureau of Catholic Indian Missions
National Anthropological Archives, Smithsonian Institution
Guides to the Papers of Robert J. Havighurst, Dorothea Leighton, and Laura
Thompson
Records of the National Congress of American Indians
National Archives and Records Service, Federal Records Center, Seattle, Wash-
ington
Salem Indian School Records
National Archives and Records Service, Washington, D.C.
Central Classified File, Flathead Agency 1907–39
Records of the Bureau of Indian Affairs, Record Group 75
Correspondence of Assistant Commissioner William Zimmerman, 1935–48
Desk File, Office of Commissioner of Indian Affairs, Commissioner Dillon
S. Myer, 1950–53

Inter-American Indian Programs
Memoranda of Assistant Commissioner William Zimmerman, 1944–50
Office File of Assistant Commissioner John H. Provinse, 1946–50
Office File of Fred H. Daiker, 1929–43
Office Files of Commissioner John Collier, 1933–45
Office Files of Joseph McCaskill, 1939–46
Office Records of Assistant Commissioner William Zimmerman, 1935–48
Records of the Works Progress Administration, Central Staff, National Coordinating Project, Record Group 69
Selected Records of the BIA Related to the Enrollment of Indians on the Flathead Reservation. Microfilm Production M1350
Newberry Library, Chicago, Illinois, Special Collections
D'Arcy McNickle Papers
Towner/McNickle Papers
Regenstein Library, University of Chicago
Sol Tax Papers
United States Office of Personnel Management, Federal Records Center, St. Louis, Missouri
McNickle Personnel File
University of Montana, Missoula
Files of the Alumni Association
Mike Mansfield Library, Special Collections
Harold G. Merriam Papers, 1904–80
University of New Mexico, Albuquerque, Zimmerman Library, Special Collections
Collier Papers
Doris Duke Project

UNPUBLISHED WORKS

Koppes, Clayton. "Oscar L. Chapman: A Liberal at the Interior Department, 1933–1953." Ph.D. Diss., University of Kansas, 1974.

Myer, Dillon. "An Autobiography of Dillon Myer." Oral History Transcript, Bancroft Library, University of California, Berkeley, 1970. (Copy also at Oberlin College Library, Oberlin, Ohio.)

Rosenthal, Elizabeth Clark. "'Indian Interest Organizations' and the American Indian Community, 1882–1982." Draft, February 1982. Copy in author's file.

Stacher, Herbert C. "History of Crownpoint, New Mexico, 1910–1935, while Samuel Franklin Stacher was in charge as Superintendent." Fellin Public Library, Gallup, New Mexico, 1986.

BOOKS

Adair, John; Deuschle, Kurt W.; and Barnett, Clifford R. *The People's Health: Anthropology and Medicine in a Navajo Community*. Albuquerque: University of New Mexico Press, 1988.

Allen, Paula Gunn, ed. *Studies in American Indian Literature: Critical Essays and Course Designs*. New York: Modern Language Assoc., 1983.

Bahr, Howard; Chadwick, Bruce A.; and Day, Robert C., eds. *Native Americans Today*. New York: Harper & Row, 1972.

Bailey, Garrick, and Bailey, Roberta. *A History of the Navajos: The Reservation Years*. Santa Fe: School of American Research, 1986.

Beatty, Willard W., and associates. *Education for Cultural Change: Selected Articles from Indian Education, 1944–1951*. Washington, D.C.: U.S. Department of Interior, Bureau of Indian Affairs, 1953.

Beuf, Ann H. *Red Children in White America*. Philadelphia: University of Pennsylvania Press, 1977.

Berkhofer, Robert, Jr. *The White Man's Indian*. New York: Alfred A. Knopf, 1978.

Bevis, William W. *Ten Tough Trips: Montana Writers and the West*. Seattle: University of Washington Press, 1990.

Brunhouse, Robert. *Pursuit of the Ancient Maya: Some Archeological Visits of Yesterday*. Albuquerque: University of New Mexico Press, 1975.

Burt, Larry. *Tribalism in Crisis: Federal Indian Policy, 1953–1961*. Albuquerque: University of New Mexico Press, 1982.

Campbell, Joseph. *The Hero with a Thousand Faces*. 2d ed. Bollinger Series, vol. 17. Princeton, N.J.: Princeton University Press, 1949.

Chamberlain, J. E. *The Harrowing of Eden: White Attitudes toward Native Americans*. New York: Seabury Press, 1975.

Clifford, James L. *From Puzzles to Portraits: Problems of a Literary Biographer*. Chapel Hill: University of North Carolina Press, 1970.

Clifton, James A., ed. *Being and Becoming Indian: Biographical Studies of North American Frontiers*. Chicago: Dorsey Press, 1989.

Cohen, Felix S. *The Legal Conscience: Selected Papers of Felix S. Cohen*. Edited by Lucy Kramer Cohen. New Haven: Yale University Press, 1960.

Collier, John. *From Every Zenith*. Denver: Sage Press, 1966.

———. *The Indians of the Americas*. New York: W. W. Norton & Co., 1947.

Colonnese, Tom, and Owens, Louis. *American Indian Novelists: An Annotated Critical Bibliography*. New York: Garland, 1985.

Costo, Rupert, ed. *Anthropology and the American Indian: A Report of the Symposium on Anthropology and the American Indian at the Meetings of the American*

Anthropological Association, San Diego, California, November 20, 1970. San Francisco: Indian Historian Press, 1973.

Daniels, Roger. *Concentration Camps, U.S.A.: Japanese-Americans and World War II*. New York: Holt, Rinehart and Winston, 1971.

Deloria, Vine, Jr. *Custer Died for Your Sins: An Indian Manifesto*. New York: Macmillan, 1969. Reprint. New York: Avon Books, 1970.

Deloria, Vine, Jr., ed. *Of Utmost Good Faith*. San Francisco: Straight Arrow Books, 1971.

DeVos, George, and Romanucci-Ross, L. *Ethnic Identity: Cultural Continuities and Change*. Palo Alto, Calif.: Mayfield, 1975.

Dippie, Brian. *The Vanishing American: White Attitudes and Indian Policy*. Middletown, Conn.: Wesleyan University Press, 1982.

Eisenhower, Milton S. *The President Is Calling*. Garden City, N.Y.: Doubleday & Co., 1974.

Erikson, Erik H. *Identity: Youth and Crisis*. New York: W. W. Norton & Co., 1968.

Fahey, John. *The Flathead Indians*. Norman: University of Oklahoma Press, 1974.

Fey, Harold. *Indian Rights and American Justice*. Chicago: Christian Century Foundation, 1955.

Fixico, Donald. *Termination and Relocation: Federal Indian Policy: 1945–1960*. Albuquerque: University of New Mexico Press, 1986.

Flanagan, Thomas. *Louis "David" Riel: Prophet of the New World*. Toronto: University of Toronto Press, 1979.

Fleckner, John A. *Native American Archives: An Introduction*. Chicago: Society of American Archivists, 1984.

Fuchs, Estelle, and Havighurst, Robert J. *To Live on This Earth: American Indian Education*. Garden City, N.Y.: Doubleday, 1972. Reprint. Albuquerque: University of New Mexico Press, 1983.

Giraud, Marcel. *Le Métis Canadien: Son rôle dans l'histoire des provinces de l'ouest*. Paris: Institut d'ethnologie, 1945. Reprint, translated. *The Métis in the Canadian West*. Lincoln: University of Nebraska Press, 1986.

Girdner, Audrie, and Loftis, Anne. *The Great Betrayal: The Evacuation of the Japanese-Americans during World War II*. New York: Macmillan, 1969.

Goldschmidt, Walter Rochs, ed. *The Uses of Anthropology*. American Anthropology Association Special Publication 11. Washington, D.C.: American Anthropological Association, 1979.

Greene, Victor R. *American Immigrant Leaders, 1800–1910: Marginality and Identity*. Baltimore: Johns Hopkins University Press, 1987.

Guthrie, A. B., Jr. *The Blue Hen's Chick: A Life in Context*. New York: McGraw-Hill Book Co., 1965.

Hallowell, A. Irving. *Culture and Experience*. Philadelphia: University of Pennsylvania Press, 1955.

Hauptman, Lawrence M. *The Iroquois and the New Deal*. Syracuse, N.Y.: Syracuse University Press, 1981.

Hertzberg, Hazel W. *The Search for an American Indian Identity: Modern Pan-Indian Movements*. Syracuse, N.Y.: Syracuse University Press, 1971.

Hobson, Geary. *The Remembered Earth: An Anthology of Contemporary Native American Literature*. Albuquerque: University of New Mexico Press, 1979.

Hofstadter, Richard. *The Progressive Historians: Turner, Beard, Parrington*. New York: Alfred A. Knopf, 1969.

Howard, Joseph Kinsey. *Strange Empire: A Narrative of the Northwest*. New York: William Morrow & Co., 1952.

Hoxie, Frederick. *Indians in American History: An Introduction*. Arlington Heights, Ill.: Harlan Davidson, 1988.

Indian Voices. The First Convocation of American Indian Scholars, 1970. San Francisco: Indian Historian Press, 1970.

Isaacs, Harold R. *Idols of the Tribe: Group Identity and Political Change*. New York: Harper & Row, 1975.

Iverson, Peter. *The Navajo Nation*. Albuquerque: University of New Mexico Press, 1979.

Joseph, Alice; Spicer, Rosamond; and Chesky, Jane. *The Desert People: A Study of the Papago Indians*. Chicago: University of Chicago Press, 1949.

Kazin, Alfred. *An American Procession*. New York: Alfred A. Knopf, 1984.

Kelly, Lawrence C. *The Assault on Assimilation: John Collier and the Origins of Indian Policy Reform*. Albuquerque: University of New Mexico Press, 1983.

Kendall, Paul Murray. *The Art of Biography*. London: George Allen & Unwin, 1965.

Kluckhohn, Clyde, and Leighton, Dorothea. *The Navajo*. Cambridge: Harvard University Press, 1946.

Kluckhohn, Clyde, and Murray, H. A., eds. *Personality in Nature, Society, and Culture*. New York: Alfred A. Knopf, 1948.

Kroeber, Karl, ed. *Traditional American Indian Literature: Texts and Interpretations*. Lincoln: University of Nebraska Press, 1981.

Kvasnicka, Robert, and Viola, Herman, eds. *The Commissioners of Indian Affairs, 1824–1977*. Lincoln: University of Nebraska Press, 1979.

Larson, Charles R. *American Indian Fiction*. Albuquerque: University of New Mexico Press, 1978.

Leacock, Eleanor Burke, and Lurie, Nancy Oestreich. *North American Indians in Historical Perspective*. New York: Random House, 1971.

Leighton, Alexander, and Leighton, Dorothea. *The Navajo Door: An Introduction to Navajo Life*. Cambridge: Harvard University Press, 1945.

Leighton, Alexander. *The Governing of Men: General Principles and Recommendations Based on Experience at a Japanese Relocation Camp*. Princeton: Princeton University Press, 1945.

Leighton, Dorothea, and Adair, John. *People of the Middle Place*. New Haven: Human Relations Area Files, 1965.

Leighton, Dorothea, and Kluckhohn, Clyde. *Children of the People: The Navajo Indian and His Development*. Cambridge: Harvard University Press, 1947.

Levine, Stuart, and Lurie, Nancy Oestreich, eds. *The American Indian Today*. Midcontinent American Studies Journal 6 (Fall 1965). Rev. and exp. ed. Baltimore: Penguin Books, 1970.

Lieuwin, Edwin. *United States Policy in Latin America: A Short History*. New York: Frederick A. Praeger, 1965.

Lippmann, Walter. *Interpretations, 1931–1932*. New York: Macmillan, 1932.

McNickle, Roma. *The Changing West: Implications for Higher Education*. Boulder, Colo.: Western Interstate Commission for Higher Education, 1965.

———. *The WICHE Student Exchange Program, 1953–54 through 1964–65*. Boulder, Colo.: Western Interstate Commission for Higher Education, 1966.

McNitt, Frank. *The Indian Traders*. Norman: University of Oklahoma Press, 1962.

McWilliams, Carey. *The Education of Carey McWilliams*. New York: Simon & Schuster, 1979.

Mourning Dove. *Cogewea, the Half Breed: A Depiction of the Great Montana Cattle Range*. Boston: Four Seasons, 1927. Reprinted. Lincoln: University of Nebraska Press, 1981.

———. *Mourning Dove: A Salishan Autobiography*. Edited by Jay Miller. Lincoln: University of Nebraska Press, 1988.

Morton, Desmond. *The Last War Drum: The North West Campaign of 1885*. Toronto: A. M. Hakkert, 1972.

Myer, Dillon. *Uprooted Americans: The Japanese Americans and the War Relocation Authority during World War II*. Tucson: University of Arizona Press, 1971.

The Native American Today: The Second Convocation of Indian Scholars. San Francisco: Indian Historian Press, 1974.

Nelson, Mary Carroll. *Annie Wauneka: The Story of an American Indian*. Minneapolis: Dillon Press, 1972.

Olson, James S., and Wilson, Raymond. *Native Americans in the Twentieth Century*. Provo, Utah: Brigham Young University Press, 1984.

Pachter, Marc, ed. *Telling Lives: The Biographers' Art*. Washington, D.C.: New Republic Books, 1979.

Parman, Donald. *The Navajos and the New Deal*. New Haven: Yale University Press, 1976.

Penkower, Monty Noam. *The Federal Writers Project: A Study in Government Patronage of the Arts*. Urbana: University of Illinois Press, 1977.

Peterson, Jacqueline, and Brown, Jennifer S. H., eds., *The New Peoples: Being and Becoming Métis in North America*. Lincoln: University of Nebraska Press, 1986.

Peyer, Bernd C. *The Singing Spirit: Early Short Stories by North American Indians*. Tucson: University of Arizona Press, 1990.

Philp, Kenneth R. *Indian Self-Rule: First-Hand Accounts of Indian-White Relations from Roosevelt to Reagan*. Salt Lake City: Howe Bros., 1986.

————. *John Collier's Crusade for Indian Reform, 1920–1954*. Tucson: University of Arizona Press, 1977.

Prucha, Francis Paul. *The Churches and the Indian Schools, 1888–1912*. Lincoln: University of Nebraska Press, 1979.

Purdy, John Lloyd. *Word Ways: The Novels of D'Arcy McNickle*. Tucson: University of Arizona Press, 1990.

Riel, Louis. *The Diaries of Louis Riel*. Edited by Thomas Flanagan. Edmonton, Alberta: Hurtig, 1976.

Roessel, Robert A., Jr. *Indian Communities in Action*. Tempe: Arizona State University, 1967.

Royce, Anya Peterson. *Ethnic Identity: Strategies of Diversity*. Bloomington: Indiana University Press, 1982.

Ruoff, A. LaVonne Brown. *American Indian Literatures: Introduction, Bibliographic Review, and Selected Bibliography*. New York: Modern Language Assoc., 1990.

Rupert, James. *D'Arcy McNickle*. Western Writers Series, no. 38. Boise: Boise State University Press, 1988.

Schusky, Ernest L. *Political Organization of Native North Americans*. Washington, D.C.: Press of America, 1980.

Slobodin, Richard. *Métis of the Mackenzie District*. Ottawa: Canadian Research Center for Anthropology, 1966.

Smith, Jane F., and Kvasnicka, Robert M., eds. *Indian-White Relations: A Persistent Paradox*. Washington, D.C.: Howard University Press, 1976.

The Social Welfare Forum, 1955. New York: Columbia University Press, 1975.

Social Contexts of American Ethnology, 1840–1984: 1984. Washington, D.C.: American Anthropological Association, 1985.

Spicer, Edward H.; Hansen, Asael T.; Luomala, Katherine; and Opler, Marvin K., joint authors. *Impounded People: Japanese-Americans in the Relocation Centers*. Tucson: University of Arizona Press, 1969.

St. Ignatius Mission. St. Ignatius, Mont.: Jesuit Fathers, 1977.

Stacher, Herbert C. *History of Crownpoint, New Mexico, 1910 to 1935, while Samuel Franklin Stacher was in Charge as Superintendent*. N.p., 1986.

Statistics of Indian Tribes, Agencies, and Schools, Compiled to July 1, 1903. Washington, D.C.: G P O, 1903. Reprint. Millwood, N.Y.: Krause Reprint Co., 1976.

Steele, Ronald. *Walter Lippmann and the American Century.* Boston: Little, Brown & Co., 1980.

Steiner, Stan. *The New Indians.* New York: Harper & Row, 1967. Reprint. Dell Publishers, 1968.

Sutton, Imre, ed. *Irredeemable America.* Albuquerque: University of New Mexico Press, 1985.

Swann, Brian, and Krupat, Arnold, eds. *Recovering the Word: Essays on Native American Literature.* Berkeley: University of California Press, 1987.

Szasz, Margaret. *Education and the American Indian: The Road to Self-Determination Since 1928.* Albuquerque: University of New Mexico Press, 1974.

Taylor, Graham. *The New Deal and American Indian Tribalism: The Administration of the Indian Reorganization Act, 1934–45.* Lincoln: University of Nebraska Press, 1980.

Thompson, Laura. *Culture in Crisis: A Study of the Hopi Indians.* New York: Harper & Bros., 1950.

Thompson, Laura, and Joseph, Alice. *The Hopi Way.* Chicago: University of Chicago Press, 1944.

Tjerandson, Carl. *Education for Citizenship: A Foundation's Experience.* Santa Cruz, Calif.: Emil Schwartzhaupt Foundation, 1980.

Trafzer, Clifford E., ed. *American Indian Identity: Today's Changing Perspectives.* Sacramento: Sierra Oaks, 1986.

Tyler, S. Lyman. *Indian Affairs: A Work Paper on Termination, with an Attempt to Show Its Antecedents.* Provo: Brigham Young University, 1964.

U.S. Department of Interior, War Relocation Authority. *Administrative Highlights of the WRA Program.* Washington, D.C.: G P O, 1946.

———. *Community Government in War Relocation Centers.* Washington, D.C.: G P O, 1946.

———. *WRA: A Story of Human Conservation.* Washington, D.C.: G P O, 1946.

Van Willigen, John. *Applied Anthropology.* South Hadley, Mass.: Bergin & Garvey, 1986.

Veninga, James F. *The Biographer's Gift: Life Histories and Humanism.* College Station: Texas A & M University Press, 1983.

Washburn, Wilcomb E. *Red Man's Land, White Man's Law: A Study of the Past and Present Status of the American Indian.* New York: Charles Scribner's Sons, 1971.

Weglyn, Michi. *Years of Infamy: The Untold Story of America's Concentration Camps.* New York: William Morrow and Co., 1976.

Whorf, Benjamin Lee, ed. *Language, Thought and Reality: Selected Writings.* Cambridge: M I T Press, 1956.

Wiget, Andrew, ed. *Critical Essays on Native American Literature.* Boston: G. K. Hall, 1985.

Witt, Shirley Hill, and Steiner, Stan, eds. *The Way: An Anthology of American Indian Literature.* New York: Alfred A. Knopf, 1972.

Woodcock, George. *Gabriel Dumont: The Métis Chief and His Lost World.* Edmonton, Alberta: Hurtig, 1975.

WPA and the Montana Historical Records Survey. *Inventory of the County Archives of Montana.* Bozeman, Mont.: 1938.

ARTICLES

Adair, John; Deuschle, Kurt; and McDermott, Walsh. "Patterns of Health and Disease Among the Navajo." *Annals of the American Academy of Political and Social Sciences* 331 (May 1957): 80–94.

Bevis, William. "Native American Novels: Homing In." In *Recovering the Word: Essays on Native American Literature,* edited by Brian Swann and Arnold Krupat, 580–620. Berkeley: University of California Press, 1987

Bigart, Robert J. "Patterns of Cultural Change in a Salish Flathead Community." *Human Anthropology* 30 (Fall 1971): 229–38.

Bonney, Rachel A. "The Role of AIM Leaders in Indian Nationalism." *American Indian Quarterly* 3 (1977): 209–24.

Brockman, C. Thomas. "Social Class and Educational Level on the Flathead Reservation." *Journal of American Indian Education* 10 (October 1970): 23–31.

Brunhouse, Robert. "William E. Gates." *In Pursuit of the Ancient Maya: Some Archeological Visits of Yesterday,* by Robert Brunhouse, Chap. 6. Albuquerque: University of New Mexico Press, 1975.

Clements, William M. "Folk Historical Sense in Two Native American Authors." *Melus* 12 (Spring 1985): 65–78.

Cohen, Felix. "The Erosion of Indian Rights, 1950–1953: A Case Study in Bureaucracy." *Yale Law Journal* 62 (February 1953): 348–90.

Collier, John. "A Permanent Institute on American Indian Life." *Indians at Work,* April 1940, 1–7.

———. "Collier Replies to Mekeel," *American Anthropologist* 46 (1944): 422–26.

Davis, Jack L. "The Whorf Hypothesis and Native American Literature." *South Dakota Review* 14 (1976): 59–72.

Dunsmore, Roger. "*Wind from an Enemy Sky* and 'Killing the Water.'" *Studies in American Indian Literature* 11 (Winter 1987): 38–53.

———. "Reflections on *Wind from an Enemy Sky.*" *Studies in American Indian Literature* 11 (Winter 1987): 28–57.

Dusenberry, Verne. "The Rocky Boy Indians." *Montana Magazine of History* 4 (Winter 1954): 1–15.

————. "Waiting for a Day That Never Comes." *Montana Magazine of History* 8 (April 1958): 26–39.

Feasin, Joe R., and Anderson, Randall. "Intertribal Attitudes among Native American Youth." *Social Science Quarterly* 54 (1973): 117–31.

Fenton, William. Review of *They Came Here First,* by D'Arcy McNickle. *American Anthropologist* 52 (1950): 546–47.

Frisch, Jack A. "'Action' Anthropology, 'Scientific' Anthropology, and American Indians." *New University Thought* 7 (1971): 12–15.

Harlin, Lois E. "The National Congress of American Indians." *Indians at Work,* November–December 1944, 20–22.

Holm, Tom. "Fighting a White Man's War: The Legacy of American Indian Participation." *Journal of American Studies* 9 (Summer 1981): 69–81.

Holmberg, Allan. "Participant Intervention in the Field." *Human Organization* 14 (Spring 1955): 23–26.

————. "The Research and Development Approach to the Study of Change." *Human Organization* 17 (Spring 1958): 12–19.

Iverson, Peter. "Building toward Self-Determination: Plains and Southwestern Indians in the 1940s and 1950s." *Western Historical Quarterly* 16 (April 1985): 163–73.

Kelly, Lawrence. "Anthropology and Anthropologists in the Indian New Deal." *Journal of the History of the Behavior Sciences* 16 (1980): 6–24.

————. "Anthropologists in the Soil Conservation Service." *Agricultural History* 59 (April 1985): 136–47.

Kluckhohn, Clyde. Review of *They Came Here First,* by D'Arcy McNickle. *New York Herald Tribune Book Reviews,* November 13, 1949, 30.

Koppes, Clayton. "From New Deal to Termination: Liberalism and Indian Policy, 1933–1953." *Pacific Historical Review* 46 (1977): 543–66.

Lurie, Nancy Oestreich. "As Others See Us." *New University Thought* 7 (Spring 1971): 2–6.

————. "The Indian Claims Commission." *Annals of the American Academy of Political and Social Science* 436 (March 1978): 97–110.

————. "Menominee Termination: From Reservation to Colony." *Human Organization* 31, no. 3 (Fall 1972): 257–70.

————. Review of *They Came Here First,* by D'Arcy McNickle. *American Anthropologist* 64 (1962): 1343–44.

————. "The Voice of the American Indian: Report on the American Indian Chicago Conference." *Current Anthropology* 2, no. 5 (December 1961): 478–500.

————. "The Will-O'-the-Wisp of Indian Unity." *Indian Historian,* Summer 1976, 19–24.

McWilliams, Carey. "Japanese Evacuation: Policy and Perspectives." *Common Ground,* Summer 1942, 65–72.

MeKeel, H. Scudder. "An Appraisal of the Indian Reorganization Act." *American Anthropologist* 46 (1944): 209–17.

Miller, Jay. "Mourning Dove: The Author as Cultural Mediator." In *Being and Becoming Indian,*edited by James A. Clifton. Chicago: Dorsey Press, 1989.

Neuberger, Richard L. "A Senator Surveys the Land of the Braves." *Saturday Review of Literature,* May 9, 1959, 14–15.

Oaks, Priscilla. "The First Generation of Native American Novelists." *Melus* 5 (Spring 1978): 57–65.

Ortiz, Alfonso. "D'Arcy McNickle (1904–1977): Across the River and up the Hill." *American Indian Journal,* April 1978, 12–16.

Ortiz, Simon. "Towards a National Indian Literature: Cultural Authenticity in Nationalism." *Melus* 8 (Summer 1981): 7–12.

Owens, Louis. "The 'Map of the Mind': D'Arcy McNickle and the American Indian Novel." *Western American Literature* 19 (February 1985): 275–83.

———. "The Red Road to Nowhere: D'Arcy McNickle's *The Surrounded* and 'The Hungry Generations.'" *American Indian Quarterly* 13 (Summer 1989): 239–48.

Parker, Dorothy R. "D'Arcy McNickle: An Annotated Bibliography of His Published Articles and Book Reviews in a Biographical Context." *American Indian Culture and Research Journal* 14 (August 1990): 55–75.

Philp, Kenneth R. "Stride toward Freedom: The Relocation of Indians to Cities, 1952–1960." *Western Historical Quarterly* 16 (April 1985): 175–90.

Provinse, John H. "Anthropology in Program Planning." *Applied Anthropology* 3 (December 1943): 1–5.

Rice, Julian. "How the Bird That Speaks Lakota Earned a Name." In *Recovering the Word: Essays on Native American Literature,* edited by Brian Swann and Arnold Krupat. Berkeley: University of California Press, 1987.

Rollings, Willard H. "D'Arcy McNickle." In *Historians of the American West,* edited by John R. Wunder, 408–25. Westport, Conn.: Greenwood Press, 1988.

Rosenthal, Harvey D. "Indian Claims and the American Conscience: A Brief History of the Indian Claims Commission." In *Irredeemable America,* edited by Imre Sutton, 35–70. Albuquerque: University of New Mexico Press, 1985.

Ruoff, A. LaVonne Brown. "Ethnicity and Literature: Old Traditions and New Forms." In *Studies in American Indian Literature: Critical Essays and Course Design,* edited by Paula Gunn Allen, 165–66. New York: Modern Language Association, 1983.

———. "The Survival of Tradition: American Indian Oral and Written Narratives." *Massachusetts Review* 27 (Summer 1986): 274–93.

Rupert, James. "Textual Perspectives and the Reader in *The Surrounded.*" In *Narrative Chance: Postmodern Discourse on Native American Indian Literature,* edited by Gerald Vizenor. Albuquerque: University of New Mexico Press, 1989.

Schrems, Suzanne H., and Wolff, Cynthia J. "Politics and Libel: Angie Debo and the Publication of *And Still the Waters Run.*" *Western Historical Quarterly* 22 (May 1991): 185–203.

Spicer, Edward. "Beyond Analysis and Explanation? Notes on the Life and Times of the Society for Applied Anthropology." *Human Organization* 35 (Winter 1976): 335–43.

Spindler, George, and Spindler, Louise. "American Indian Personality Types and Their Sociocultural Roots." *Annals of the American Academy of Political and Social Sciences* 331 (May 1957): 147–57.

Stewart, Omer C. "The Indians in Chicago." *Delphian Quarterly* 45 (Spring 1962): 9–14.

Tax, Sol. "The Fox Project." *Human Organization* 17 (Spring 1958): 17–19.

Taylor, Graham. "Anthropologists, Reformers, and the Indian New Deal." *Prologue* 7 (Fall 1975): 156–57.

Thompson, Laura. "Action Research among American Indians." *Scientific Monthly* 70 (1950): 34–40.

———. "Is Applied Anthropology Helping to Develop a Science of Man?" *Human Organization* 24 (1965): 277–87.

———. "Some Perspectives in Applied Anthropology." *Applied Anthropology* 3 (June 1944): 12–16.

Trosper, Ronald L. "Native American Boundary Maintenance: The Flathead Indian Reservation, Montana, 1860–1970." *Ethnicity* 3 (1976): 256–74.

Warren, Dave. "Why Tribal Archives?" In *Native American Archives: An Introduction*, edited by John A. Fleckner. Chicago: Society of American Archivists, 1984.

Washburn, Wilcomb. "Ethical Perspectives in North American Ethnology." In *Social Contexts of American Ethnology, 1840–1984: Proceedings of the American Ethnological Society, 1984*. Washington, D.C.: American Anthropological Association, 1985.

———. "A Fifty-Year Perspective on the Indian Reorganization Act." *American Anthropologist* 86 (June 1984): 279–89.

CONGRESSIONAL DOCUMENTS

U.S. Congress. House. Committee on Indian Affairs. *Wheeler-Howard Act, Exempt Certain Indians, Hearings on S.2130*, 76th Cong., 3rd sess.

———. Special Committee on Un-American Activities. *Investigation of Un-American Propaganda Activities in the United States, Report and Minority Views.* 78th Cong., 1st sess.

U.S. Congress. Senate. Committee on Appropriations. *Interior Department Appropriations Bill for 1950, Part I, Hearings on H.R. 3838.* 81st Cong., 1st sess.

————. Committee on Interior and Insular Affairs. "Report of Proceedings, April 17, 1950." 81st Cong., 2nd Sess.

U.S. Congress. Senate and House. Joint Committee on Interior and Insular Affairs. Subcommittee on Indian Affairs. *Termination of Federal Supervision over Certain Tribes of Indians, Part 7, Hearings Pursuant to Jont Resolution 108, on S.2750 and H.R. 7319,* 83rd Cong., 1st sess.

NEWSPAPERS AND PERIODICALS

Americas
Boston Transcript
Frontier (Frontier and Midland: A Literary Magazine after 1932) 1923–43
Indian Truth
Library Journal
Missoula Missoulian
Gallup (N. Mex.) *Navajo Times*
New Republic
New York Herald Tribune
New York Herald Tribune Book Review
New York Times
Saturday Review of Literature (Saturday Review after 1954)
Survey
World Literature Today

Index